AF580063

BIRDS OF VANCOUVER ISLAND

A Photographic Journey

Glenn Bartley

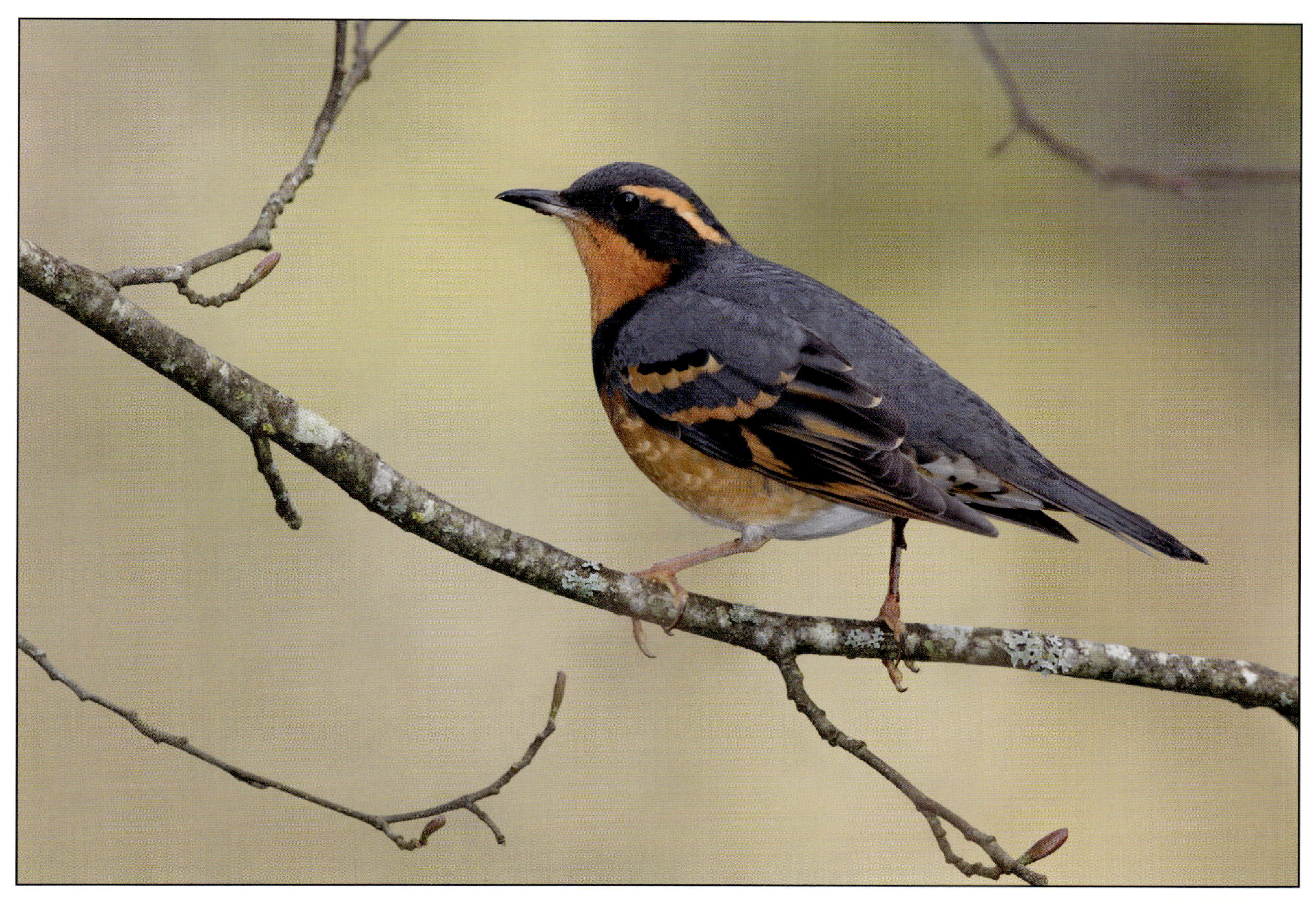

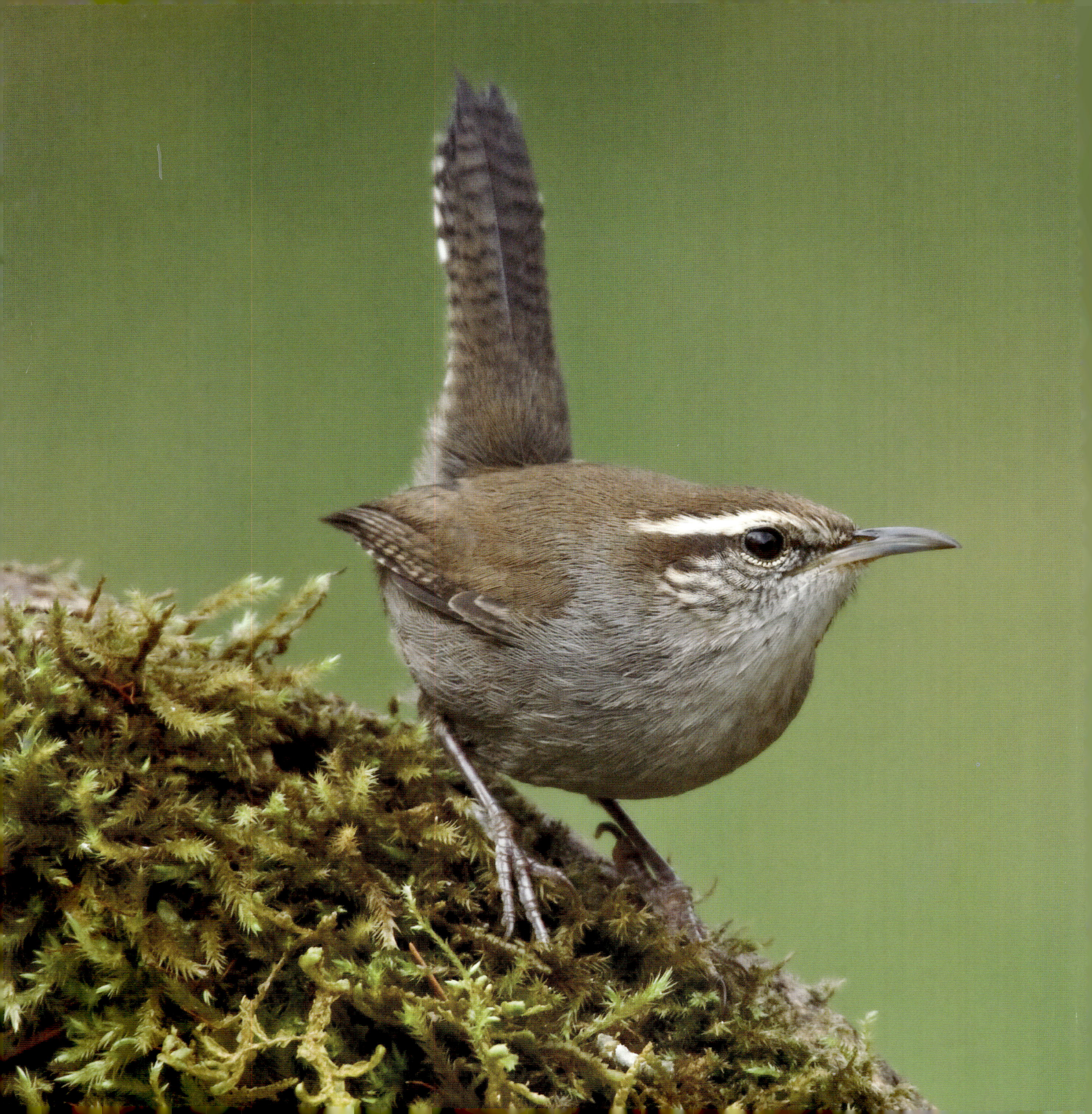

CONTENTS

Bewick's Wrens are small, expressive birds whose cheerful song can be heard throughout a variety of habitats on Vancouver Island.

REFLECTIONS ON THE BIRDS OF VANCOUVER ISLAND

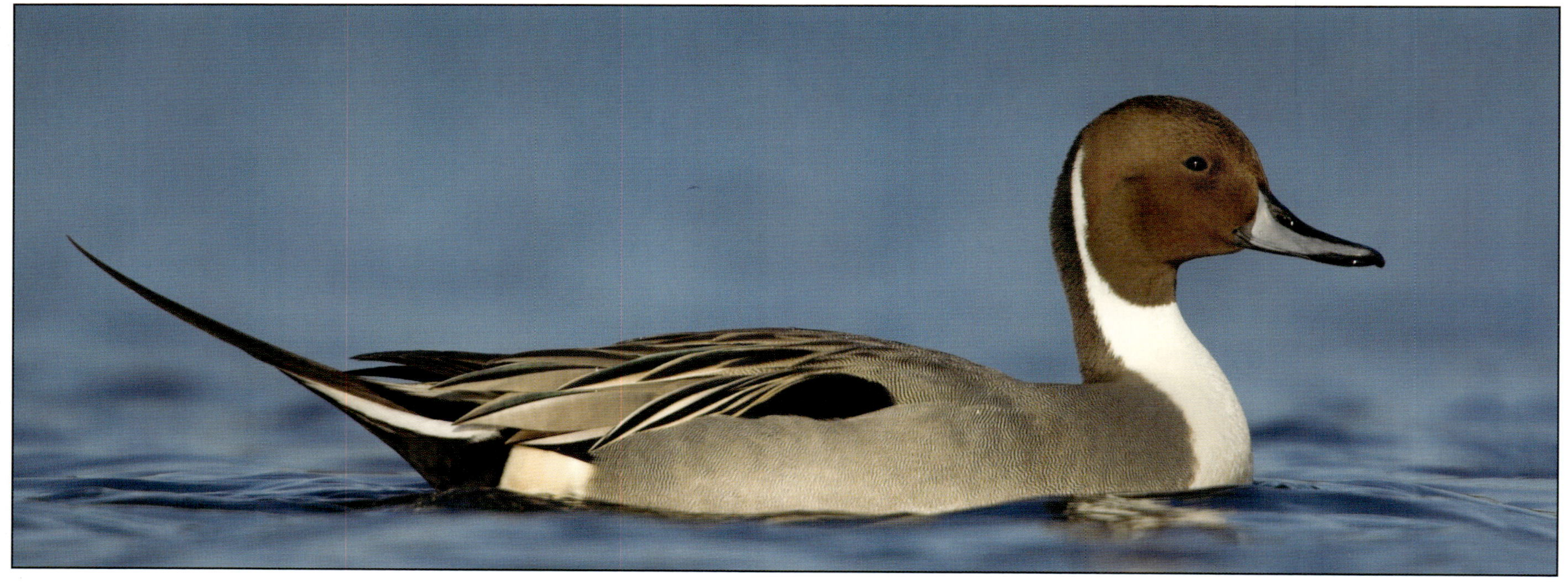

BIRDS OF THE RAINFOREST: I find myself walking down a familiar path this morning - one that leads its way through a majestic place where towering cedar and fir trees force my gaze upwards in awe. The air is damp and cool – yet the lush, mossy forest has a warm and welcoming feel to it. Off in the distance a Winter Wren is singing and, as I catch a glimpse of it, I am amazed that such a small bird can produce such an impressive song. High above, Townsend's Warblers sing to one another, proclaiming the extent of their territories and searching for mates. Approaching a small stream I watch as an American Dipper bobs up and down before eagerly jumping into the water to search for a quick meal. The persistent "tap-tap-tap" sound from a nearby tree redirects my attention towards a Red-breasted Sapsucker that is working hard for an early morning snack...

BIRDS OF THE SEA: On a clear morning in July I wake at 4:30am. A quick bite-to-eat and a short drive to the waterfront and I am on the water in my kayak by 5:30. I paddle out into the bay as the sun rises over the Olympic Mountains in the distance and the raucous sounds of Harbour Seals make it clear that there is life all around me. Twenty minutes of paddling later and I am now a few kilometres off-shore. The water is calm - as calm as I have ever seen it - and there is something about this morning that makes it feel special. In the distance I can hear gulls squawking and starting to converge in an area where bait fish are "balling up" at the surface. I race towards them to see what I can find. Glaucous-winged and Heerman's Gulls are everywhere making lots of noise and attracting even more birds from miles around. Among the new arrivals are plenty of Rhinoceros Auklets that are diving into the bait ball and emerging with their bills full of shiny silver sand lance. Pigeon Guillemots are also joining in the rapidly growing flock. The Guillemots are excitedly calling to one another revealing their brilliant vermillion colored mouths as they coordinate their attack on the helpless baitfish just inches below the surface. Just outside of this oceanic swarm of birdlife I spot two birds that seem distinctly different. Raising my binoculars to my eyes I feel a surge of adrenaline and excitement as I immediately recognize these two birds to be a gorgeous pair of Marbled Murrelets...

SONGBIRDS: Emerging at a viewpoint after a lengthy hike up the side of a mountain I look out towards the horizon. From where I now stand the towering Douglas Firs have given way to gnarled Garry Oaks. In the distance I can see an Olive-sided Flycatcher sallying up from a conspicuous open perch and snatching insects out of thin air. The trill songs of Orange-crowned Warblers ring out from the scrubby habitat that surrounds me. Just then, a flash of colour catches my eye. In the early morning sunlight the brilliance of the red and yellow plumage of this bird is beyond belief. And yet here he is: a too-beautiful-for-words male Western Tanager that I simply cannot take my eyes off...

WATERFOWL: On a warm spring afternoon I am sitting quietly next to a small sheltered pond. Reflected colours from the Yellow Dogwoods that surround the shoreline have given the water an attractive golden glow. American Widgeons, Hooded Mergansers, Wood Ducks and the ubiquitous Mallards are excitedly quacking and calling back and forth to one another. A mated pair of Northern Shovellers are swimming around and around one another as they feed by filtering water through their oversized bills. Ring-necked ducks group together in the middle of the pond and dive for food over and over again. Before long, a gorgeous male Bufflehead swims by showing off his brilliant white flanks and rainbow coloured head...

SHOREBIRDS: The inter-tidal zone along the coast of Vancouver Island always seems to be teeming with life. Low tide exposes resources to birds who flock to these areas to feed. Among my favourite are the Black Oystercatchers whose raucous calls announce their presence from far off. I love watching them as they work their way along the shoreline picking off chitons and mollusks from the rocks that low tide has recently uncovered. Nearby, a small group of Black Turnstones and Surfbirds are also picking their way along the seaweed covered rocks. When a large Gull flies over, one of the birds becomes wary and flies off. All of his companions follow close behind; calling as they select a safer area to feed...

BIRDS OF PREY: It is fall now. The long days of the summer months are beginning to fade away and, for me, the seasonal transition is accentuated by the abundance of migratory shorebirds heading south. As I walk along the oceanfront towards a large group of shorebirds they erupt into flight. Even before I see it, I know what must be nearby. Before I can appreciate what I am witnessing a Merlin has snatched a Short-billed Dowitcher from mid-air. I watch as this efficient predator devours the smaller bird and am captivated by the beauty and ferocity of Mother Nature...

BACKYARD BIRDS: Returning home from a fine day in the field I glance out the window to see the hummingbird feeder buzzing with activity. Anna's and Rufous Hummingbirds compete for their sought-after supply of nectar and whiz through the air with a speed and precision that mesmerizes me. Looking beyond the window and into the backyard I see a group of birds busily feeding. The Juncos, Chickadees, Sparrows and Towhees may have individual intentions – but when a Cooper's Hawk appears from nowhere to try for an easy meal it becomes clear that these birds are indeed working together...

These brief reflections represent but a few of my memories of the beautiful birds of Vancouver Island. Over the past four years I have spent as much time as possible out in nature finding and photographing birds. I feel fortunate to have been able to see such wonderful creatures, and even more so to be able to share the memories of these treasured birds in this book. I hope that you will enjoy "The Birds of Vancouver Island".

All the best!

Glenn Bartley, 2010

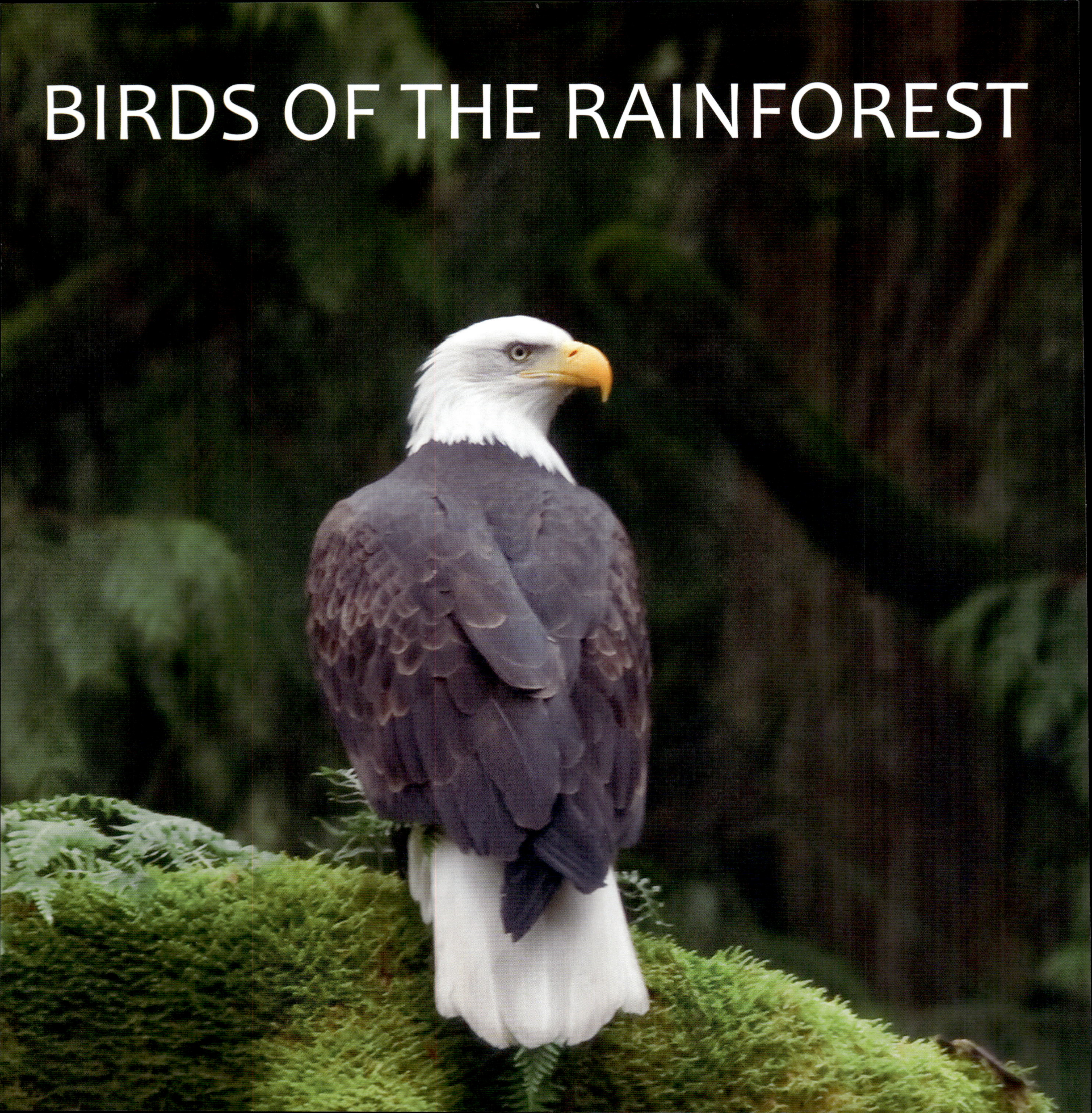
BIRDS OF THE RAINFOREST

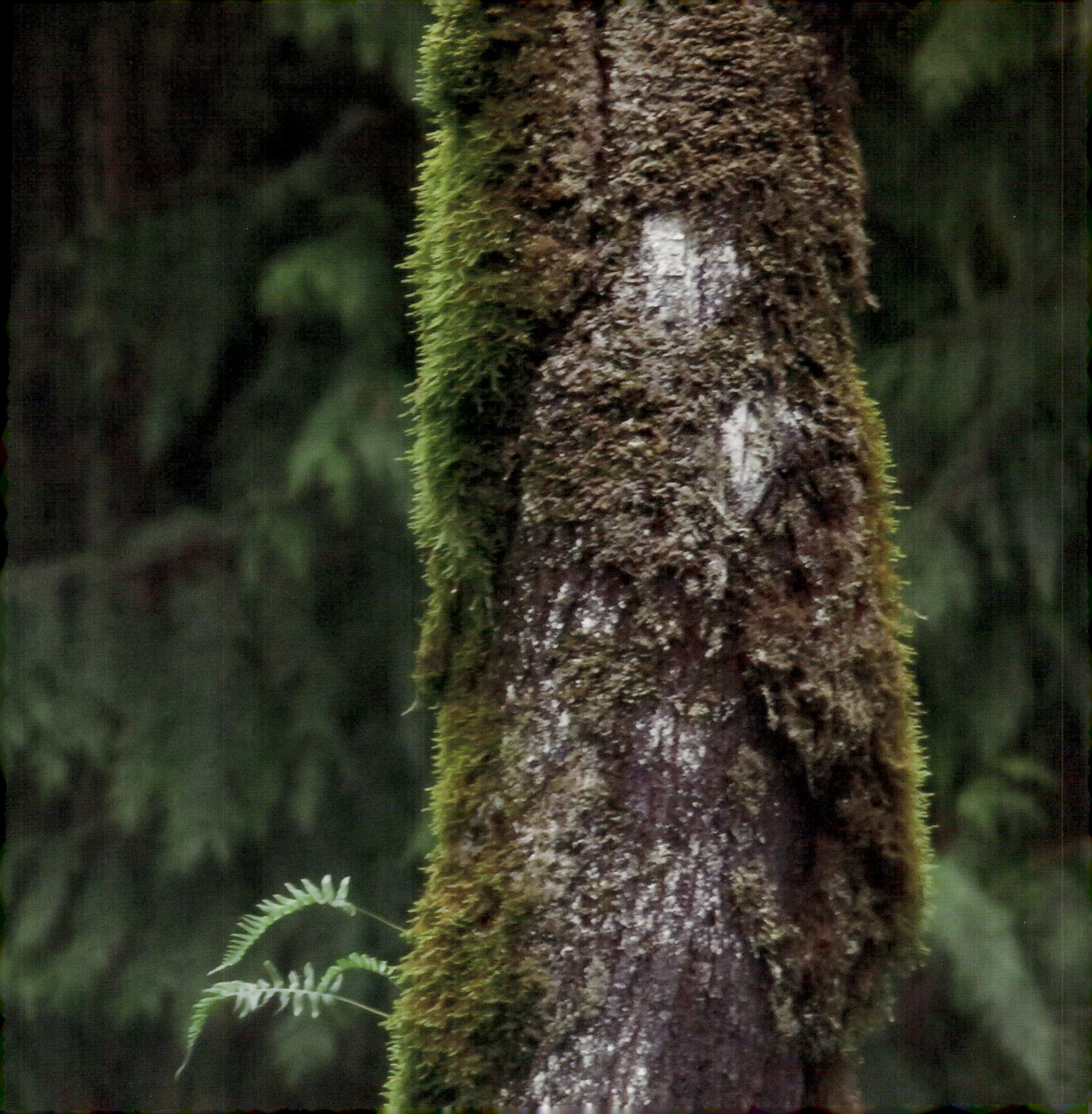

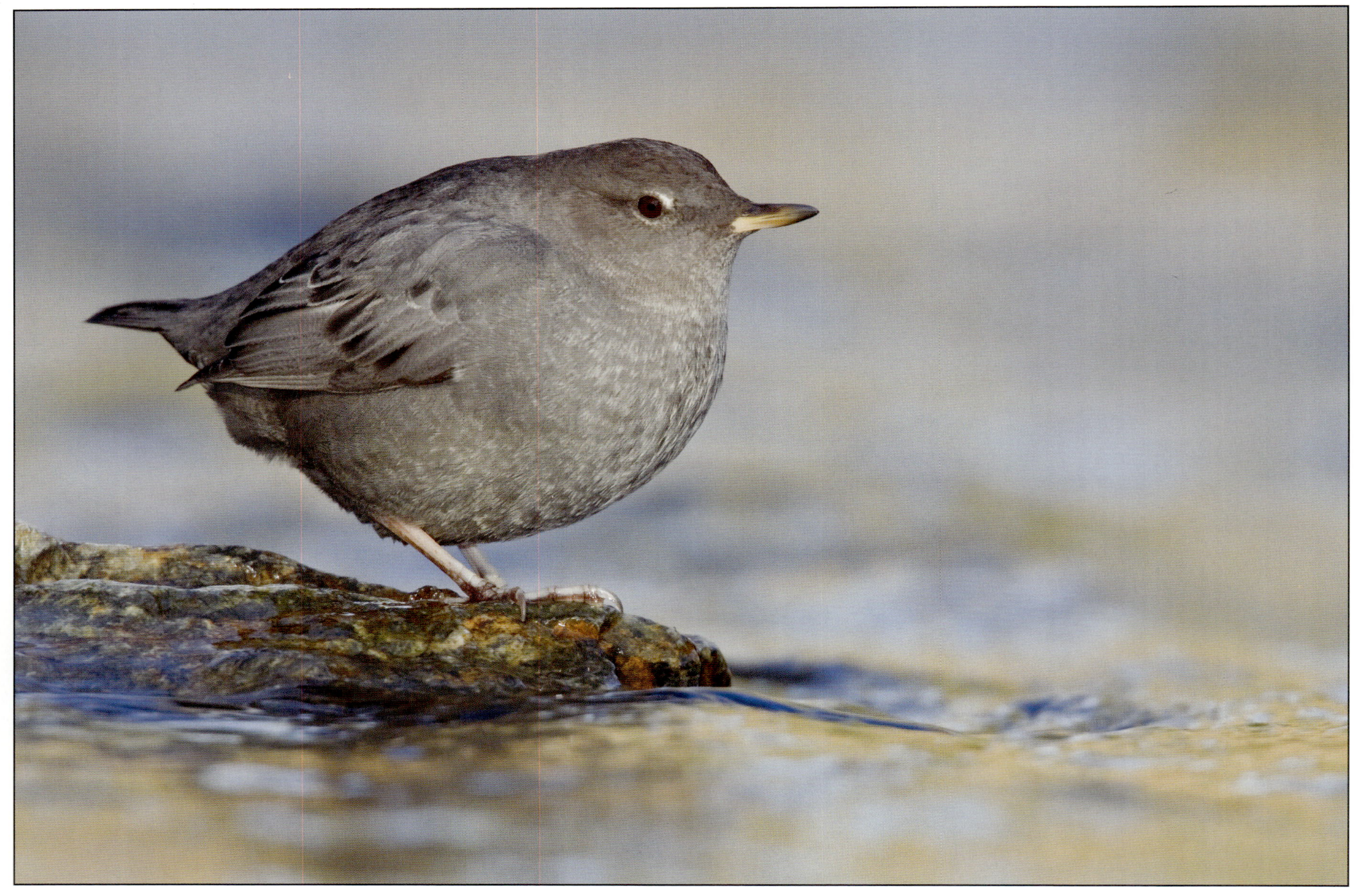

The highly aquatic American Dipper can be found patrolling small streams in the rainforest where it dips and dives into the water in search of food such as salmon eggs and aquatic invertebrates.

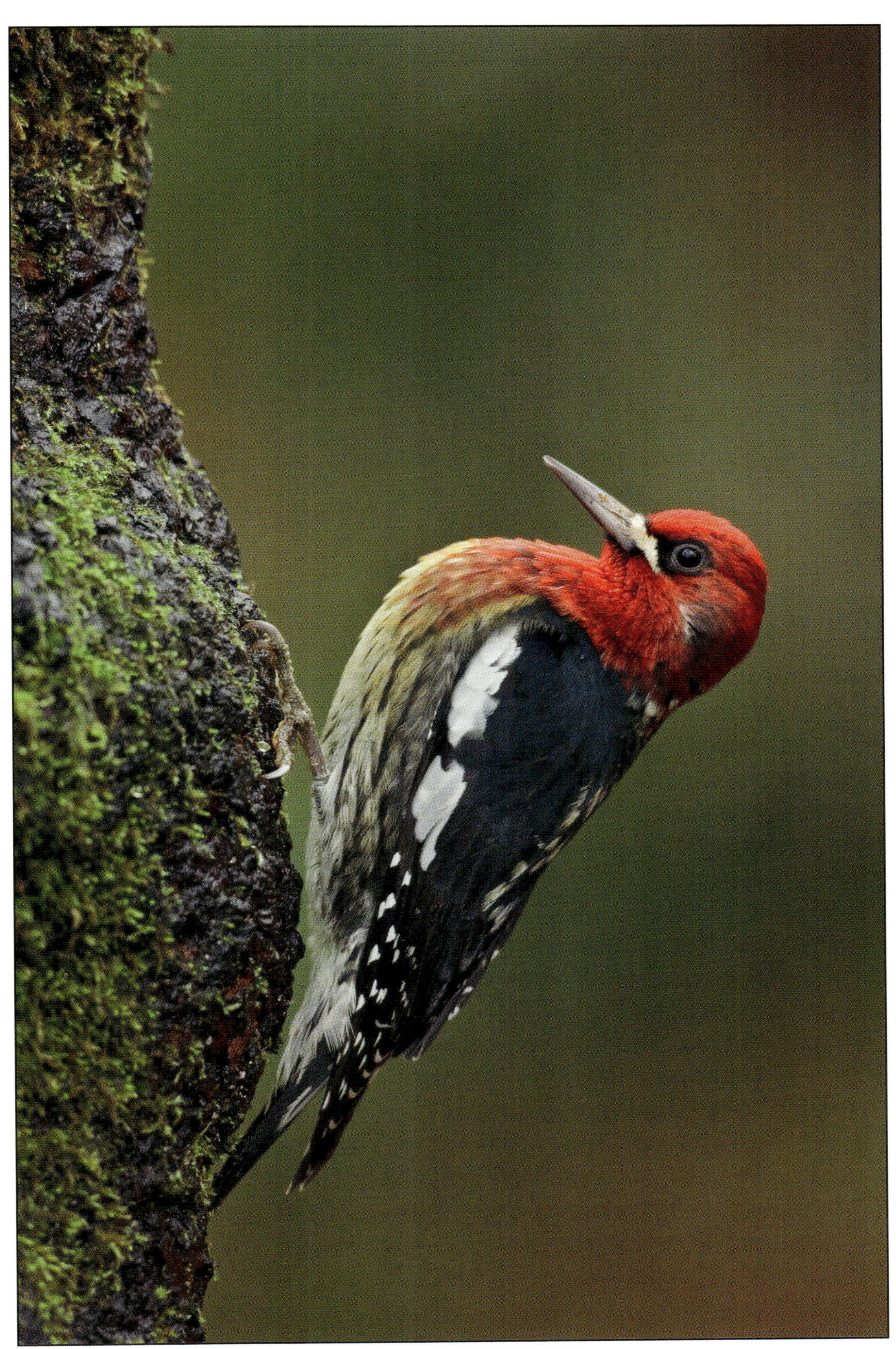

The beautiful red plumage of Red-breasted Sapsuckers can be seen in flashes as they tap-tap-tap their way around trees and devour the sap that oozes from the holes they create.

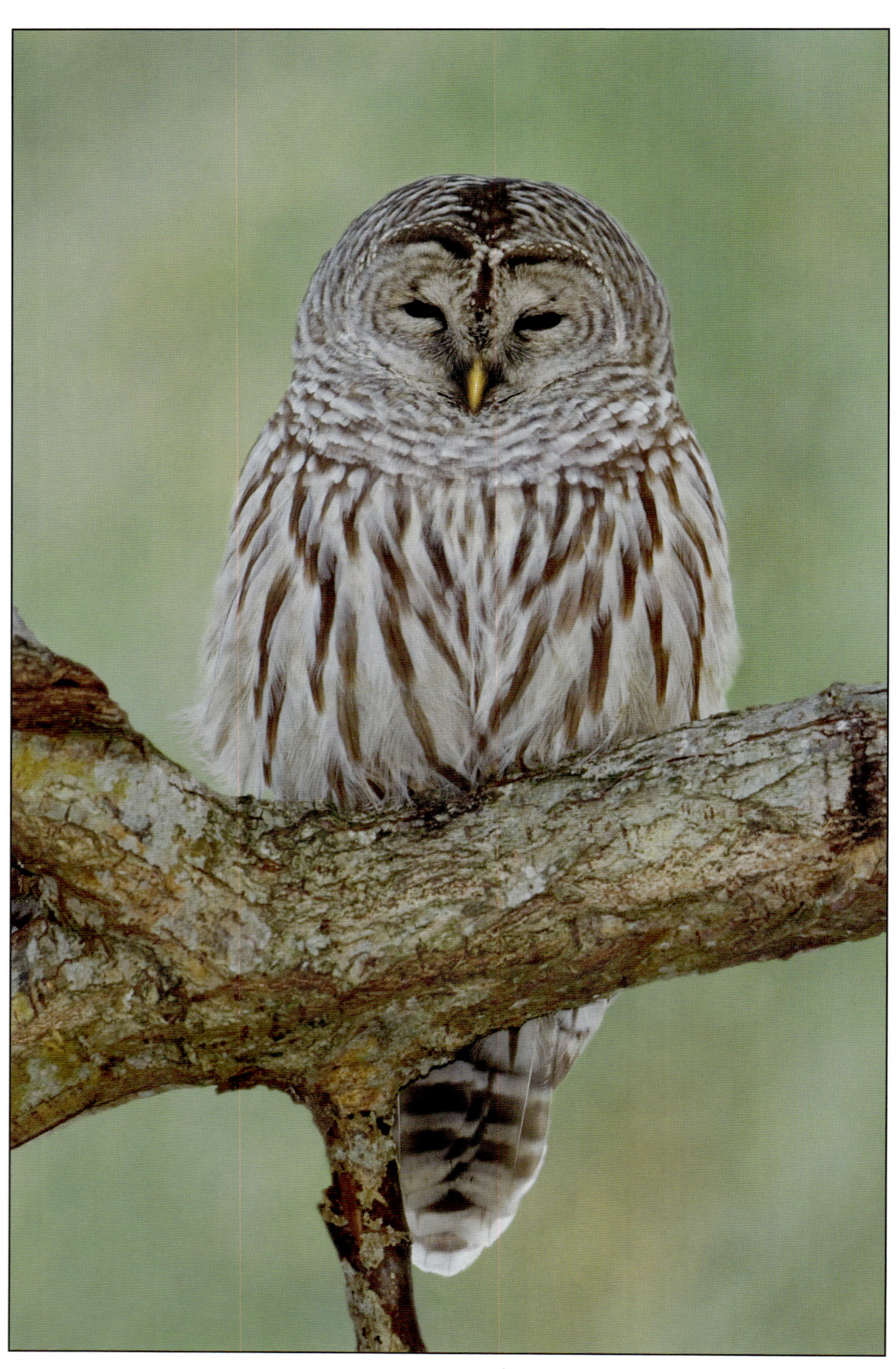

A sleepy looking Barred Owl roosts during the day before becoming a silent but deadly hunter each night.

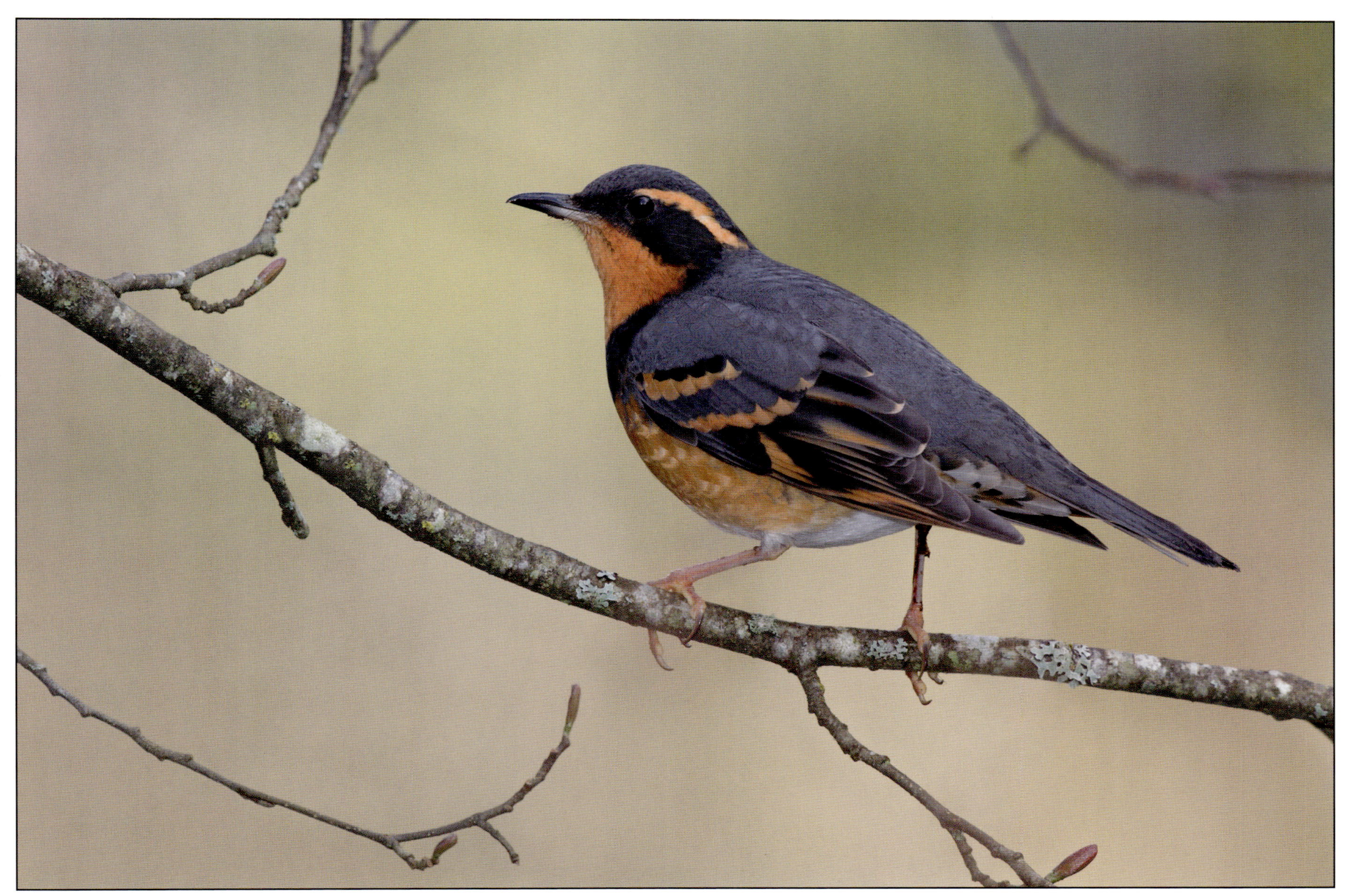

The Varied Thrush is a shy and often solitary bird whose long metallic song rings out through the rainforest in spring.

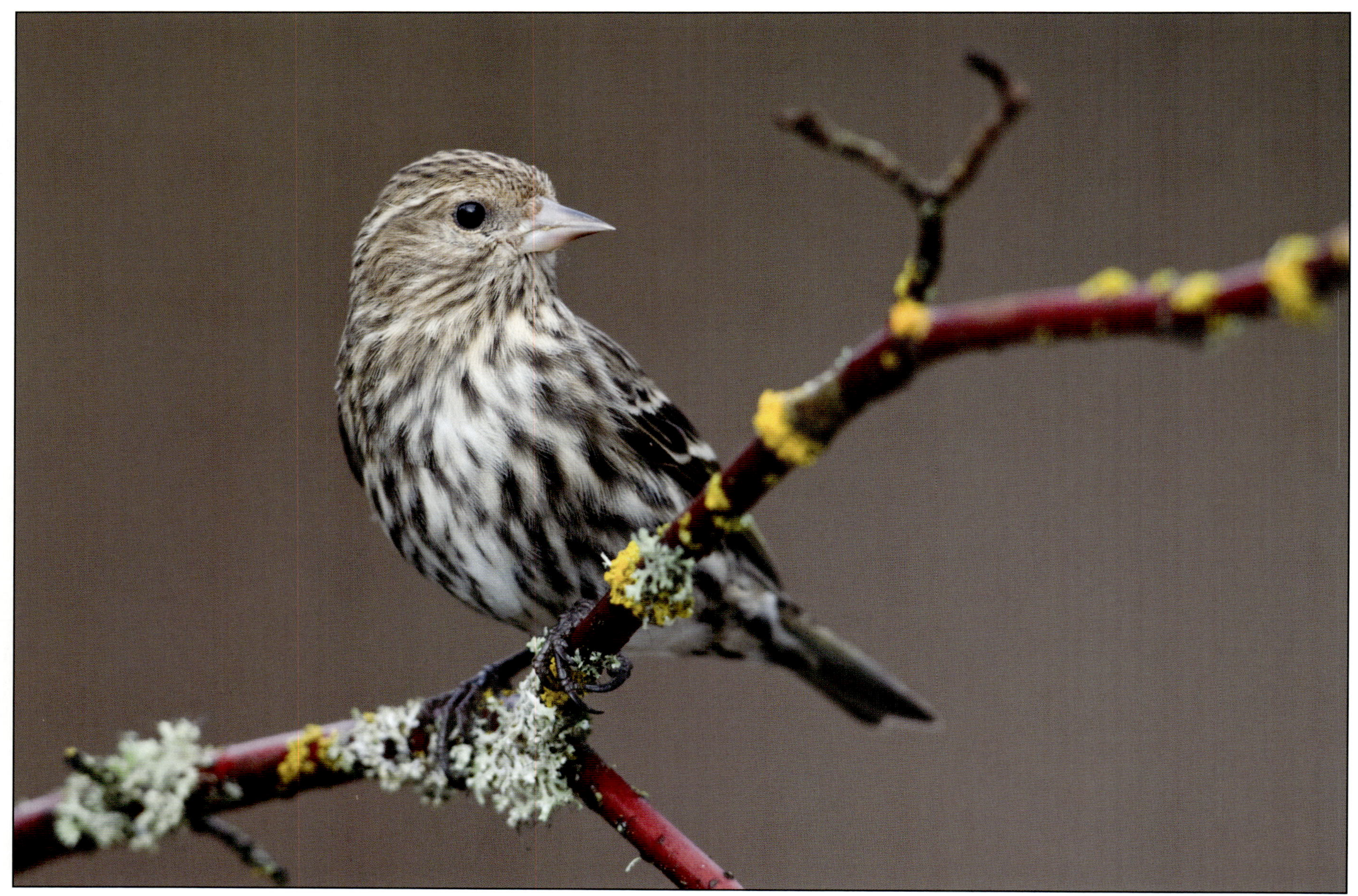

Almost always encountered in large flocks, the Pine Siskin inhabits the upper realms of the forest canopy.

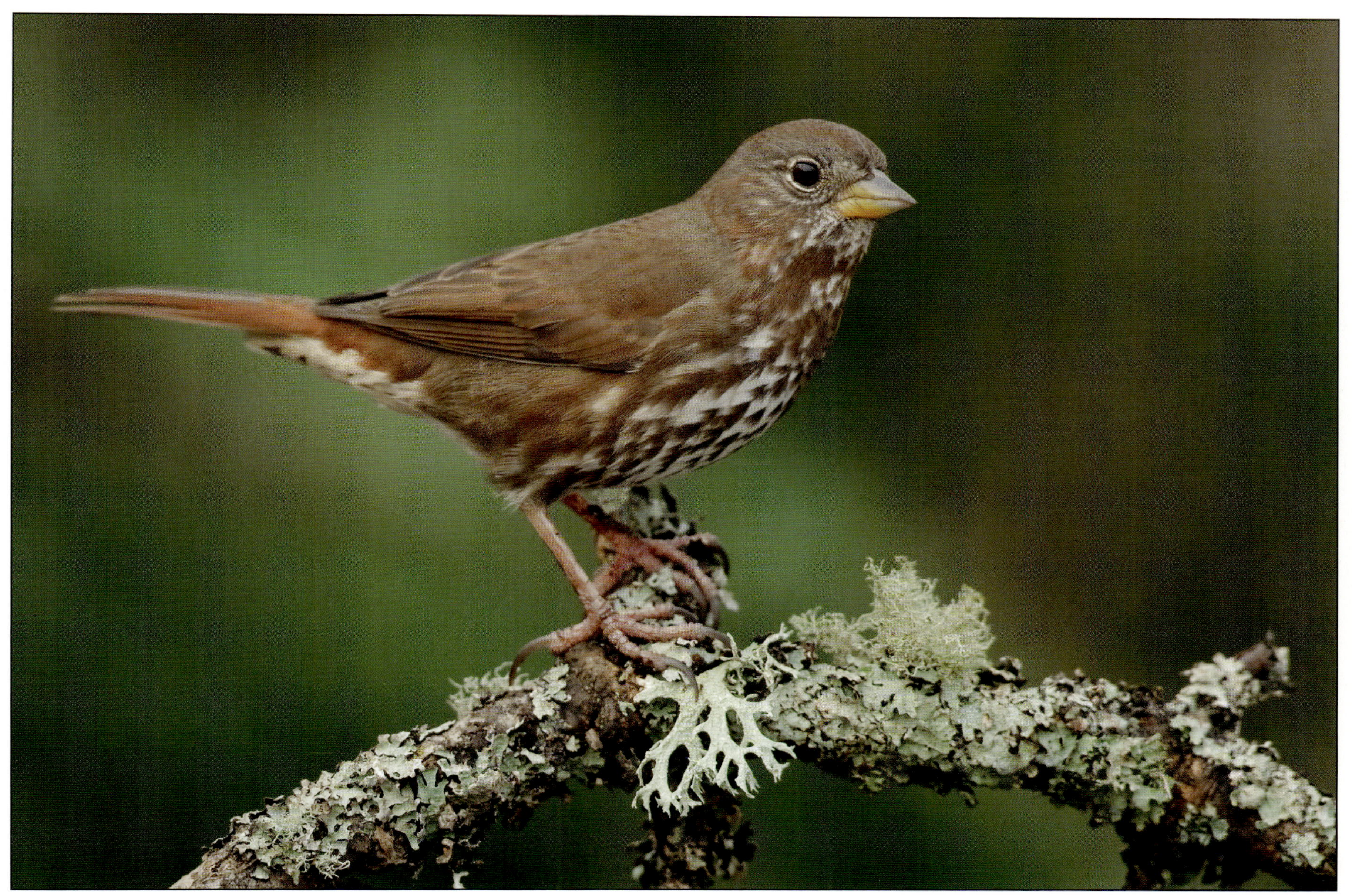

A handsome red Fox Sparrow perches atop a lichen covered branch. This species is highly variable in appearance across North America.

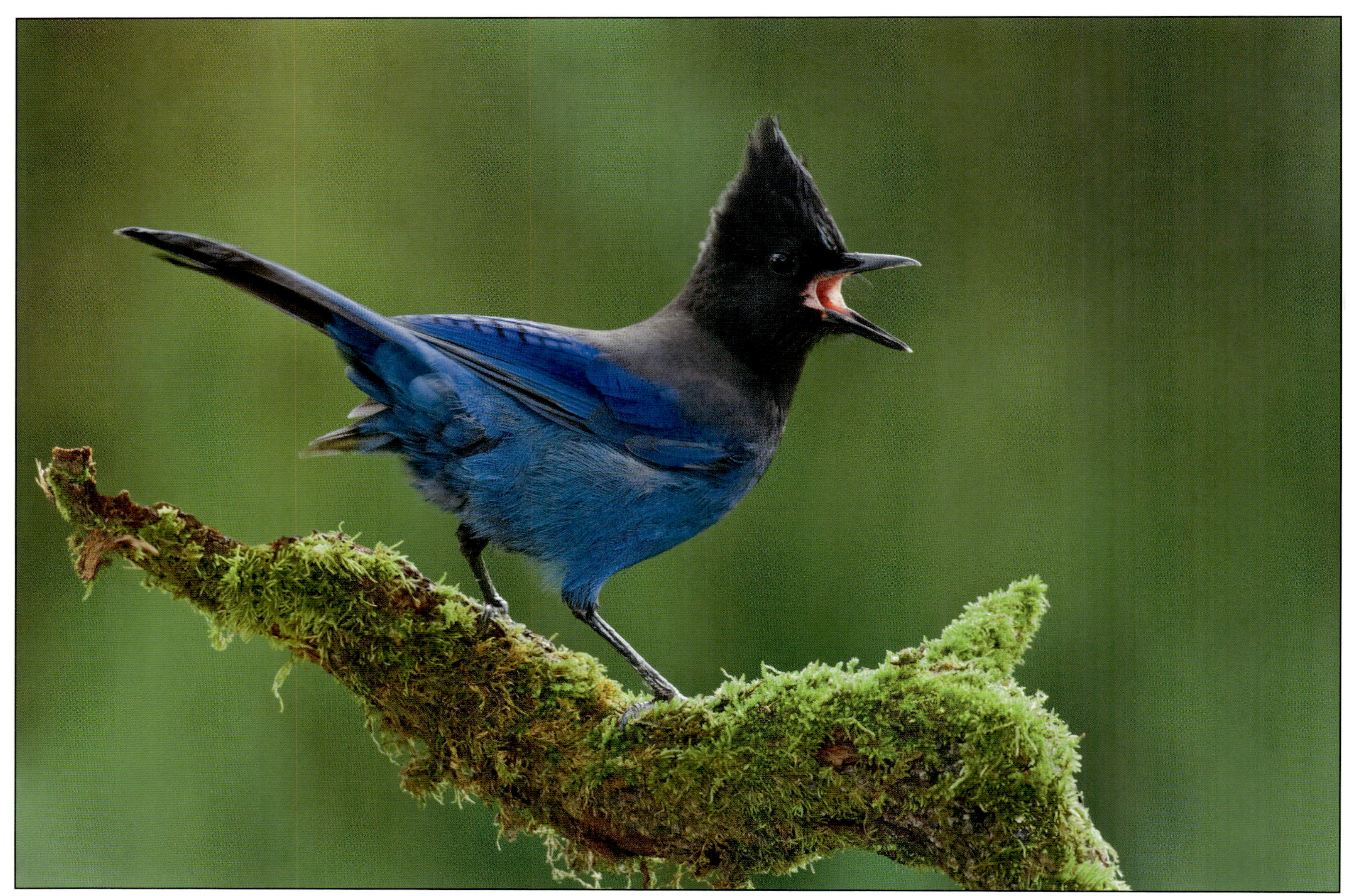

A curious and often "cheeky" bird, the Steller's Jay is easily identified by its intense blue colour or by its raucous calls.

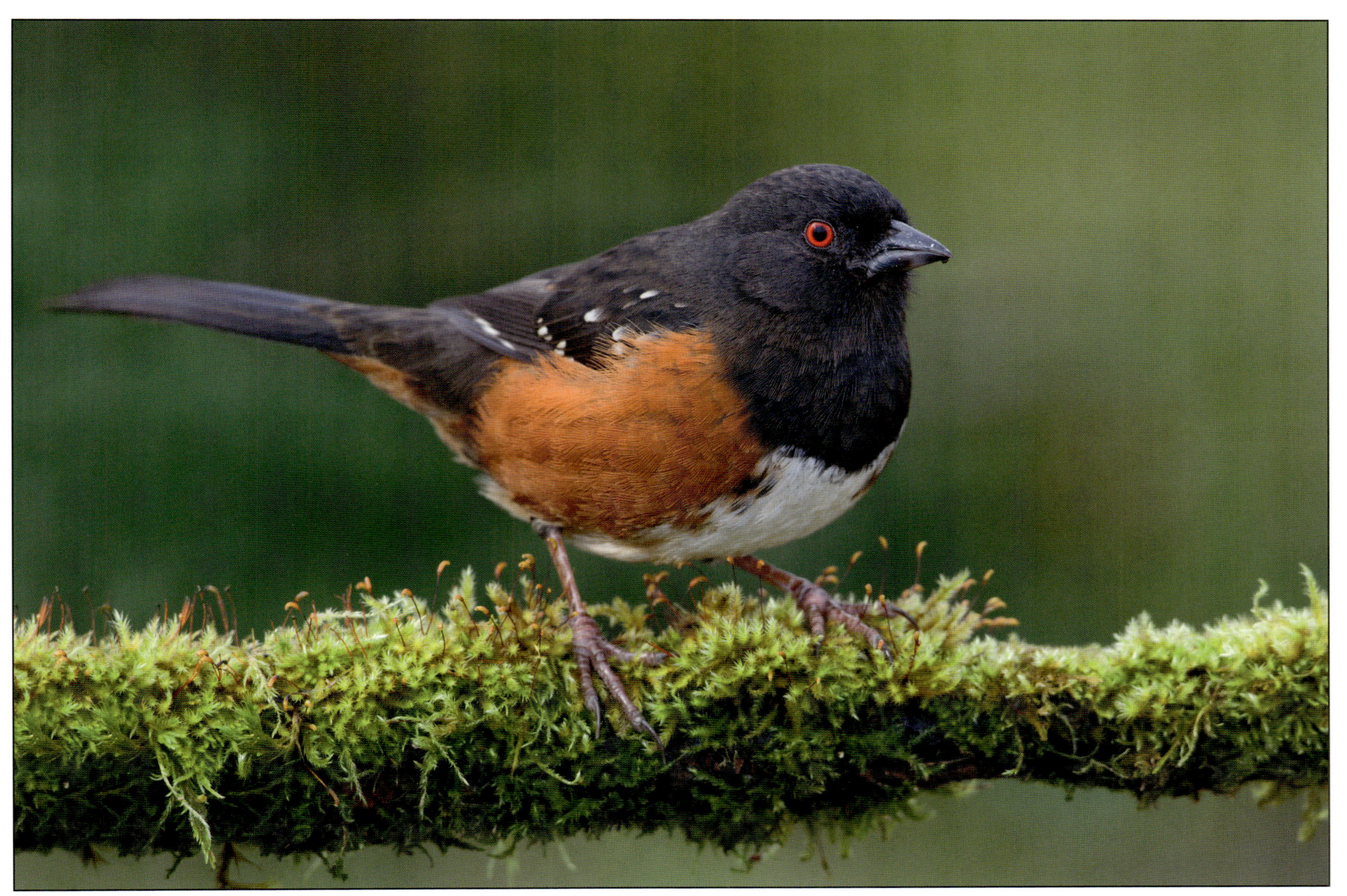

A Spotted Towhee freezes on a mossy branch before scurrying back into a thicket.

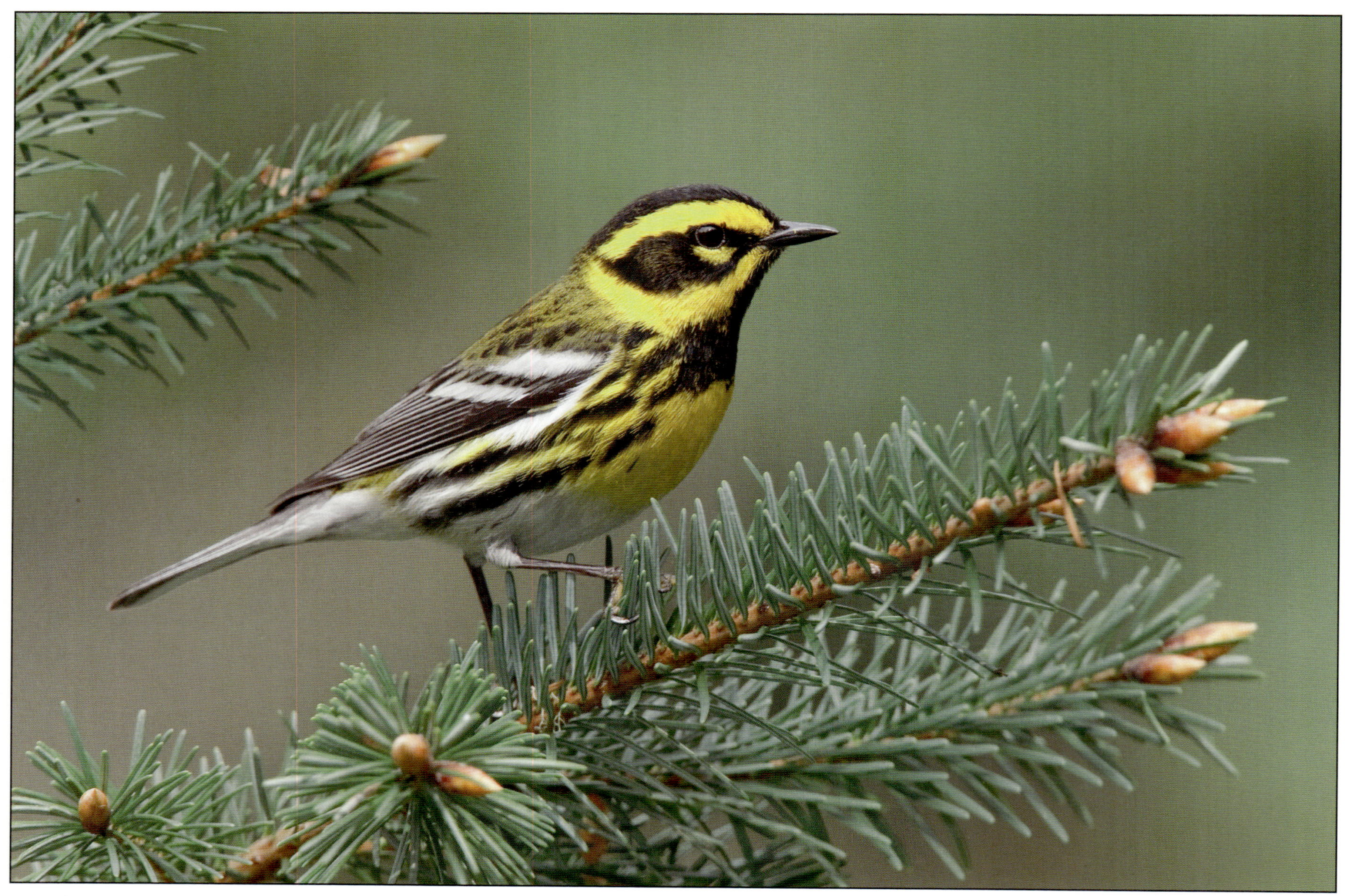

A male Townsend's Warbler poses momentarily upon a low-hanging branch before returning to the upper realms of its Douglas Fir oasis.

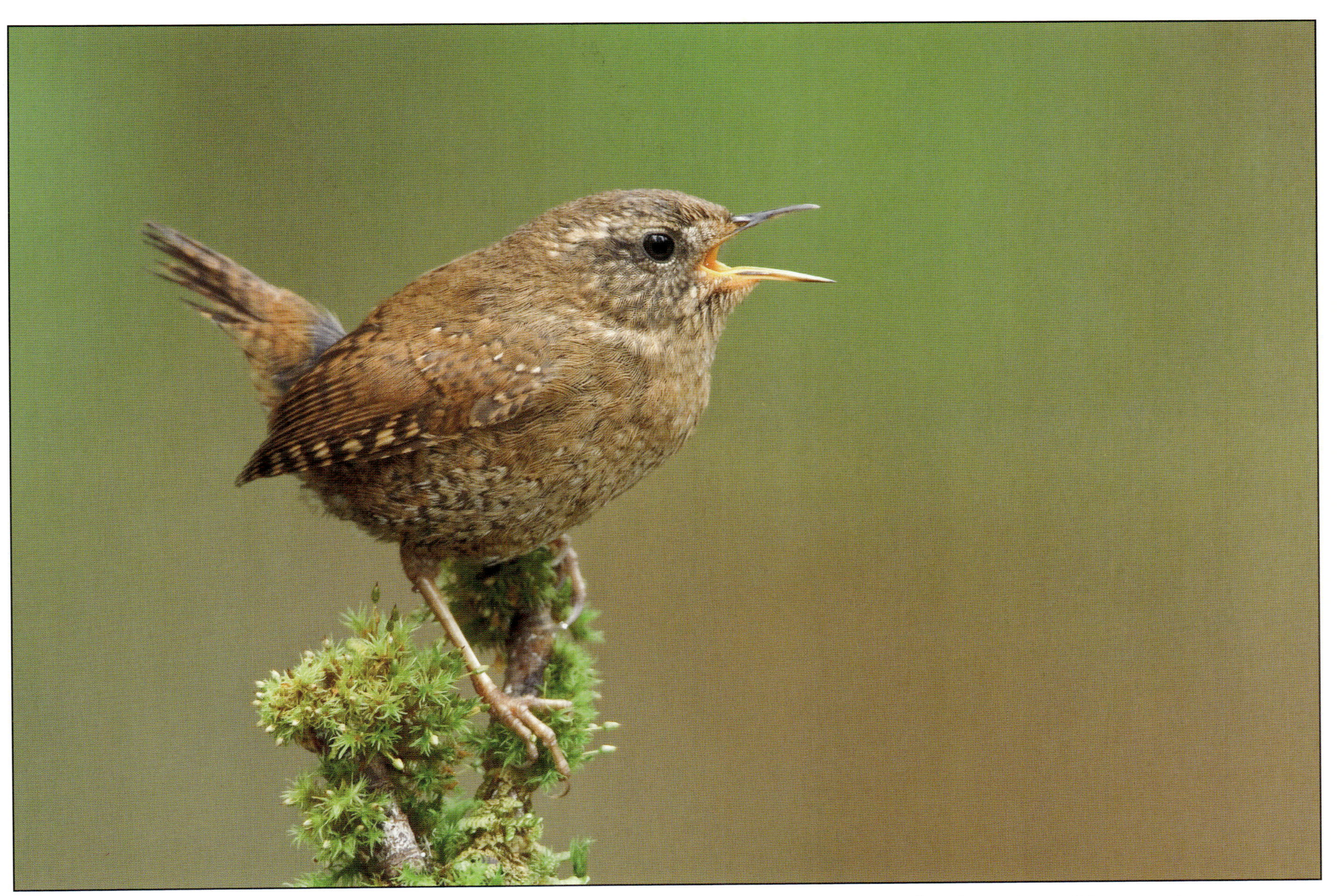

The tiny Winter Wren produces an impressively loud and lengthy song.

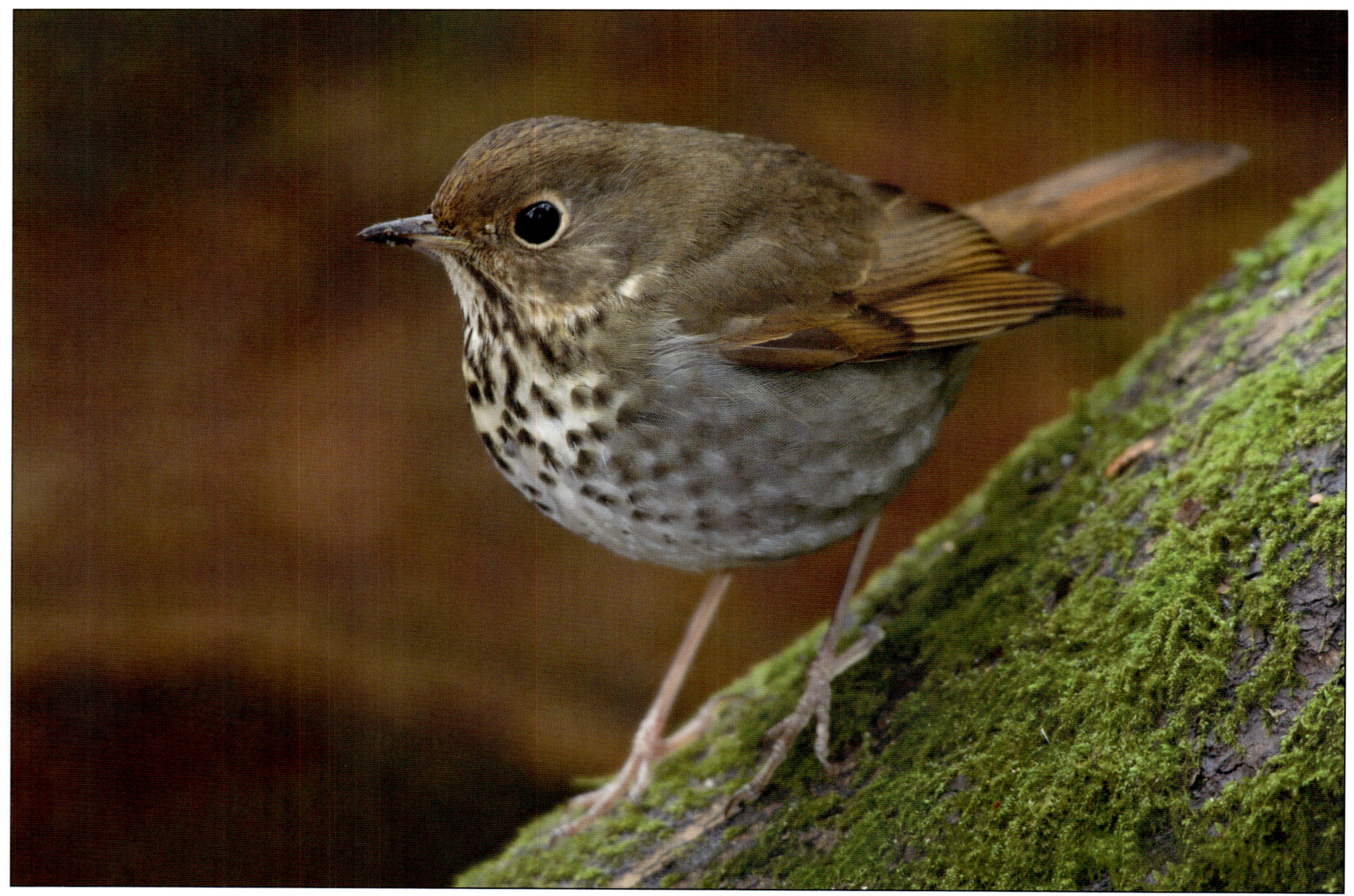

A shy Hermit Thrush poses for a photo and then quickly zips back into the understorey of its rainforest haven.

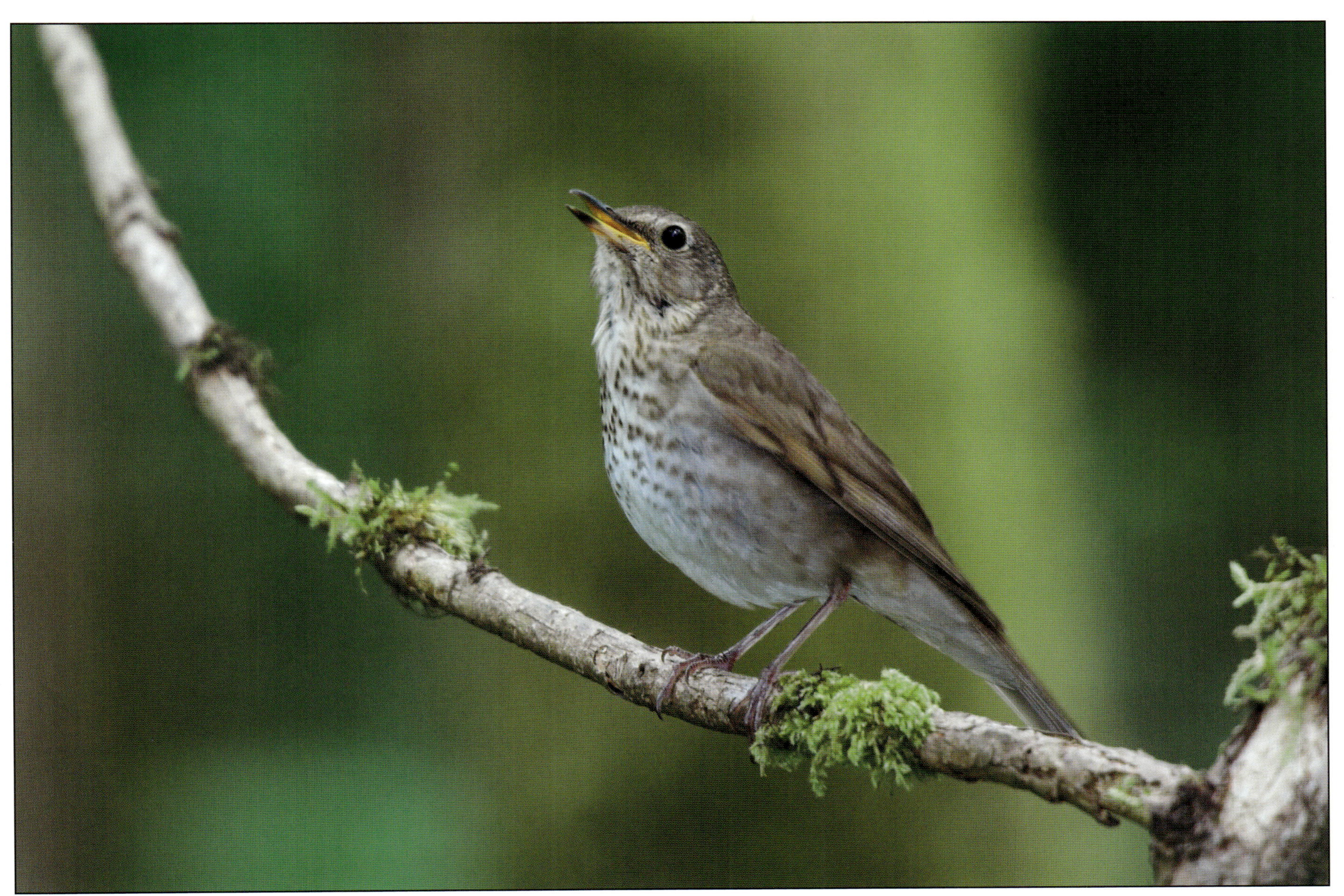

Some First Nation groups on Vancouver Island call the Swainson's Thrush the "salmonberry bird" because it sings its song during the time when the berries ripen.

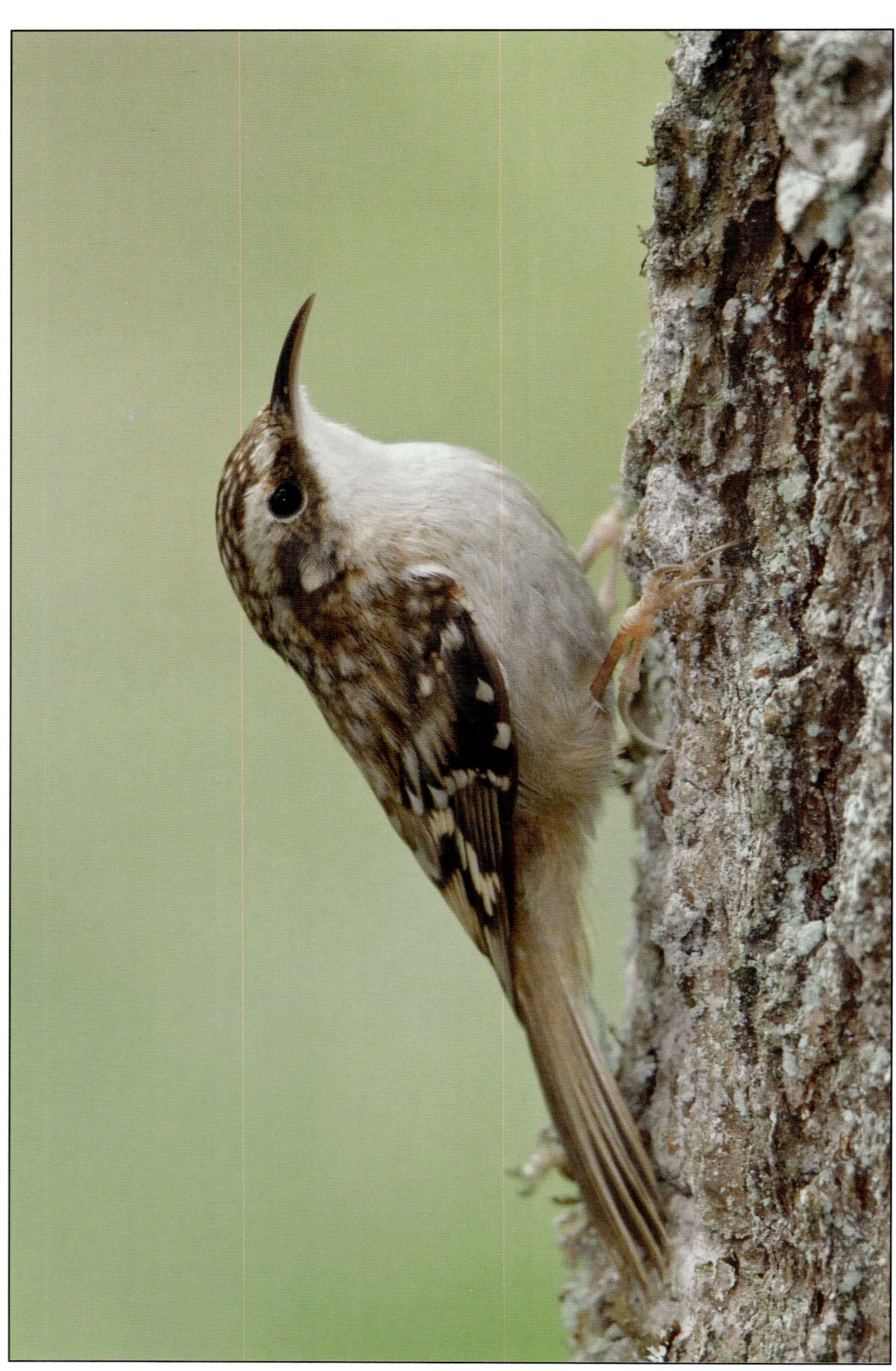

Blending in with the trees on which it lives, the Brown Creeper is most often seen spiraling its way up trees in search of insects , spiders and other food.

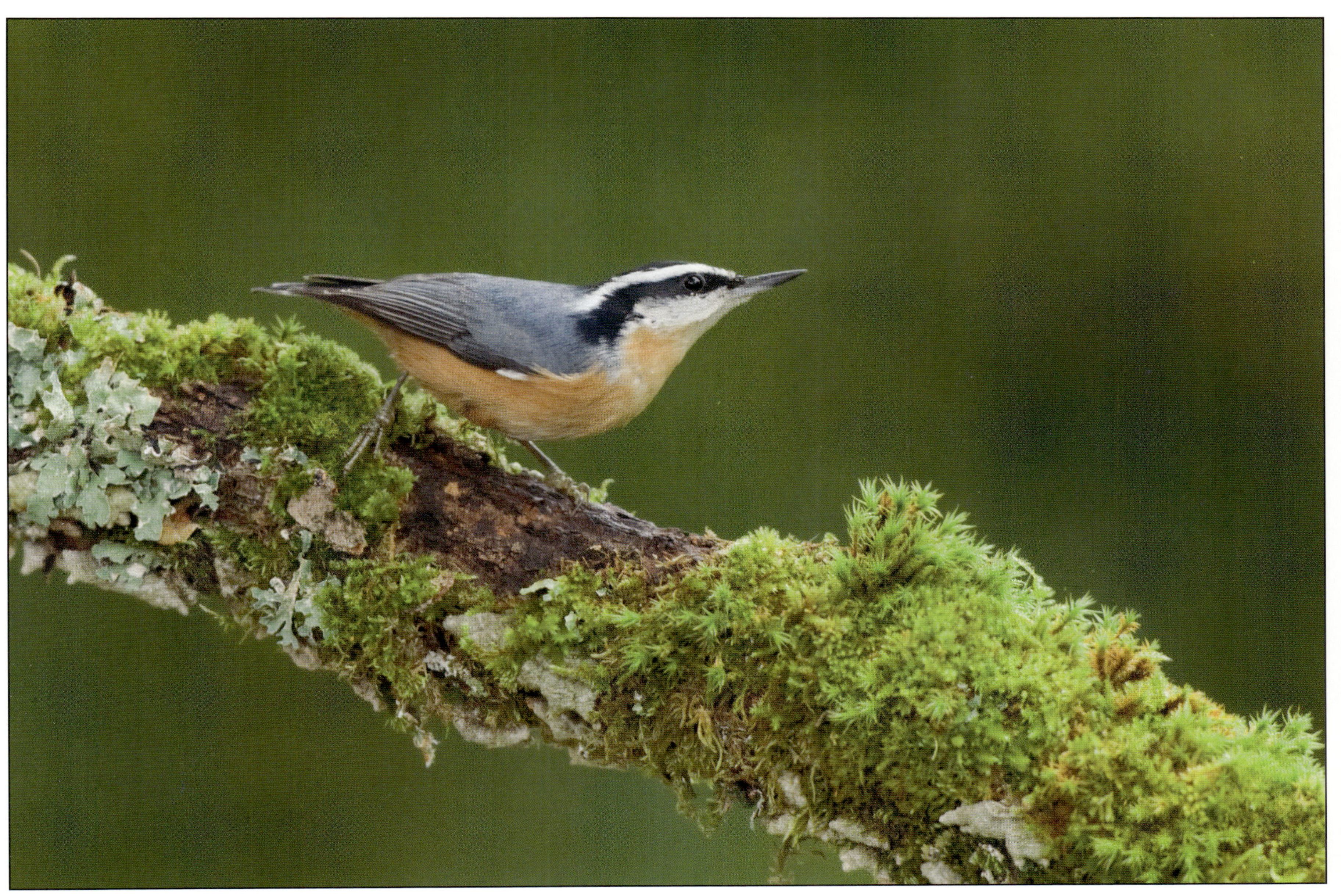

Unlike the Brown Creeper which works its way up the tree, the Red-breasted Nuthatch works its way from top to bottom finding food that other birds are likely to miss.

BIRDS OF THE OCEAN

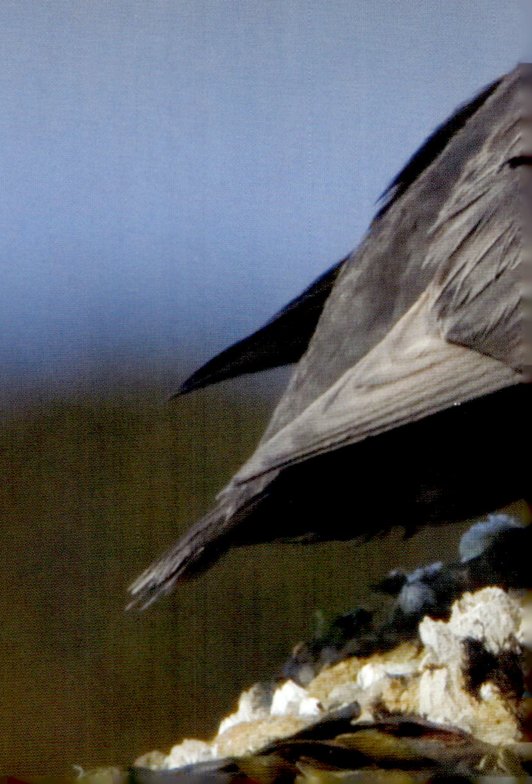

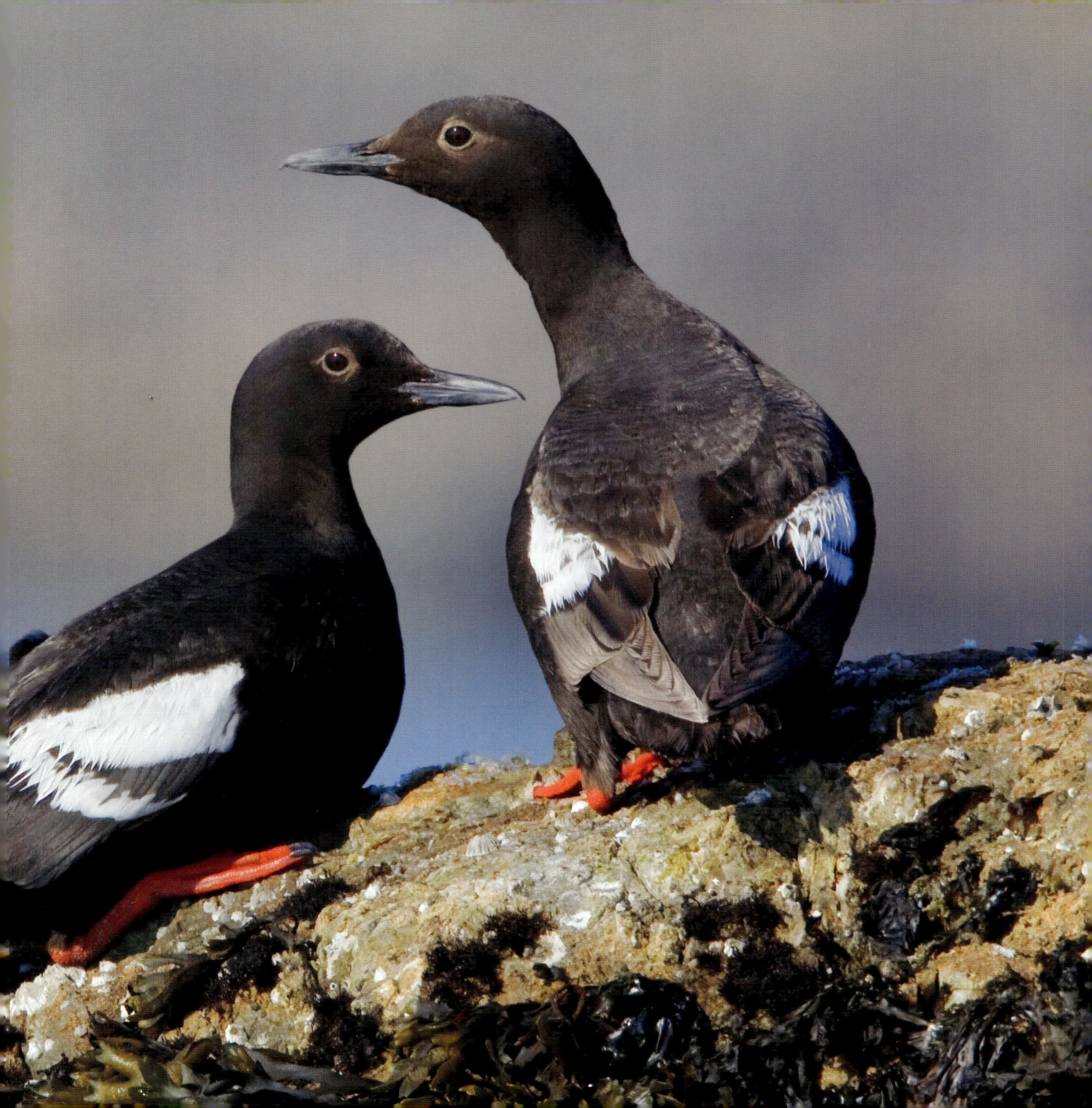

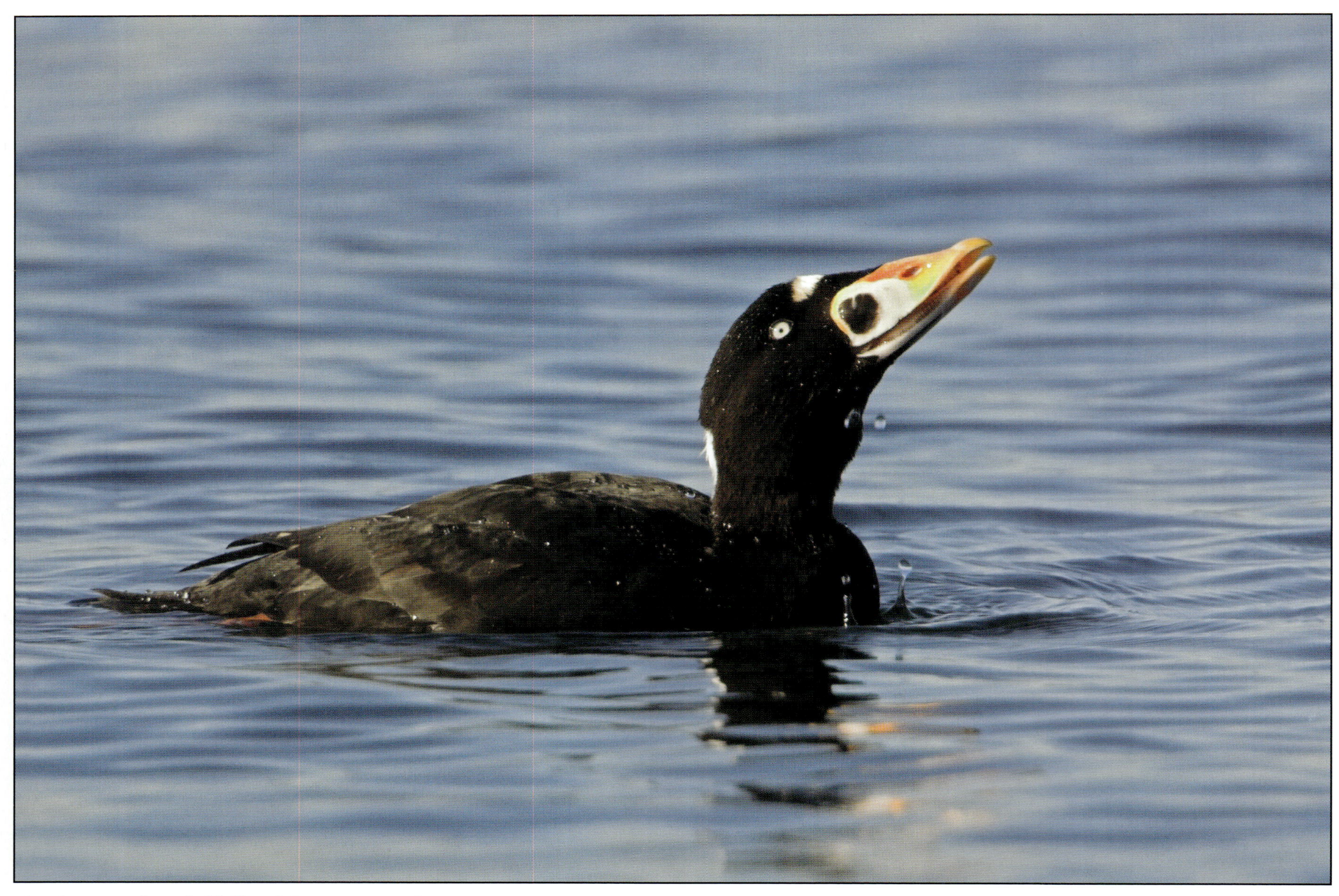

The large colourful bill, white nape and white eye of the Surf Scoter make it easily identifiable as it inspects offshore waters around Vancouver Island.

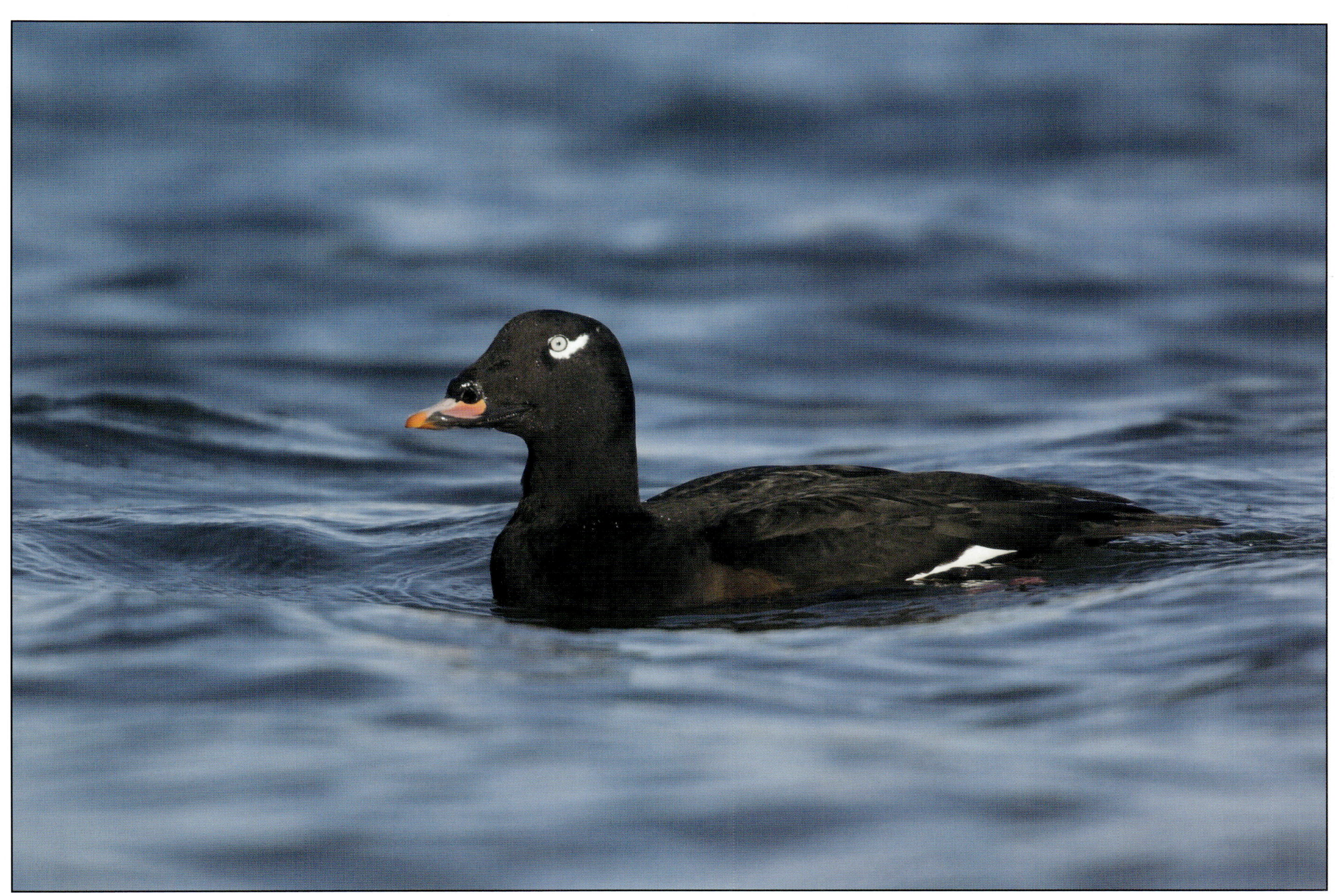

Another species of Scoter is the White-winged Scoter. These birds can be seen all along the coast of Vancouver Island where they dive for mollusks along the ocean floor.

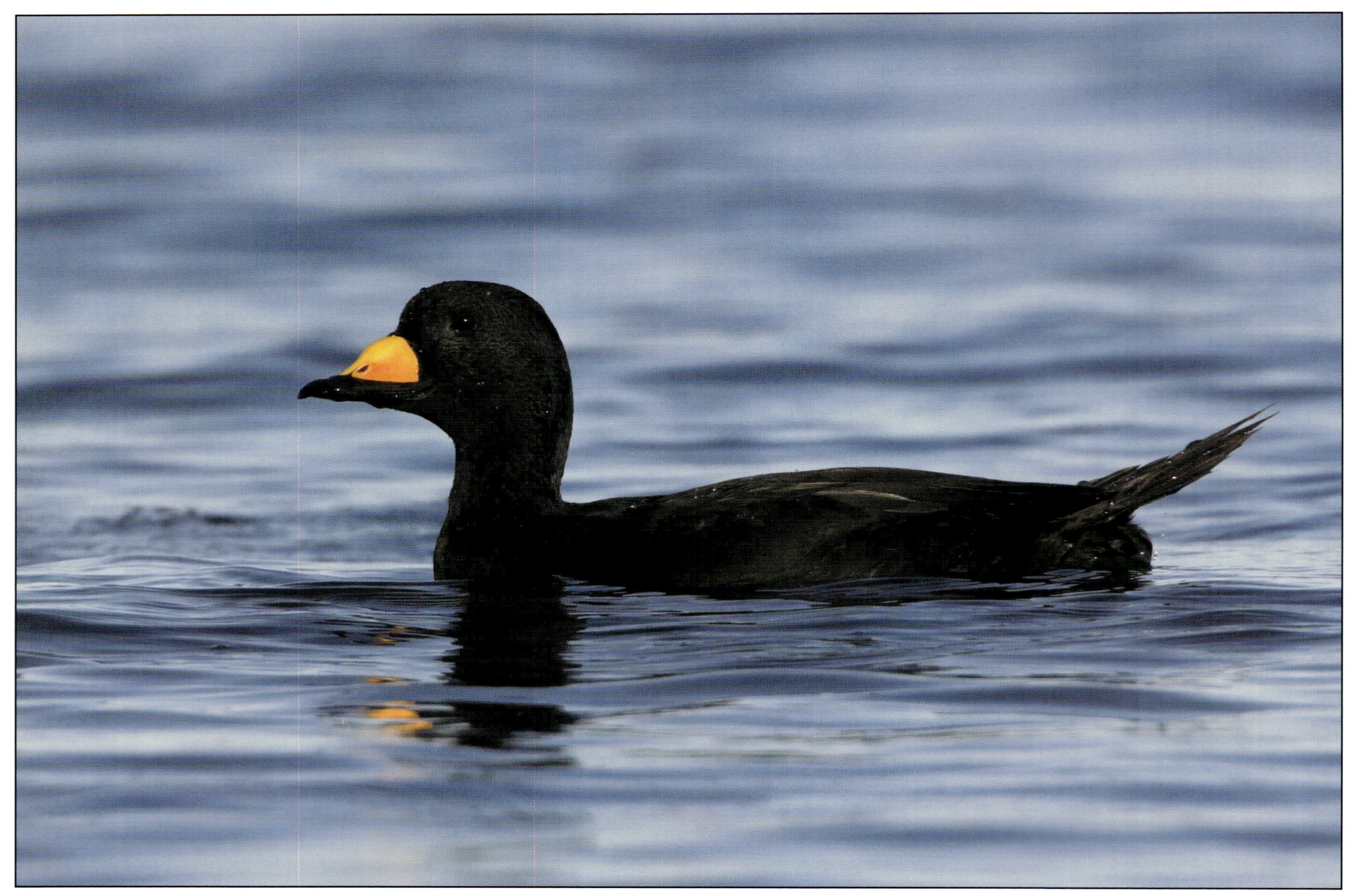

The Black Scoter is easily distinguished from other scoter species by its bright yellow nose and crisp black plumage.

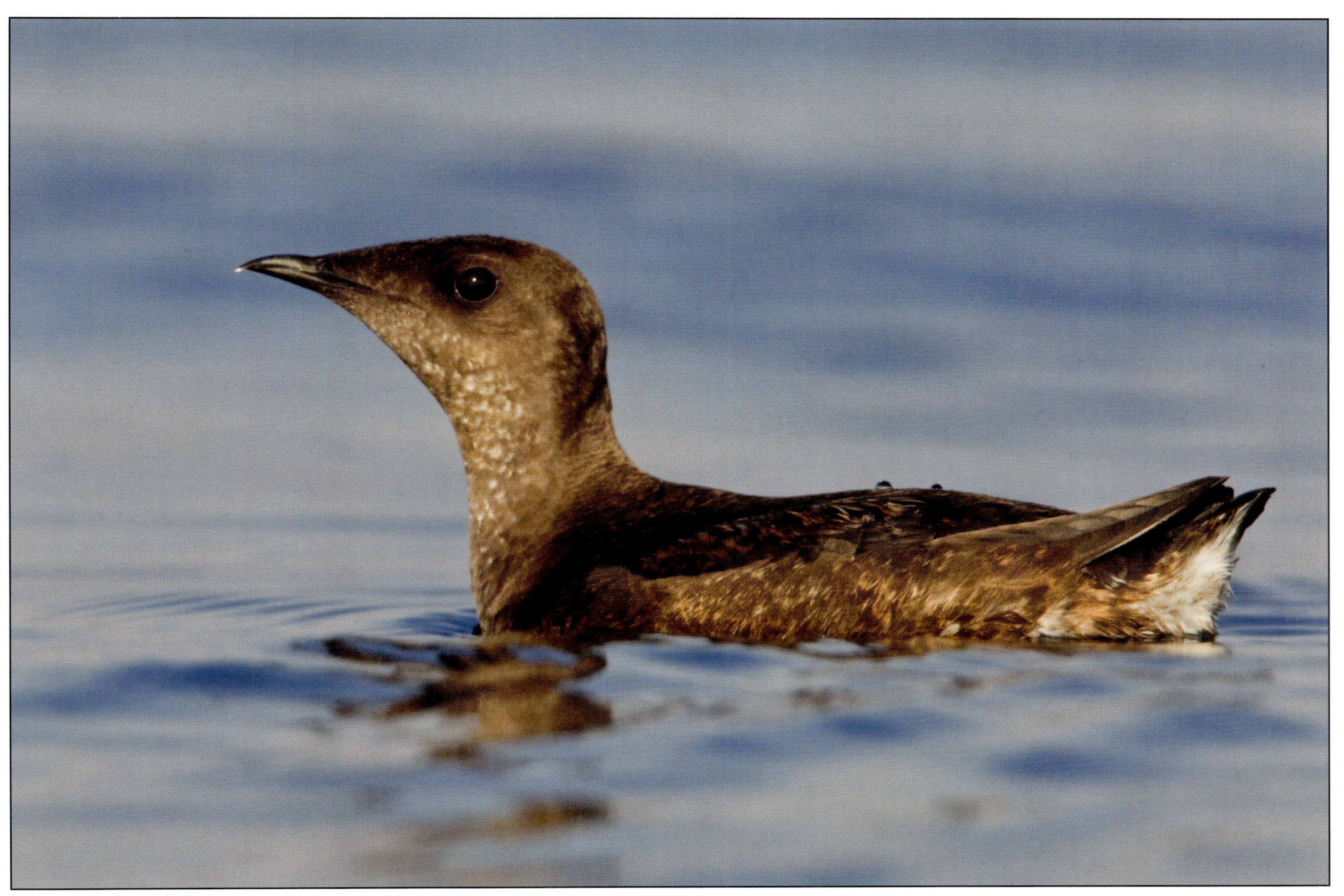

The Marbled Murrelet feeds at sea before retreating to its old-growth forest nest sites for the night. They are the only species of seabird known to nest in trees.

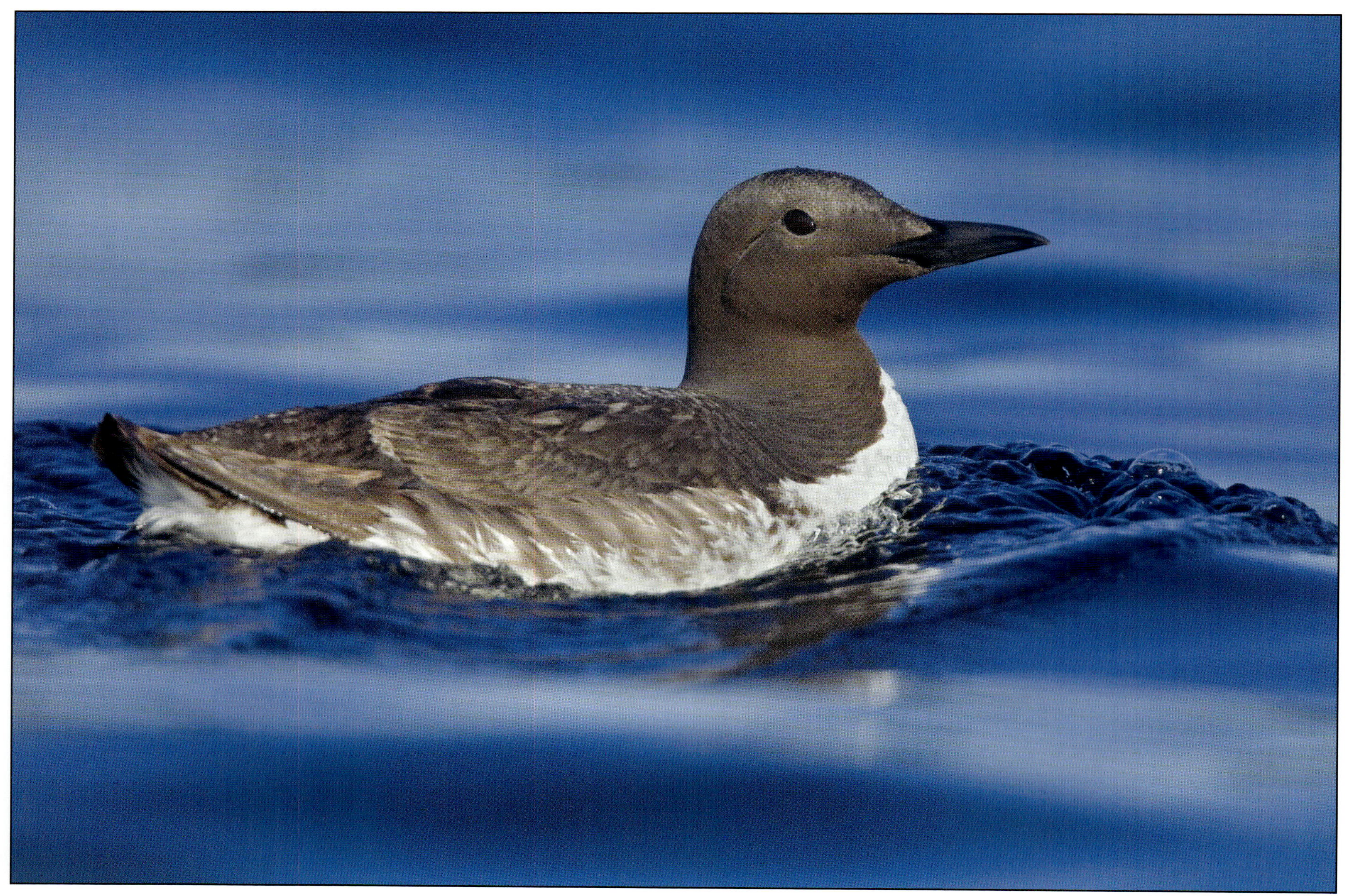

A handsome Common Murre in breeding plumage in the Juan de Fuca Strait. These birds can dive to incredible depths of over 150 metres in search of food.

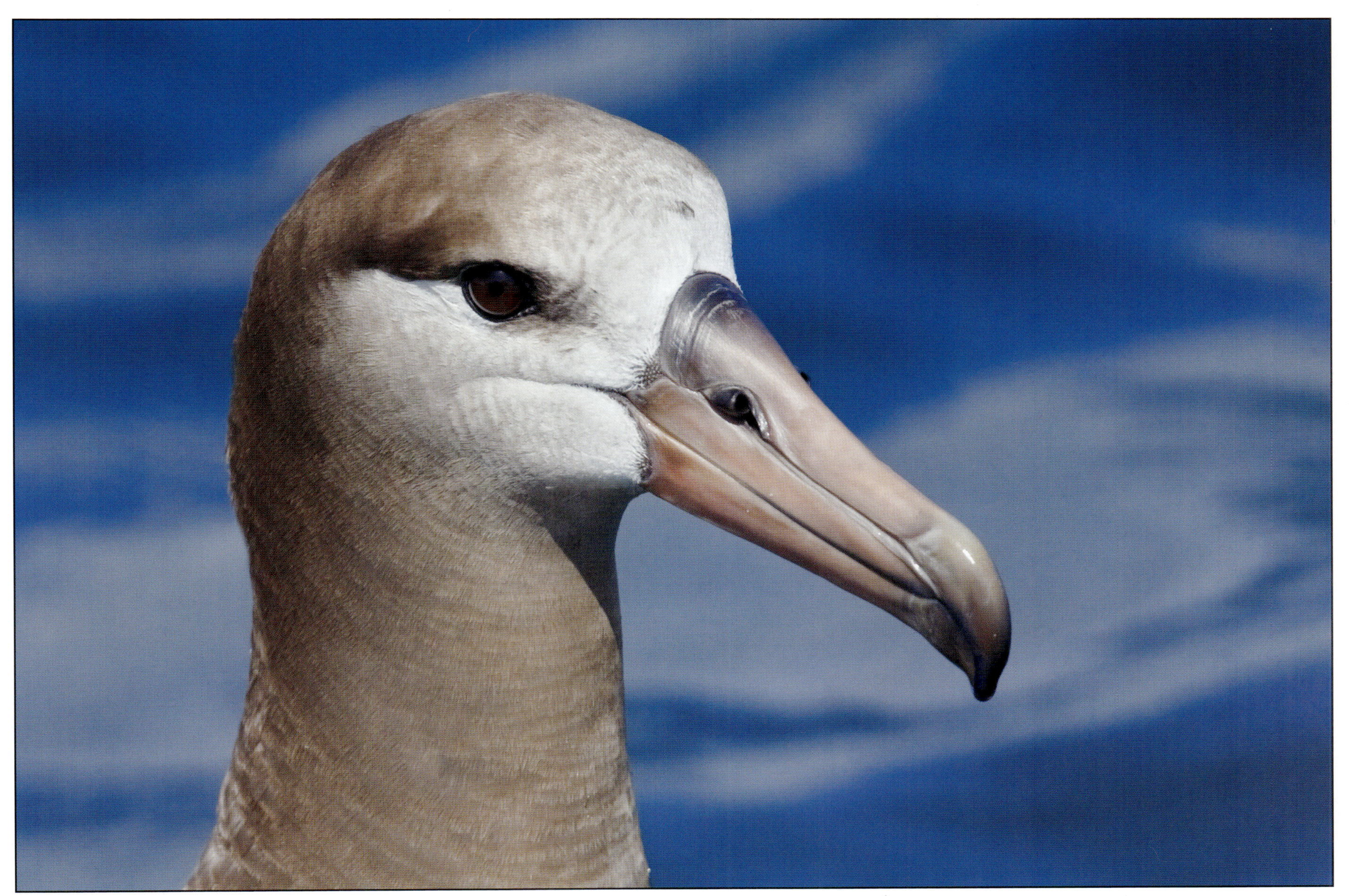

A Black-footed Albatross clearly shows why it belongs to the group of birds known as "tube noses". These birds use their nasal passages to excrete salt from their bodies.

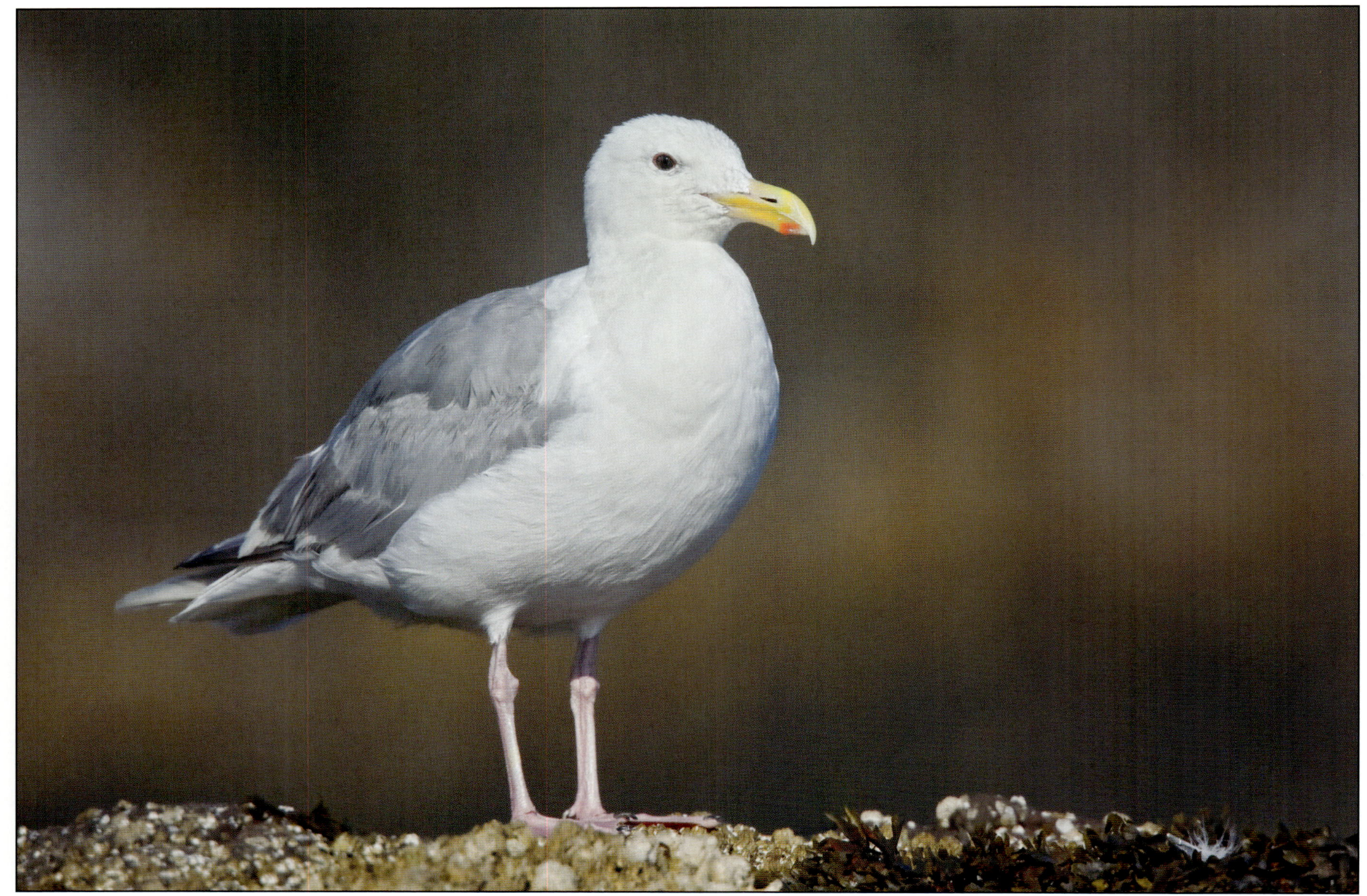

The Glaucous-winged Gull is a large gull that is common throughout Vancouver Island.

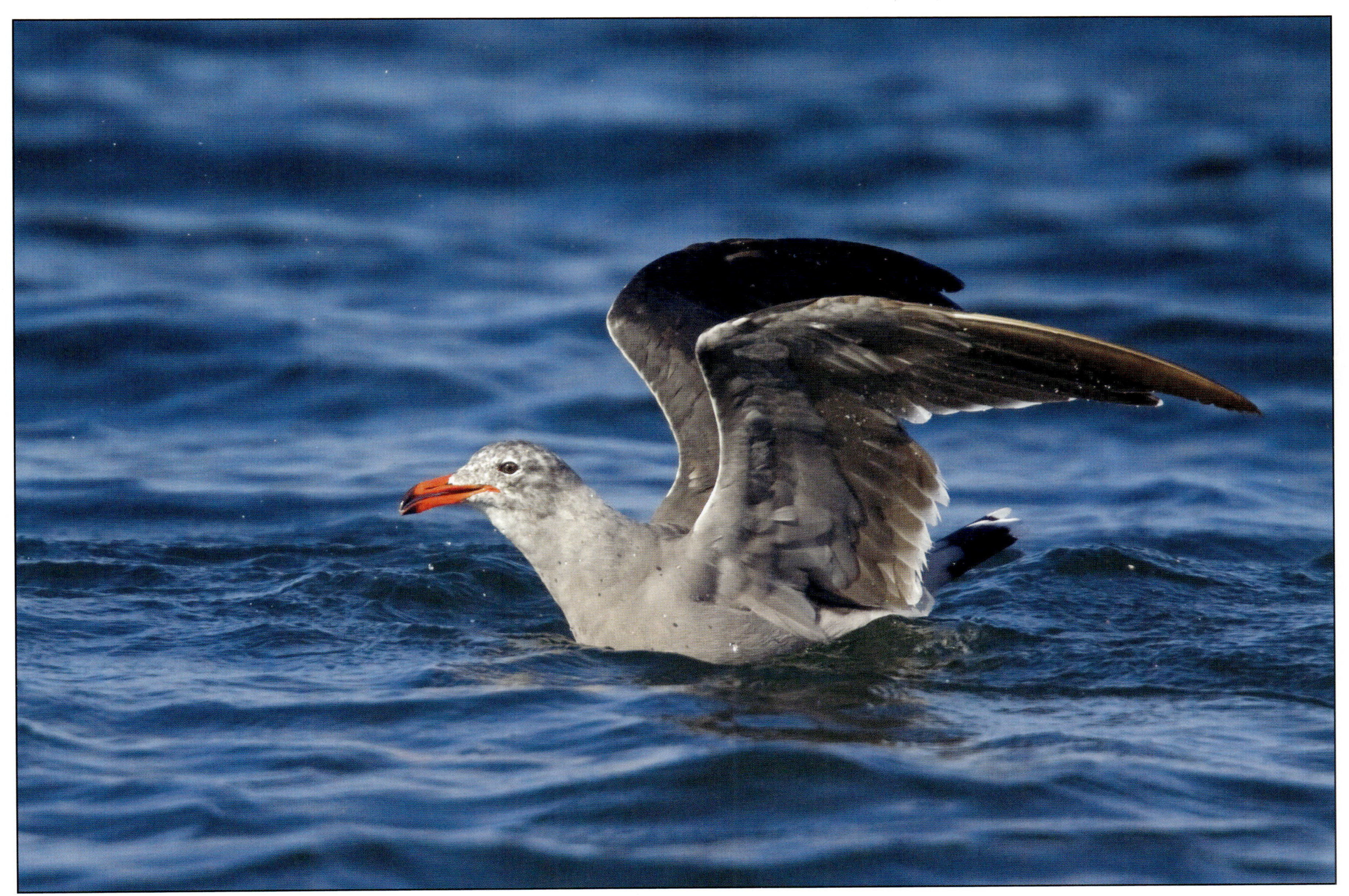

A Heerman's Gull raises its wings as it devours a recent catch near Cordova Bay on the Saanich Peninsula.

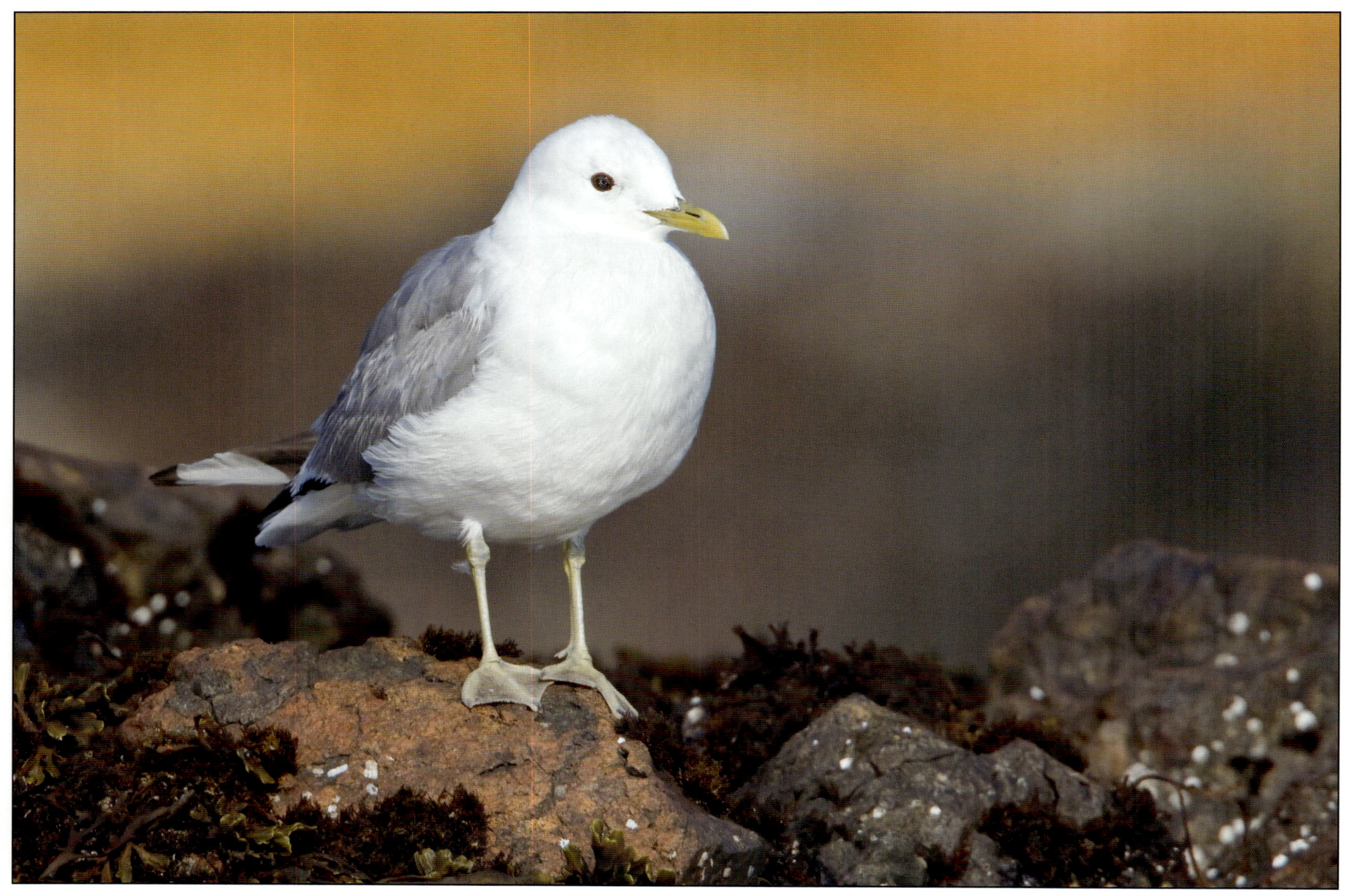

Mew Gulls are easily distinguished from other gulls on Vancouver Island by their small size and delicate bill.

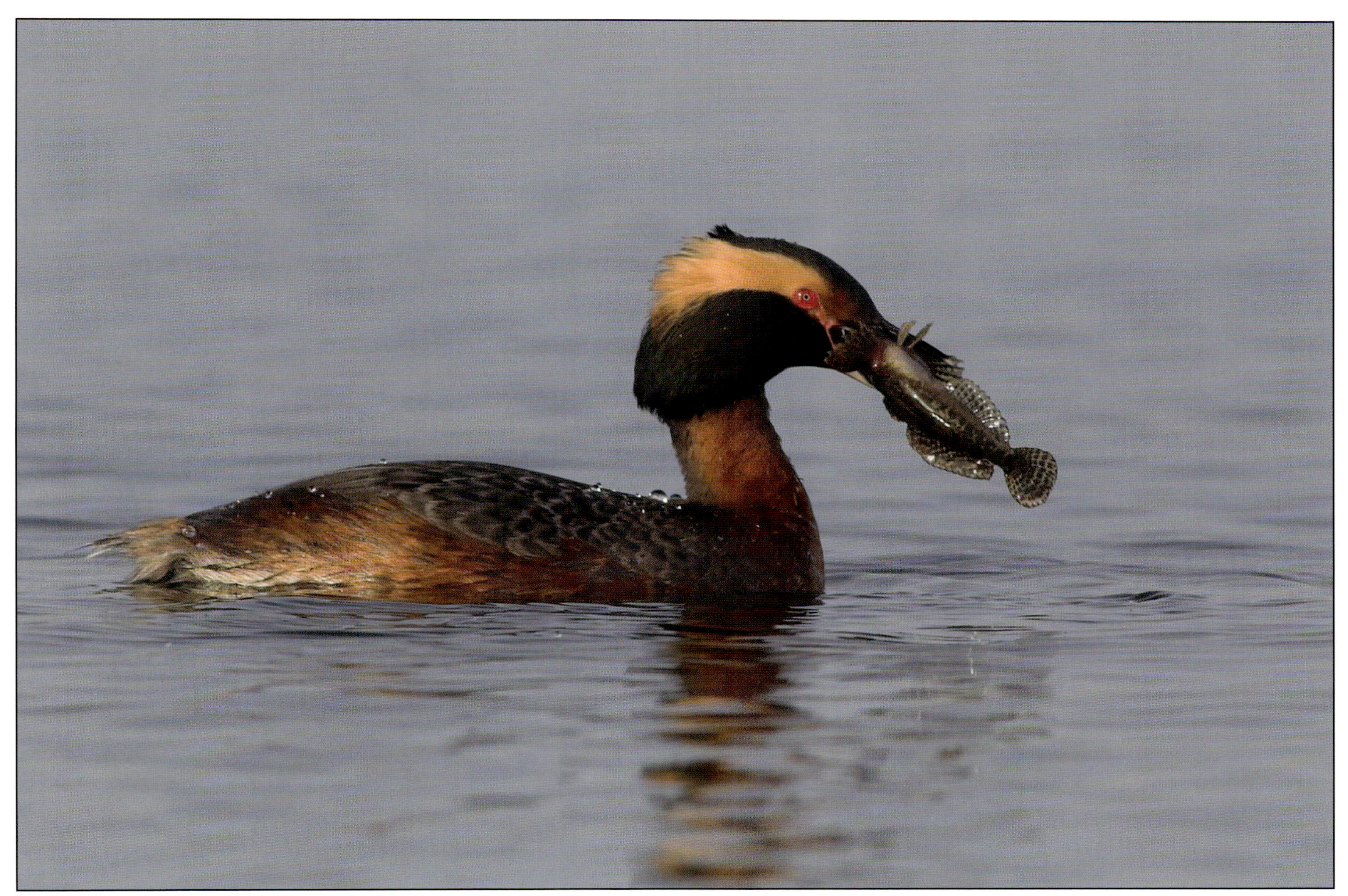

A Horned Grebe feeds on a fresh catch. This species is often found during the winter months off the coast of Vancouver Island.

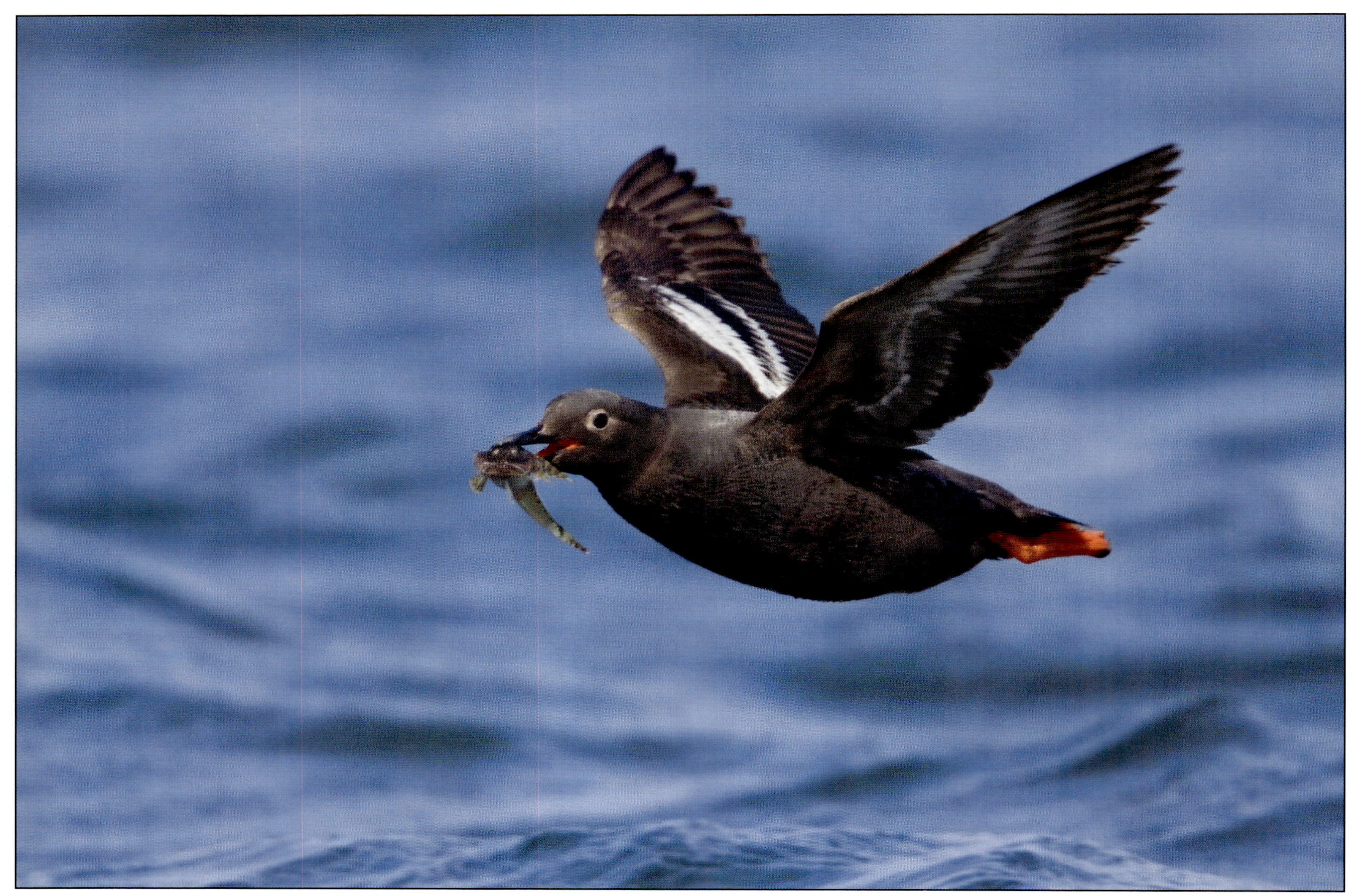

A Pigeon Guillemot returns from sea with a fresh catch to feed its young offspring who await its return.

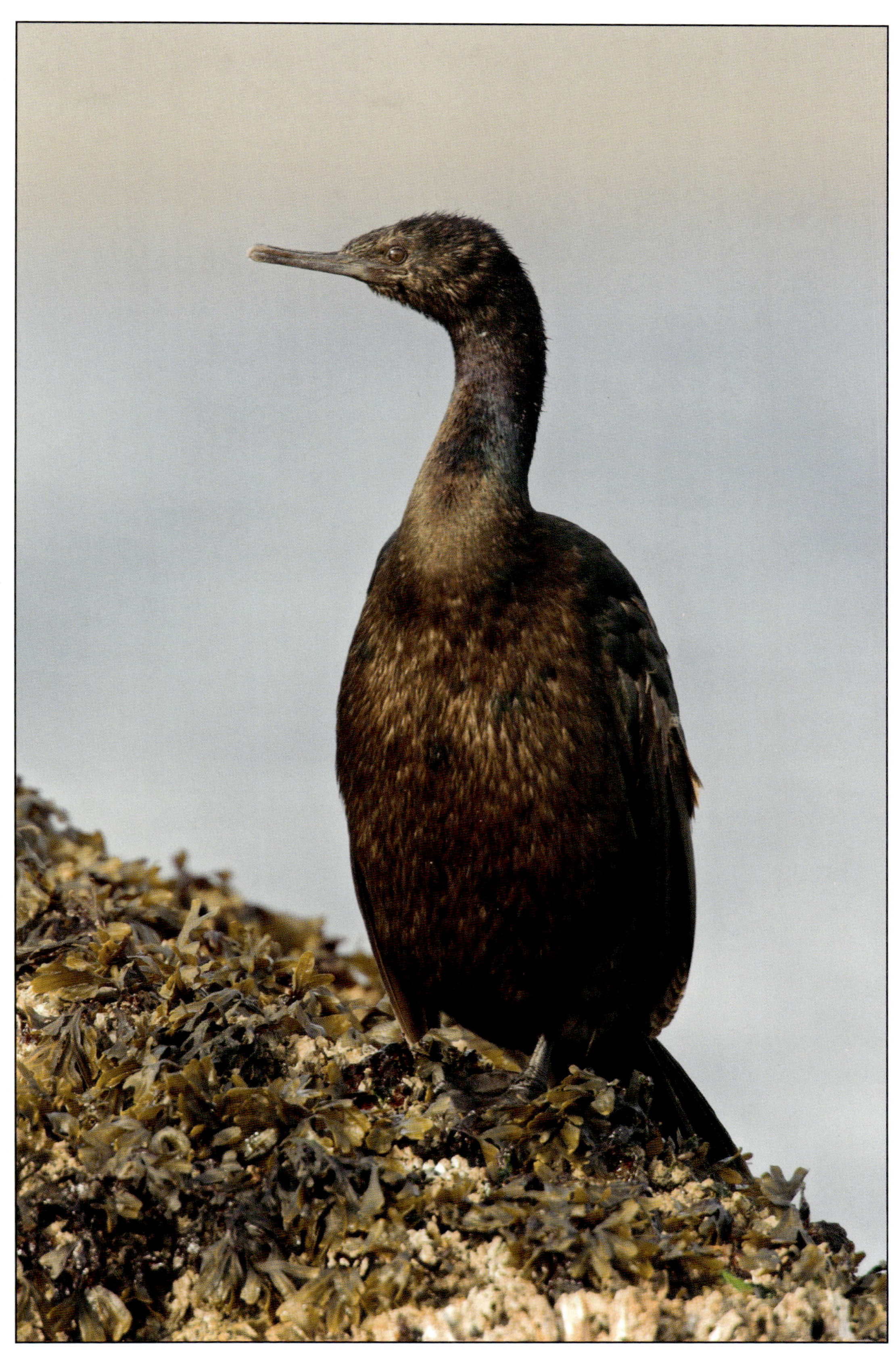

Pelagic Cormorants are also called snake birds because of their long necks and scaled pattern along their backs.

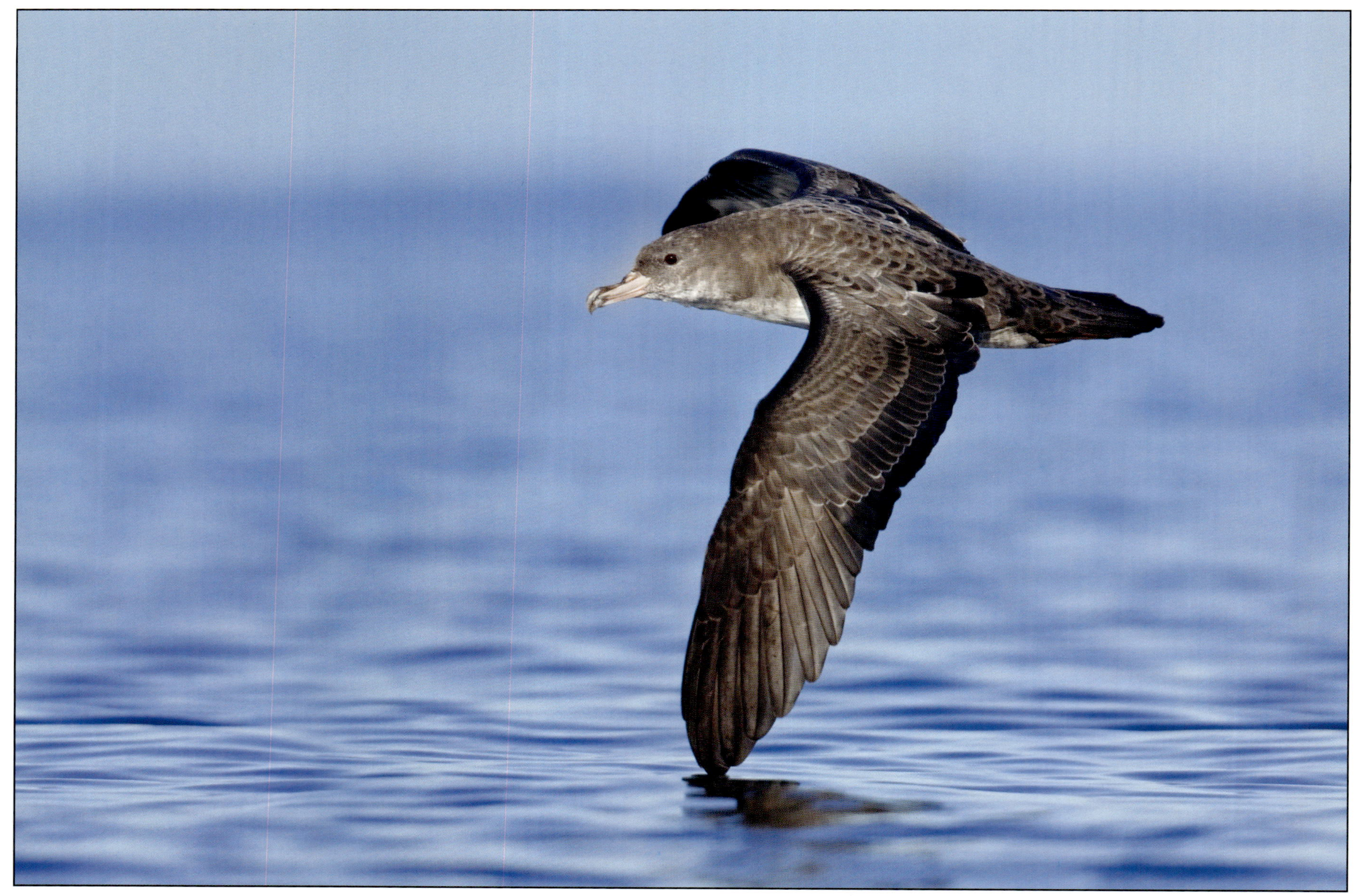

A Pink-footed Shearwater skims the surface of the water in the Juan de Fuca Strait.

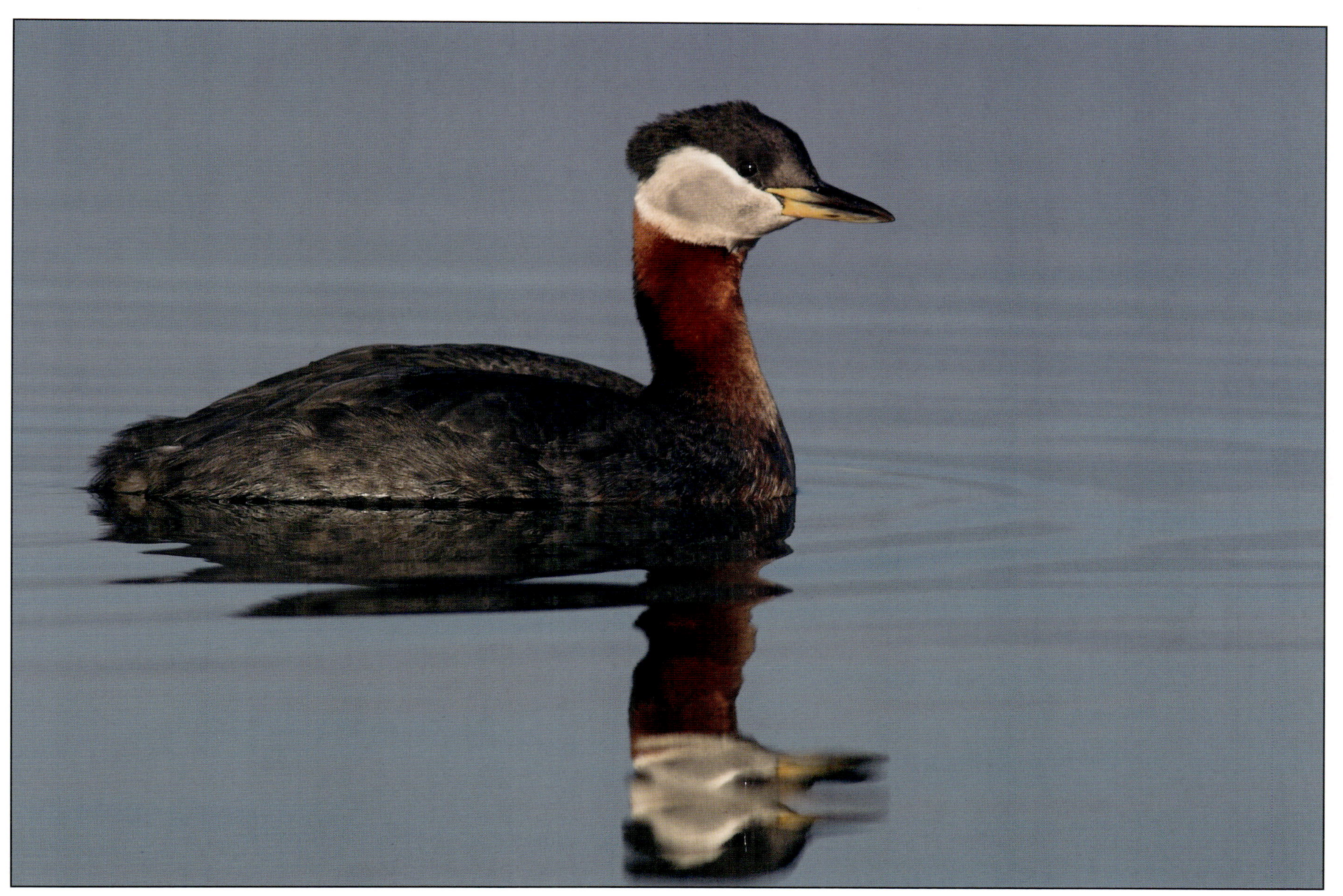

Red-necked Grebes winter off the coast of Vancouver Island before returning inland to breed on shallow lakes each spring.

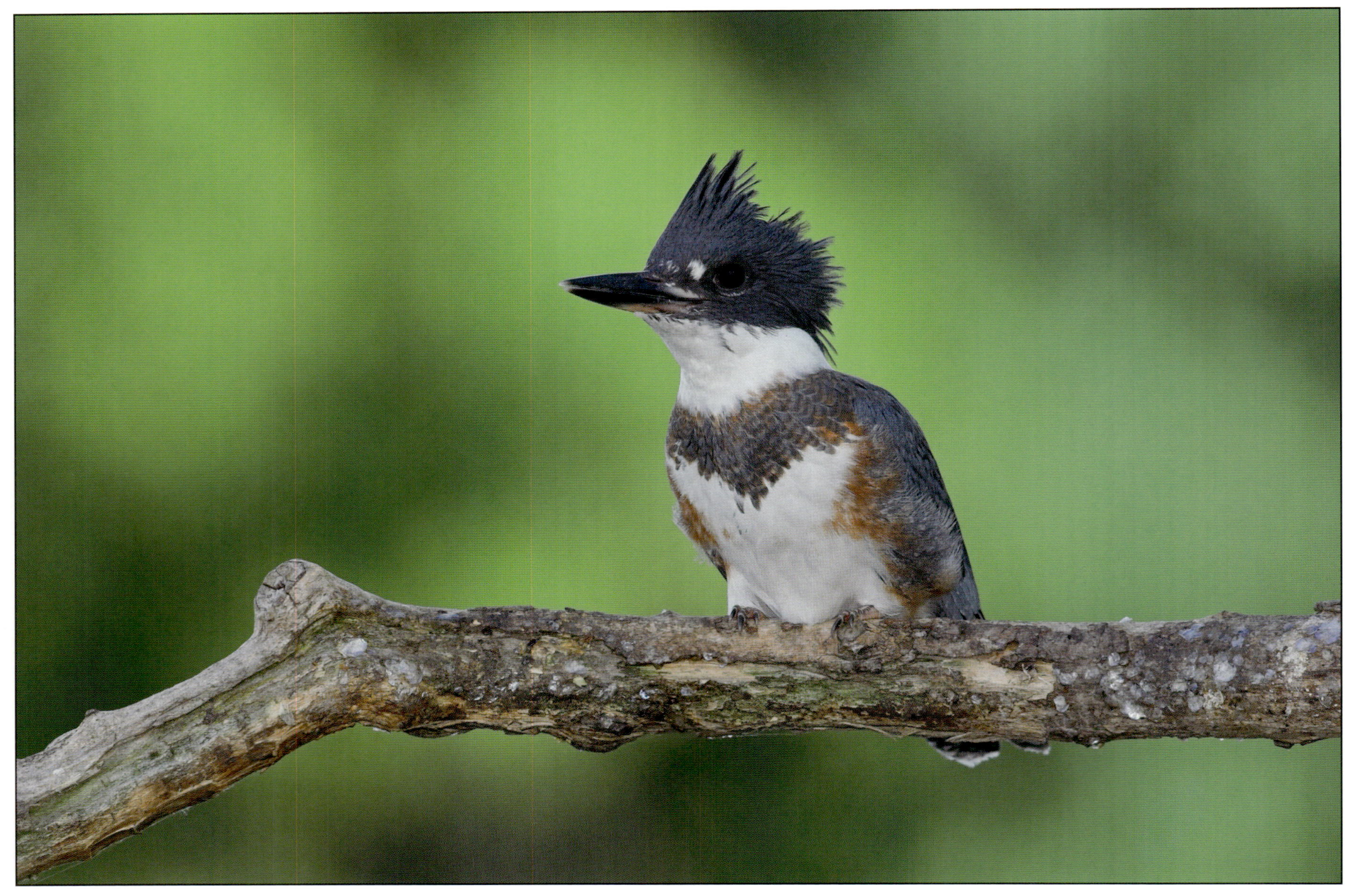

Belted Kingfishers are often seen perched above ponds and lakes searching for small fish to feed on.

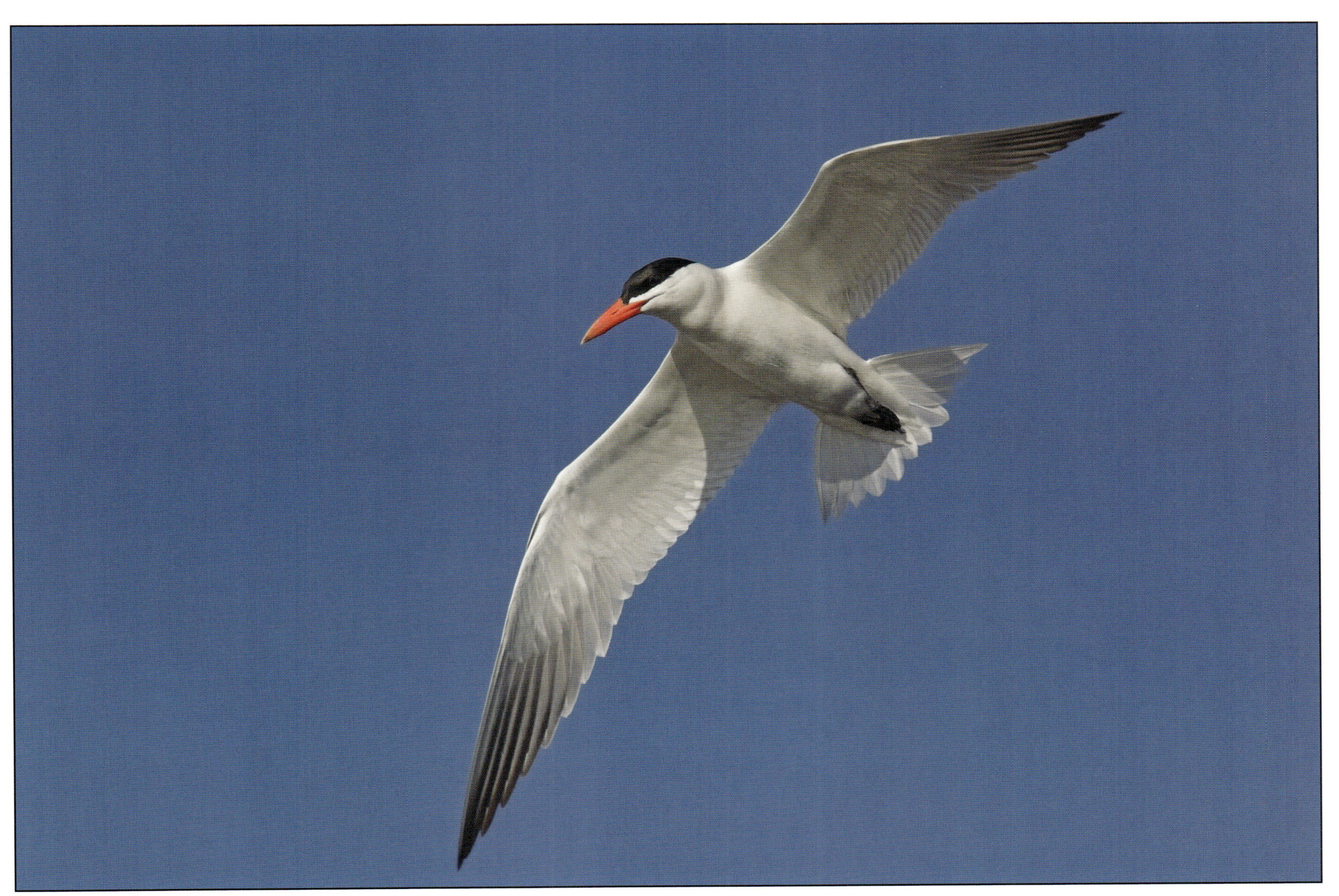

A Caspian Tern peruses the shallow waters of the shoreline in search of small baitfish.

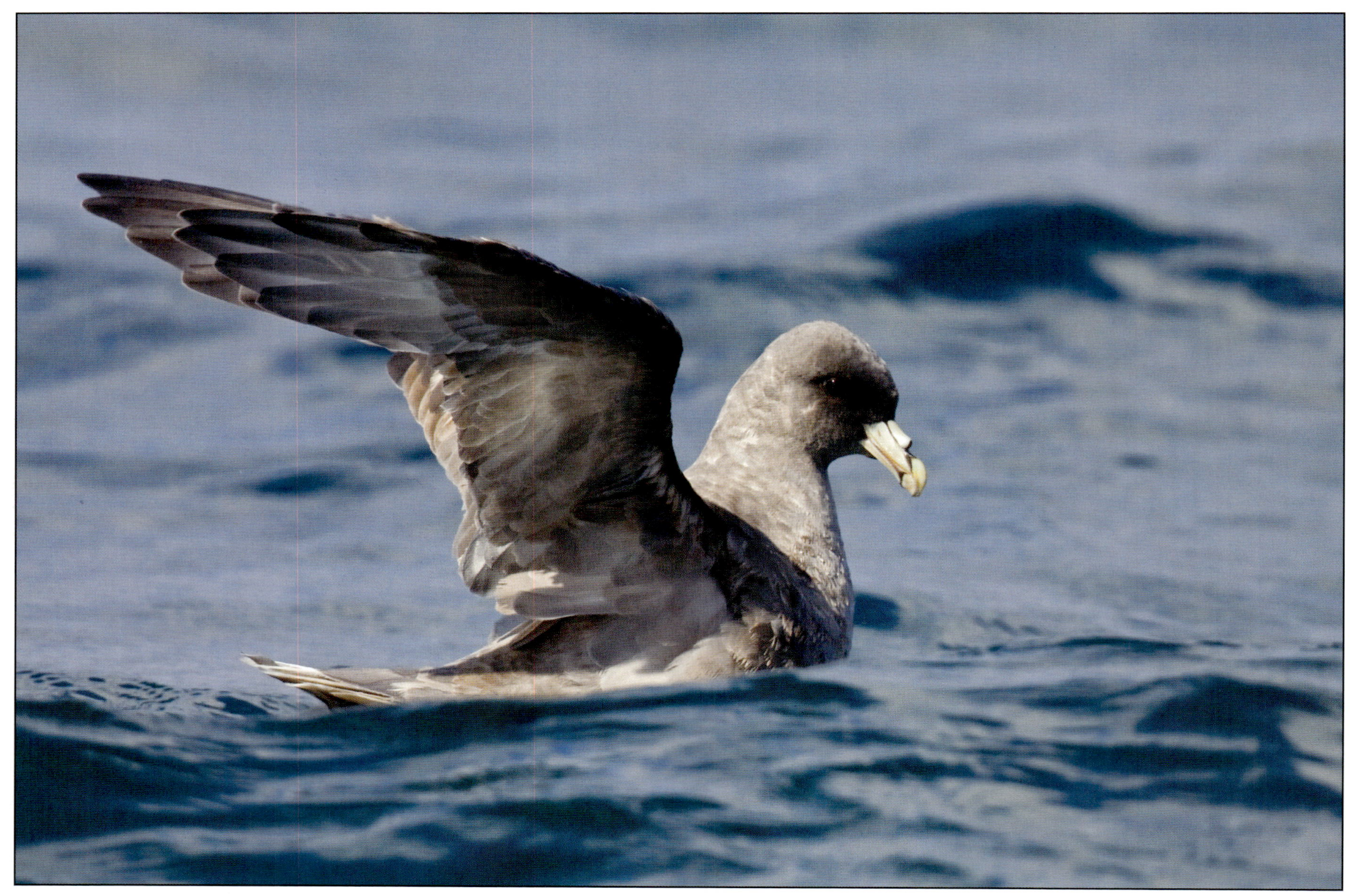

A Northern Fulmar stretches its wings far off the coast of Vancouver Island. These pelagic birds are rarely seen from shore except with a high-powered spotting scope.

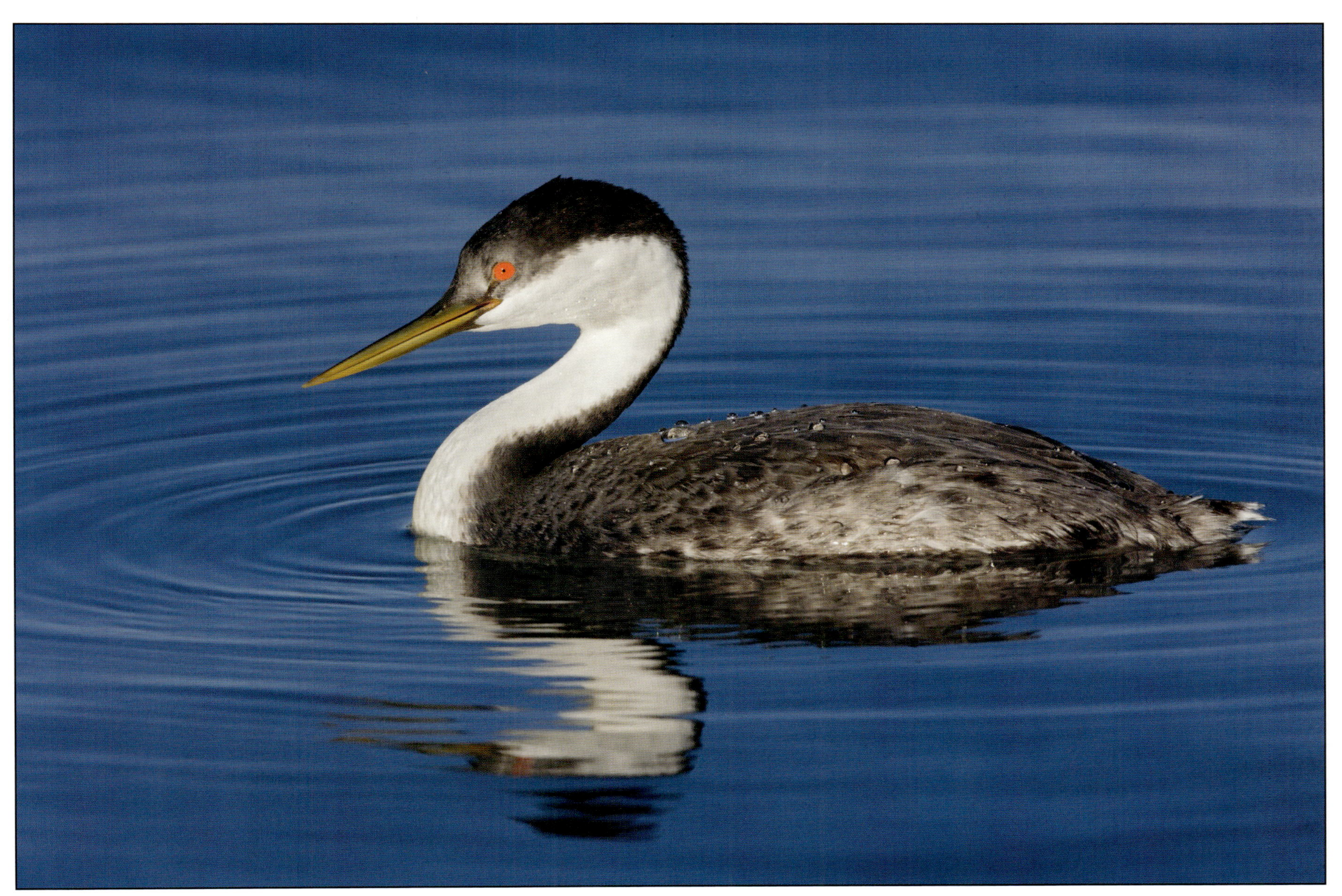

A Western Grebe pauses in between dives on a calm winter morning.

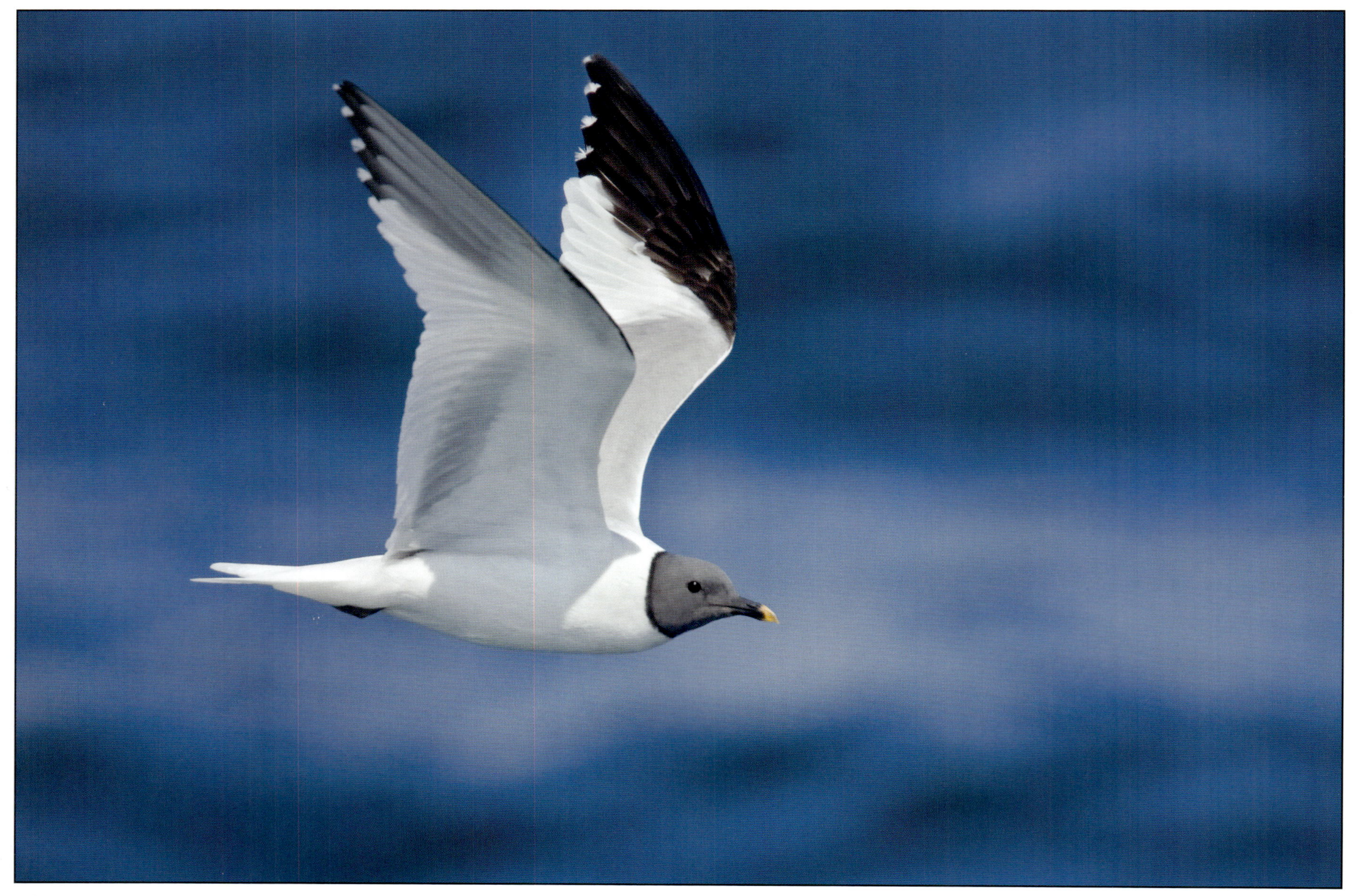

After breeding in the high Arctic, Sabine's Gulls migrate south along the west coast. They tend to stay far offshore, however, and are rarely seen from land.

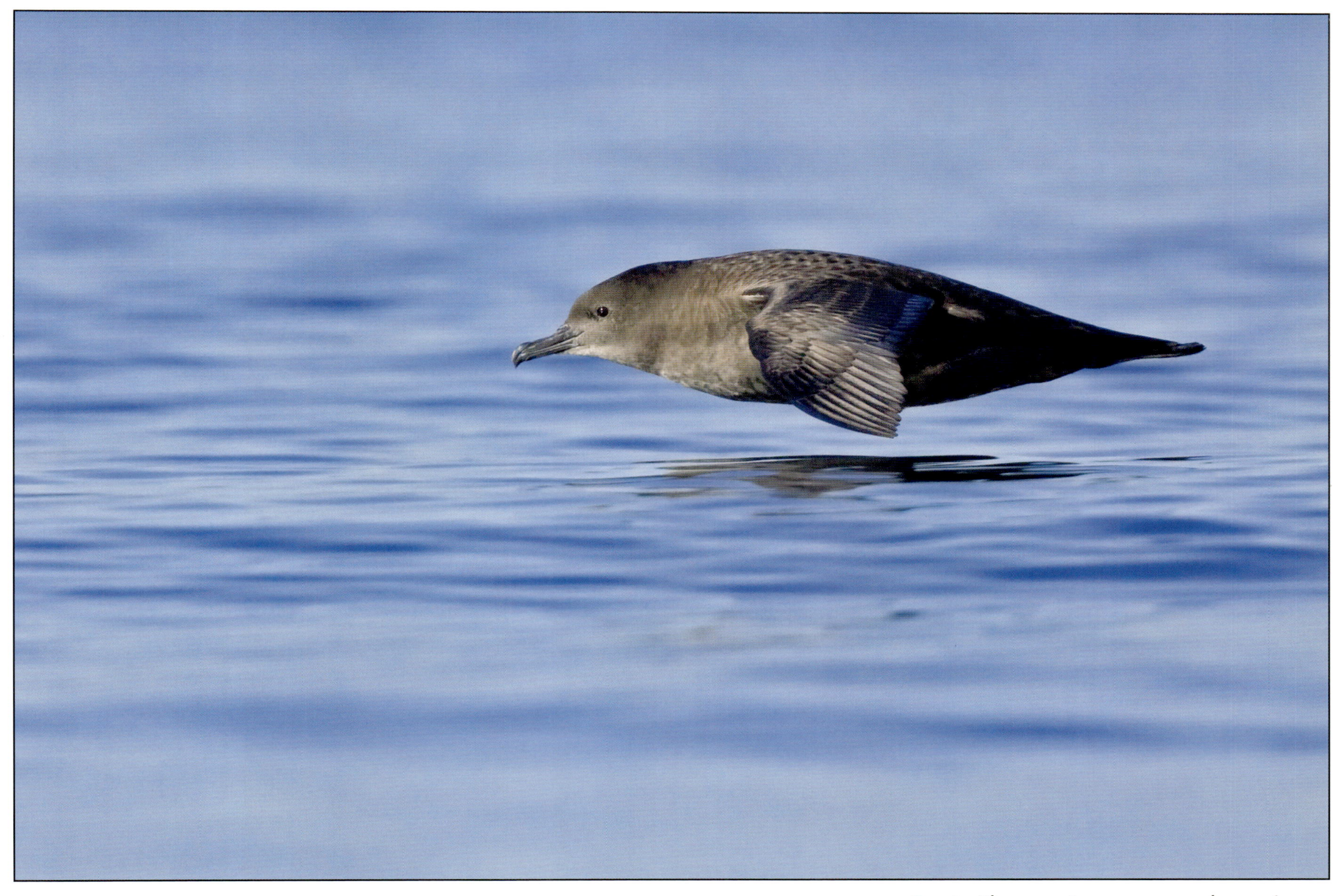

Sooty Shearwaters are aerodynamic birds that skim the surface of the ocean in flight. They can travel over 60,000 km each year, making them one of the champions of long distance flight.

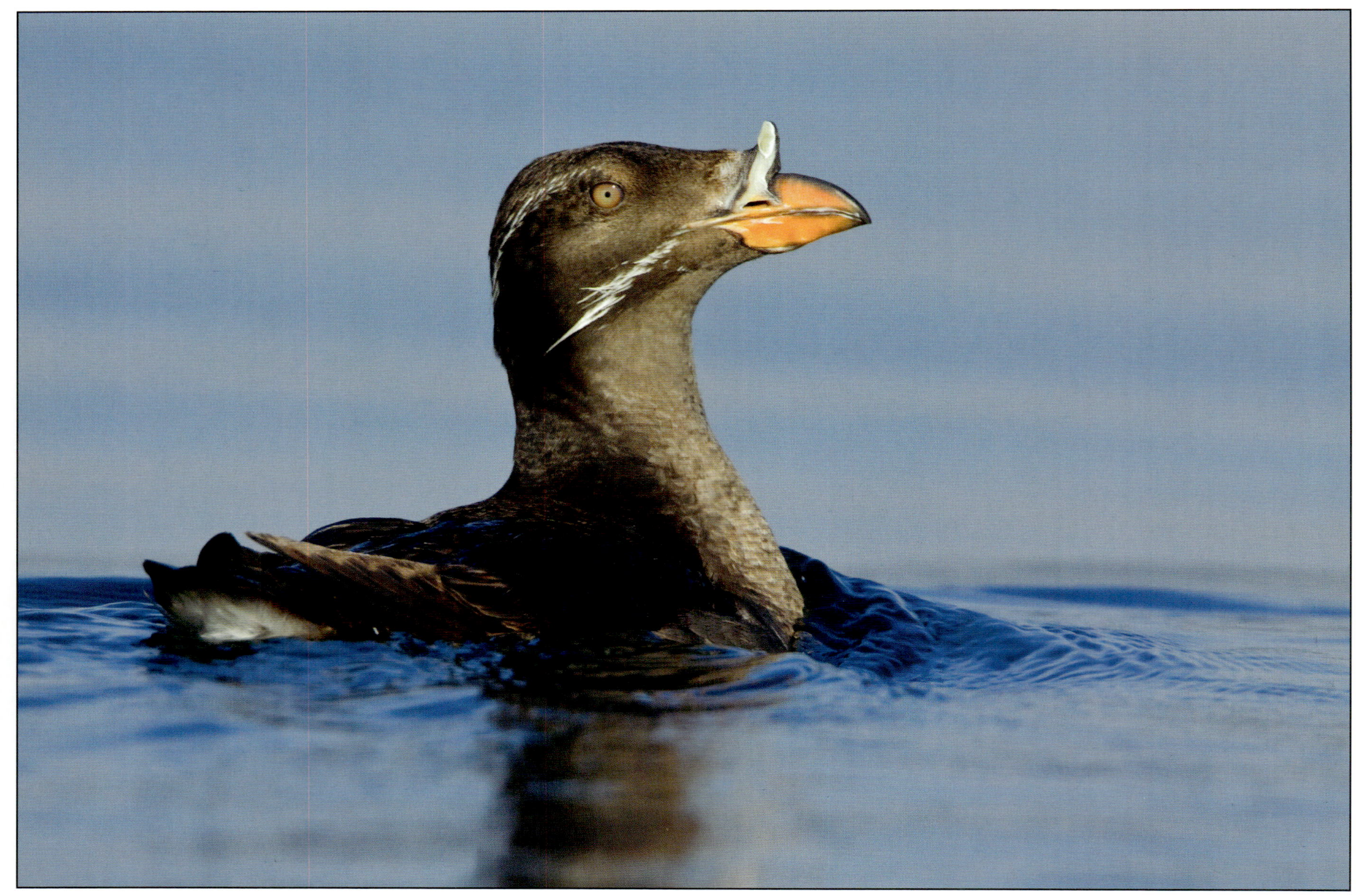

A Rhinoceros Auklet proudly displays its horn during the breeding season.

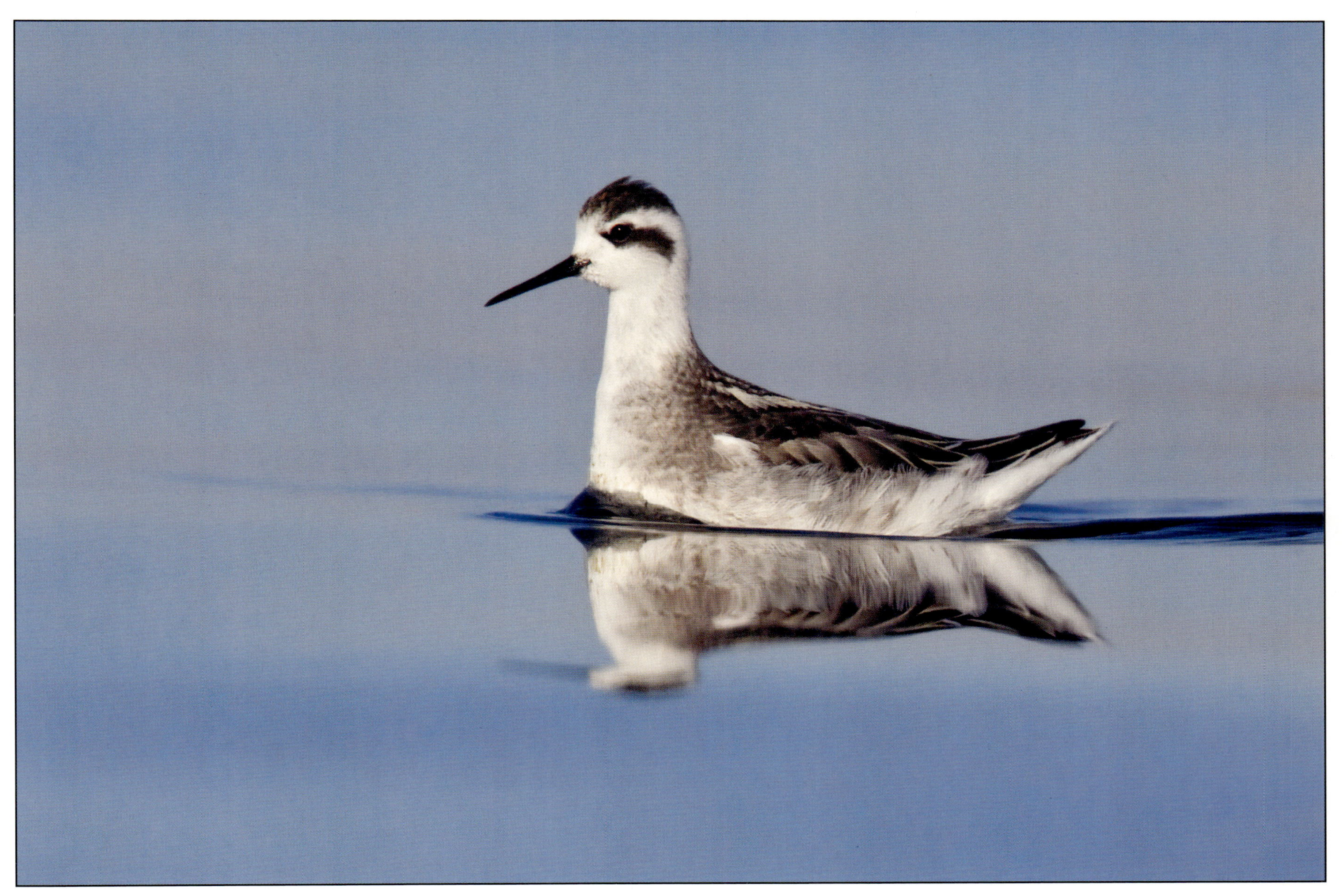

Red-necked Phalaropes migrate along the west coast of Vancouver Island in the fall from their breeding grounds in the Arctic to their wintering grounds in the Southern Hemisphere.

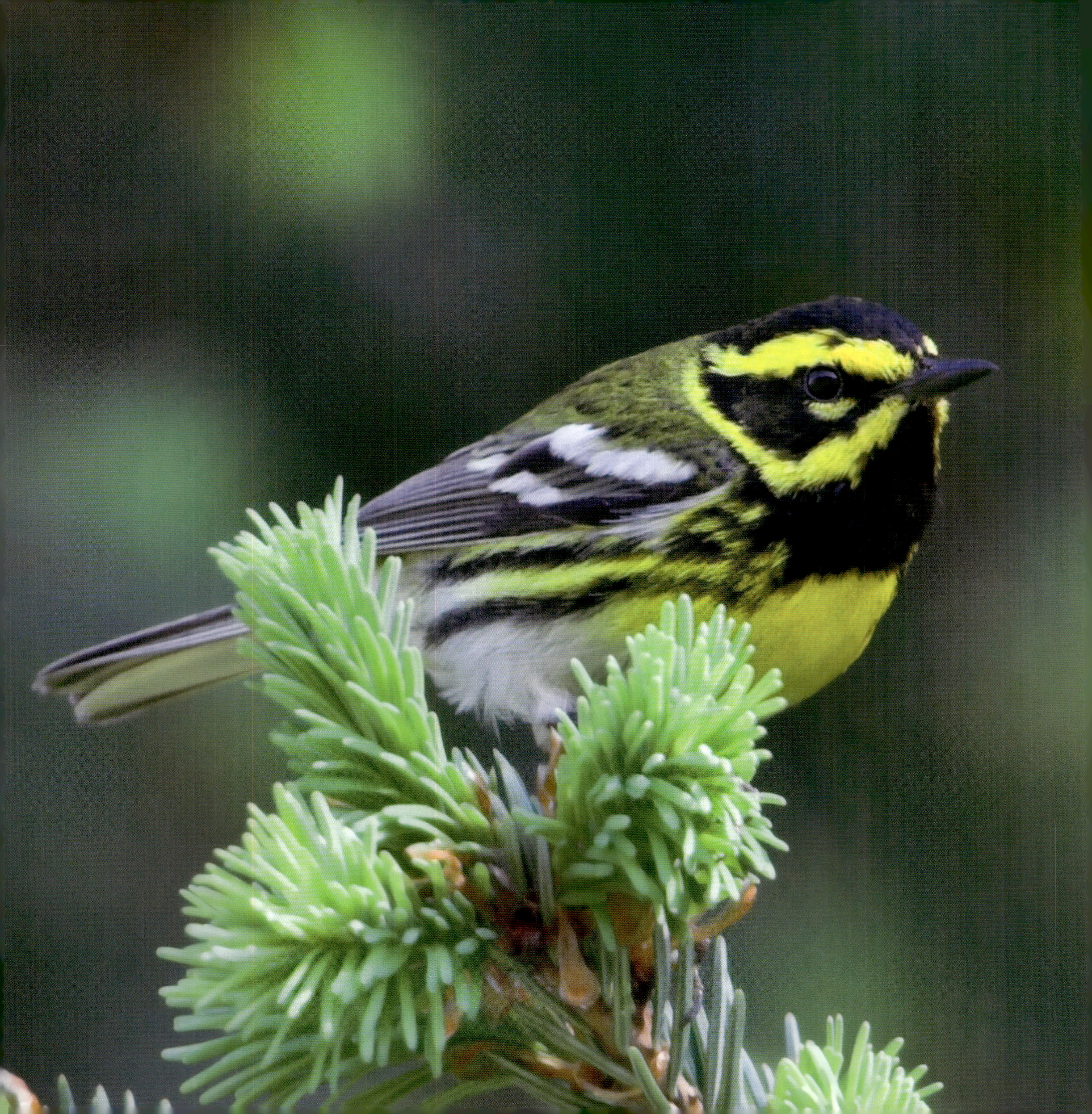

SONGBIRDS

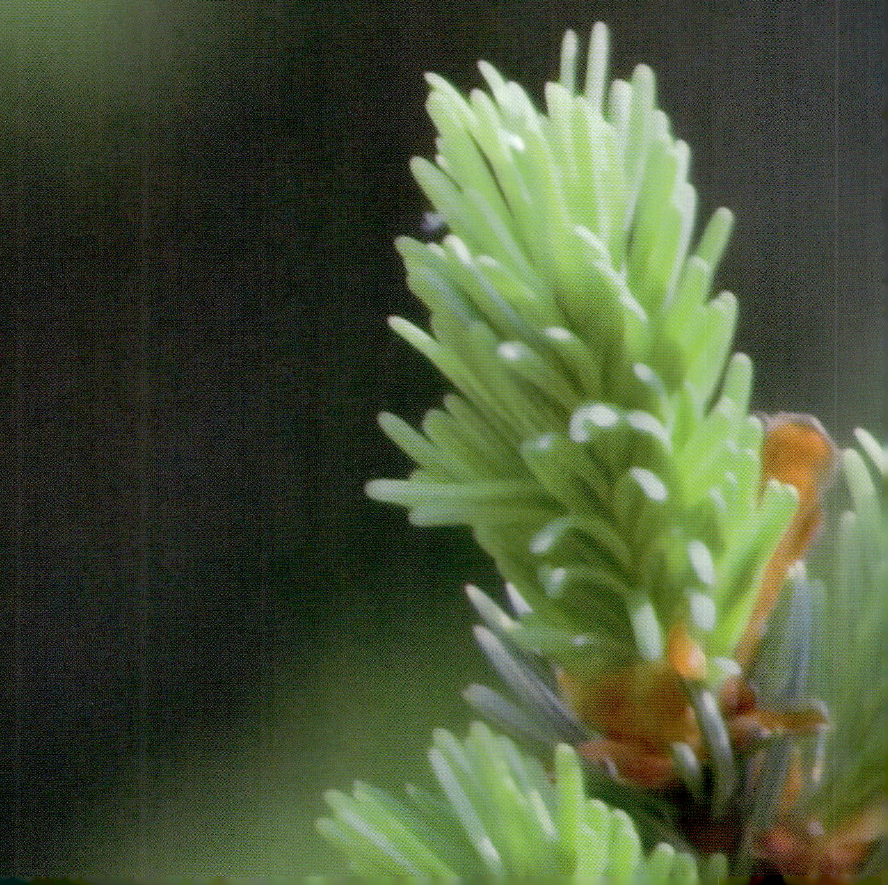

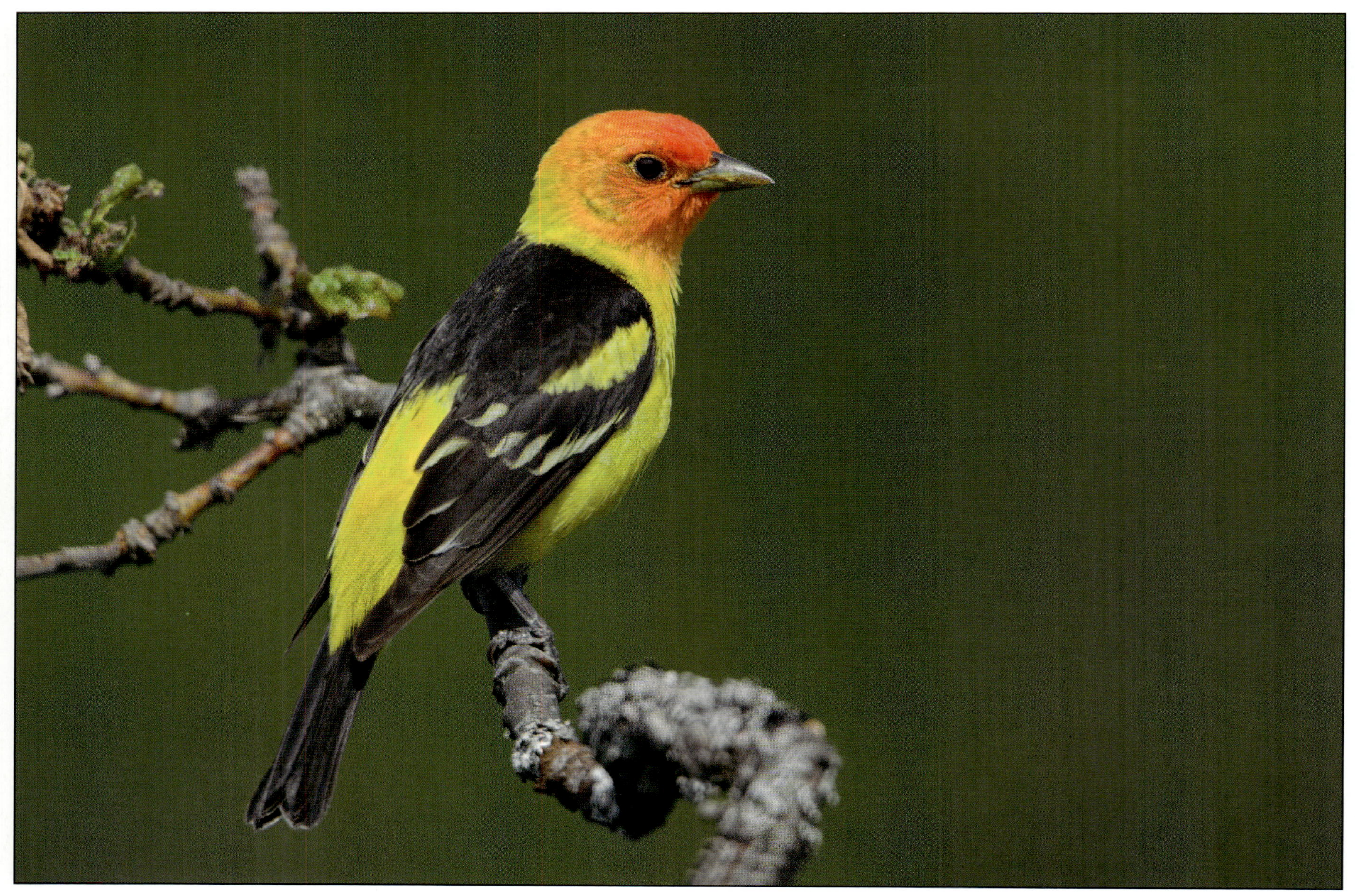

A striking male Western Tanager proudly perches atop a Garry Oak near Victoria.

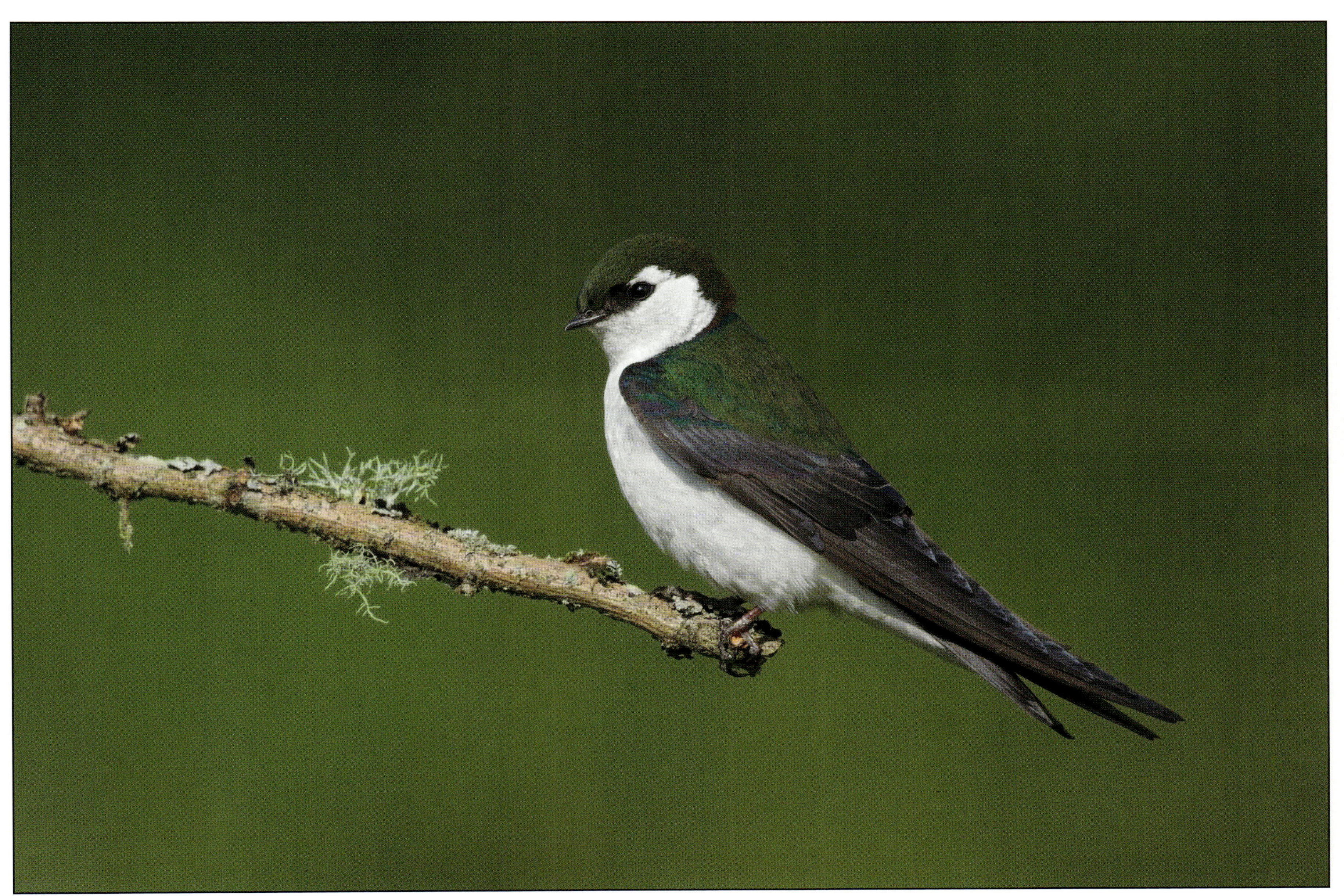

A Violet-green Swallow perches above a nest box overseeing the nest-building activities of his mate.

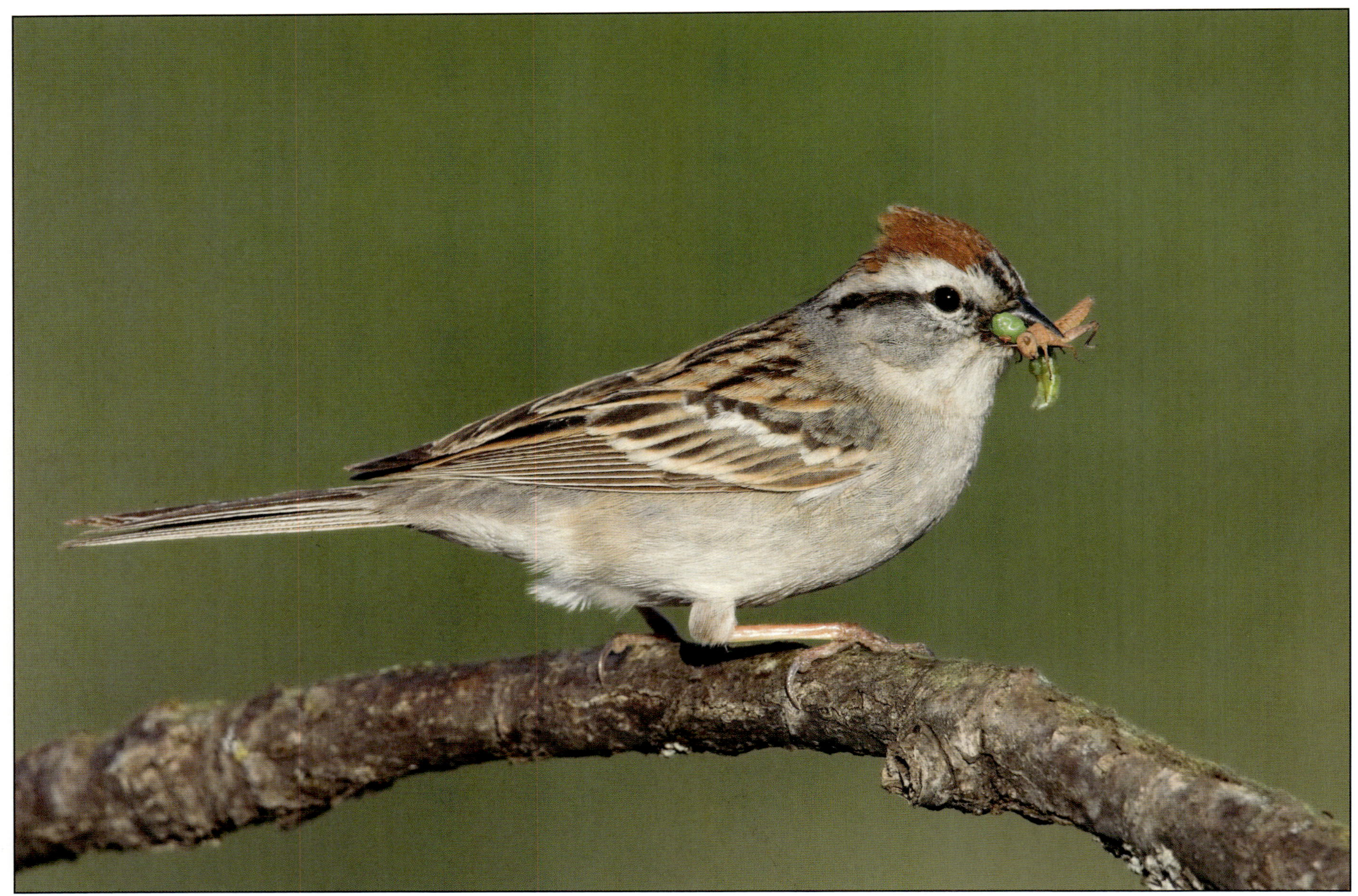

A Chipping Sparrow gathers food to satisfy the insatiable appetite of its recently hatched young.

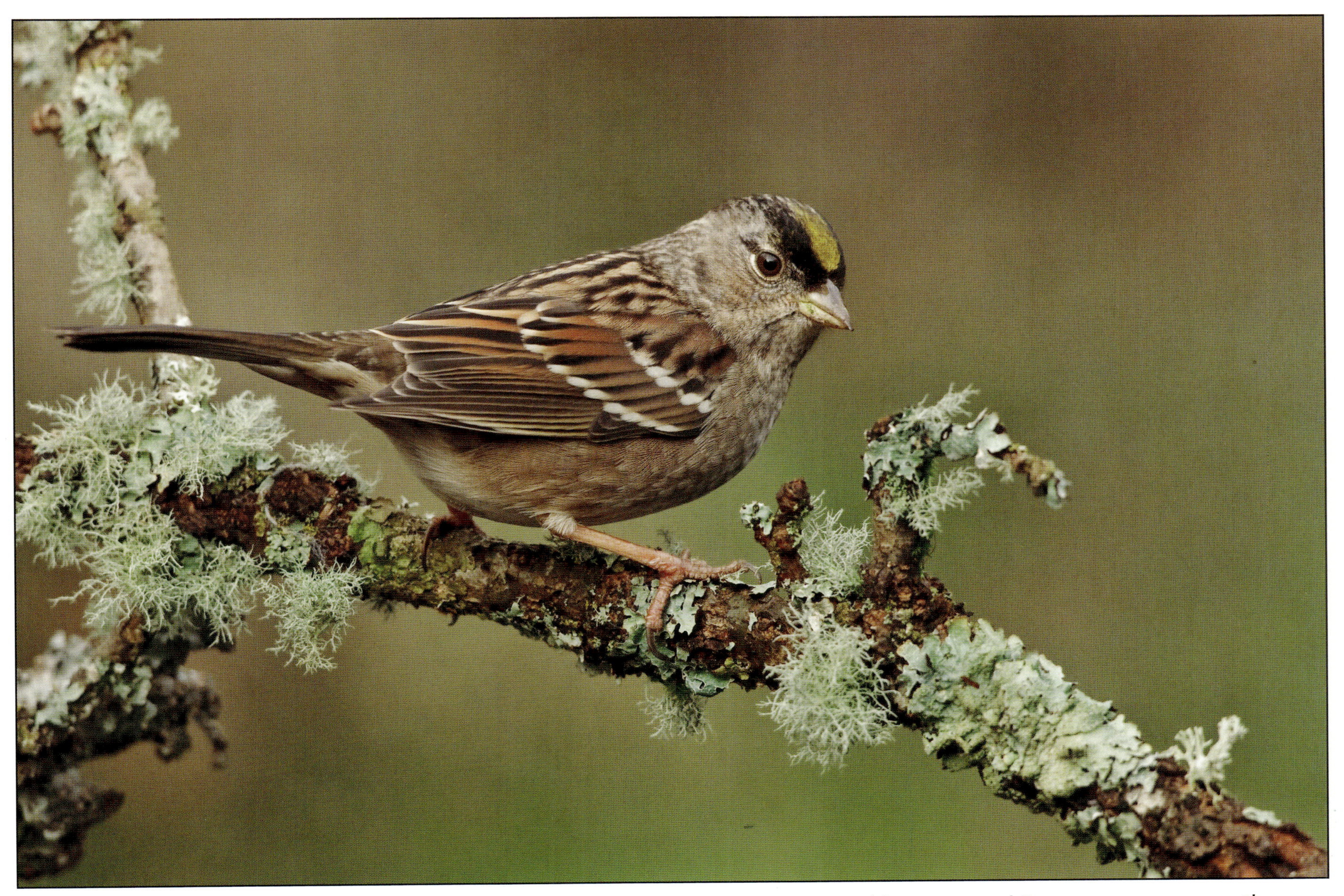

Golden-crowned Sparrows are among the most common sparrows on Vancouver Island during the winter months.

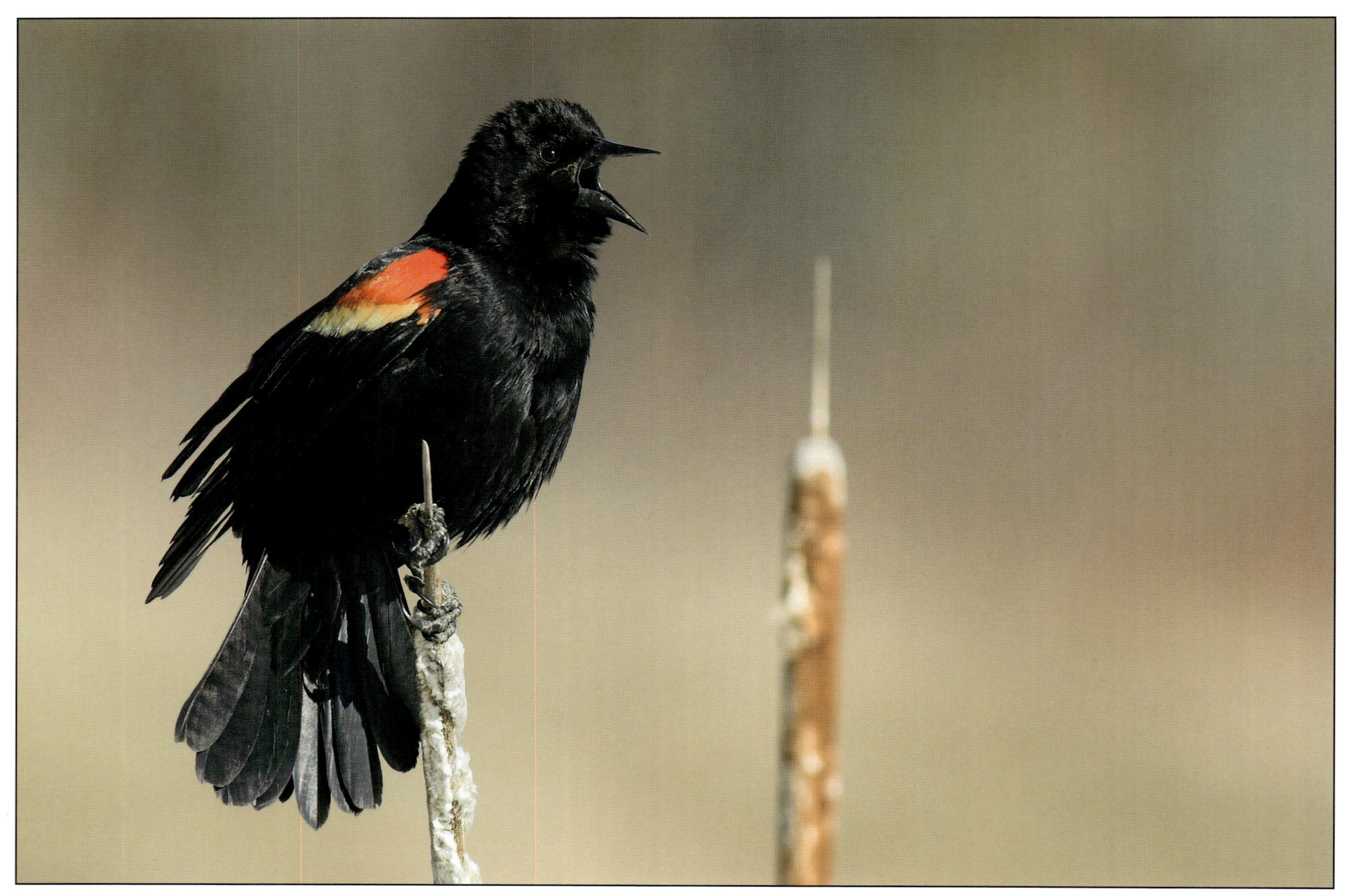

Nothing signifies the arrival of spring like the shrill calls of Red-winged Blackbirds emanating from a wetland.

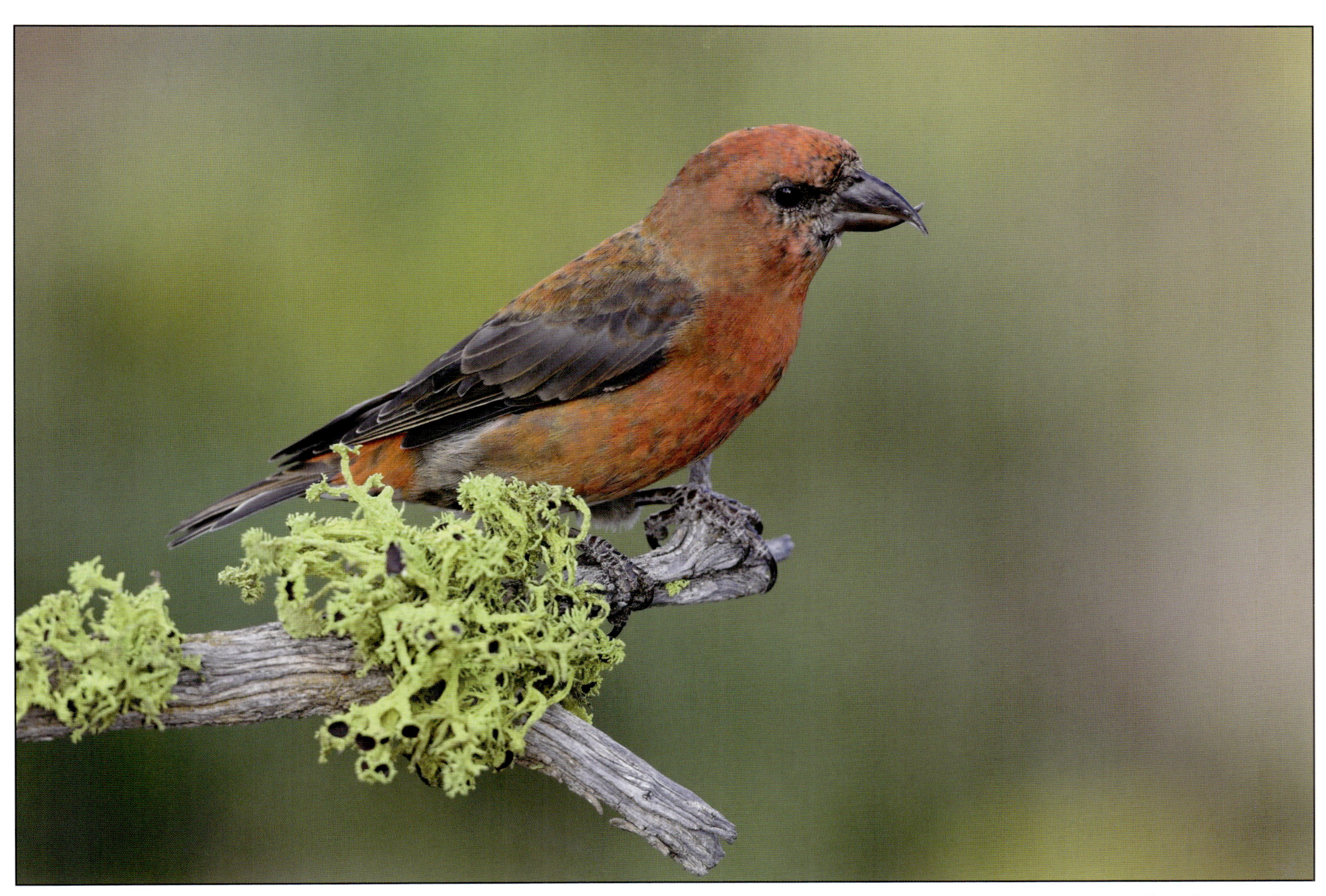

The bill of the Red Crossbill is designed to extract seeds from pinecones. These birds are most often seen in flocks as they fly between the tops of coniferous trees.

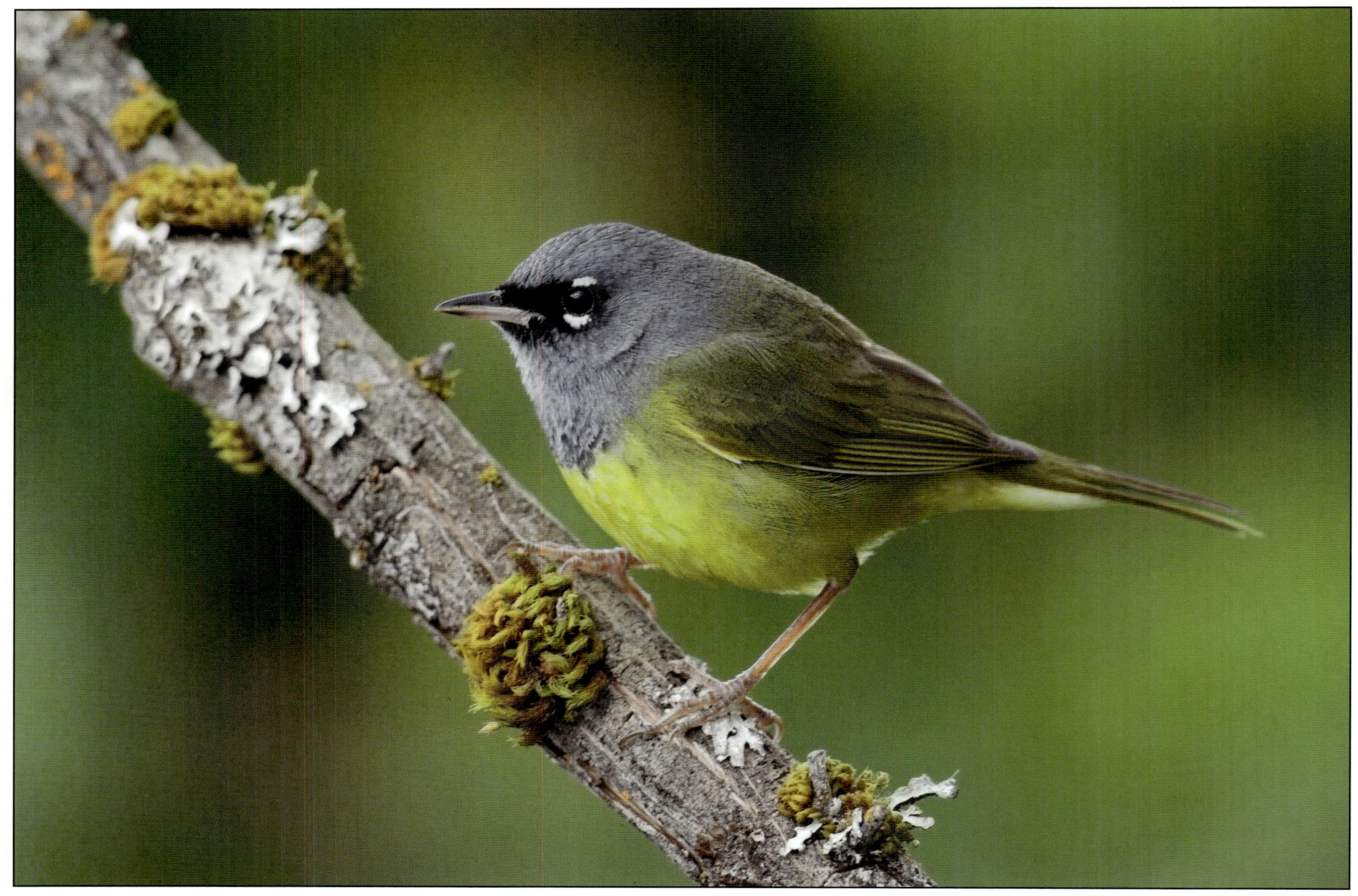

Among the more secretive of the West Coast warblers is the MacGillivray's who are most likely to be seen skulking about in thickets and forest clearings.

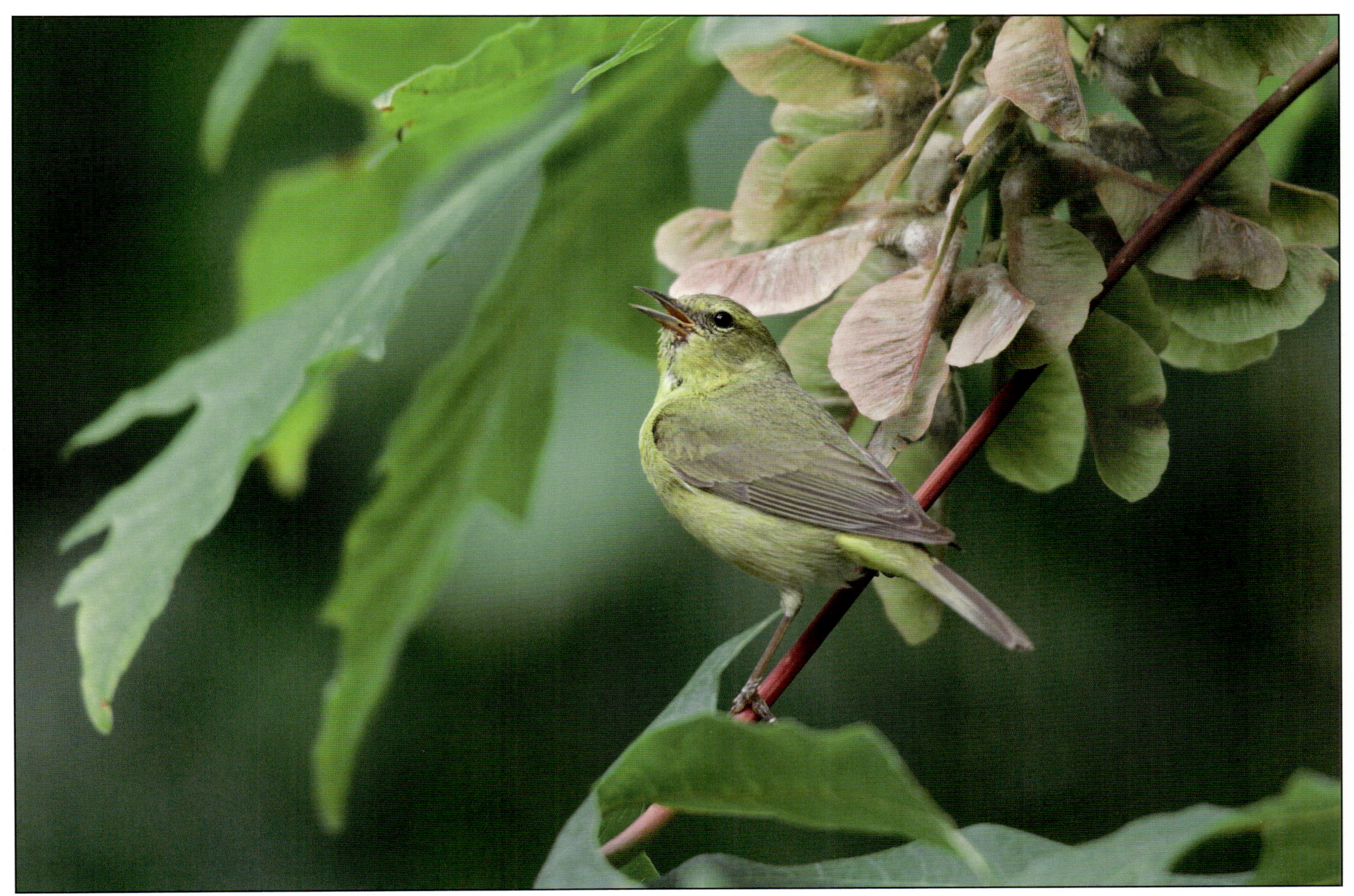

An Orange-crowned Warbler proudly sings from a branch of a Big Leaf Maple.

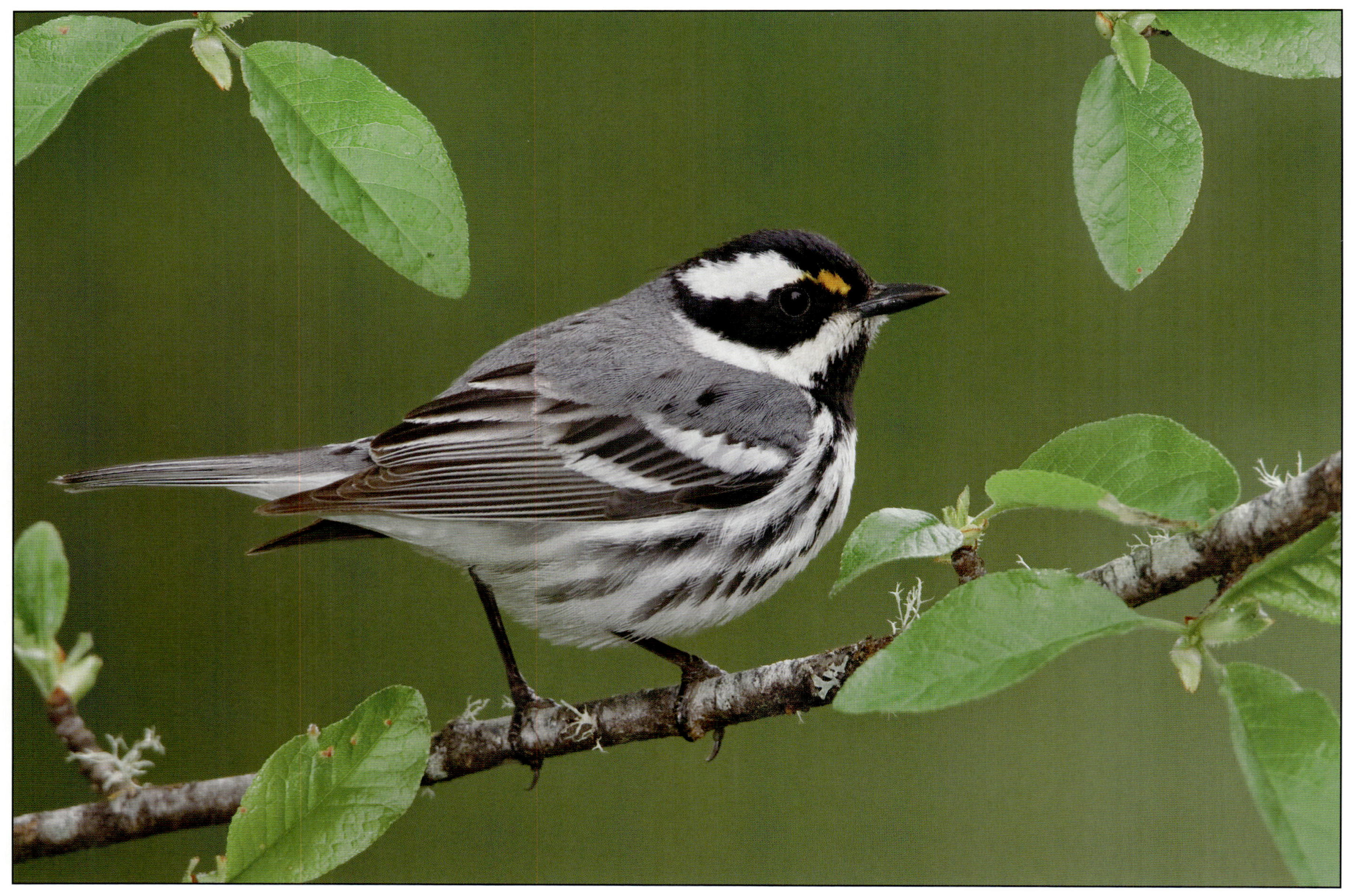

In spring and early summer the wheezy call of Black-throated Gray Warblers rings out through the woodlands of Vancouver Island.

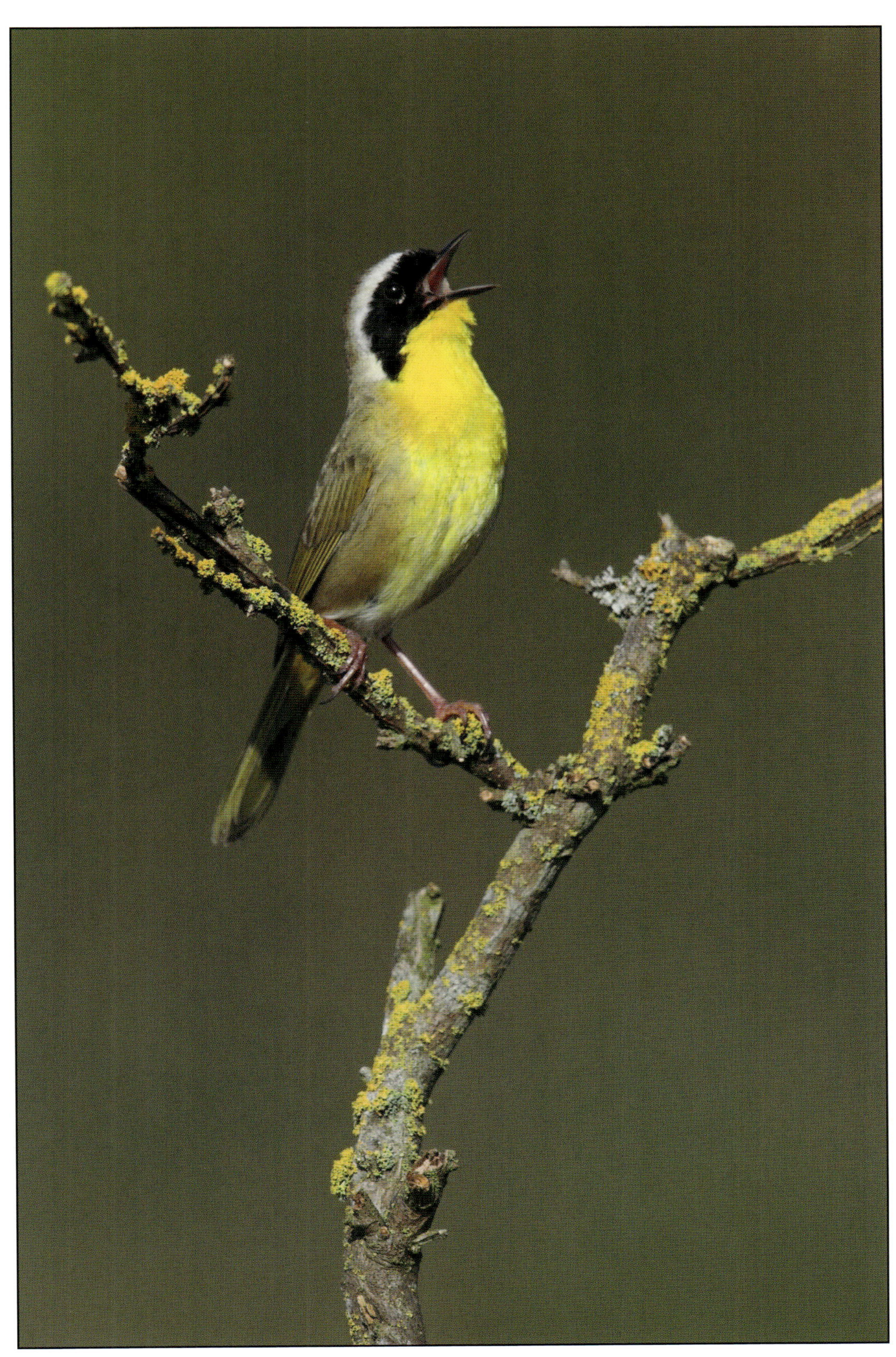

A Common Yellowthroat perches on an open branch to sing for a mate before retreating into a more sheltered shrub.

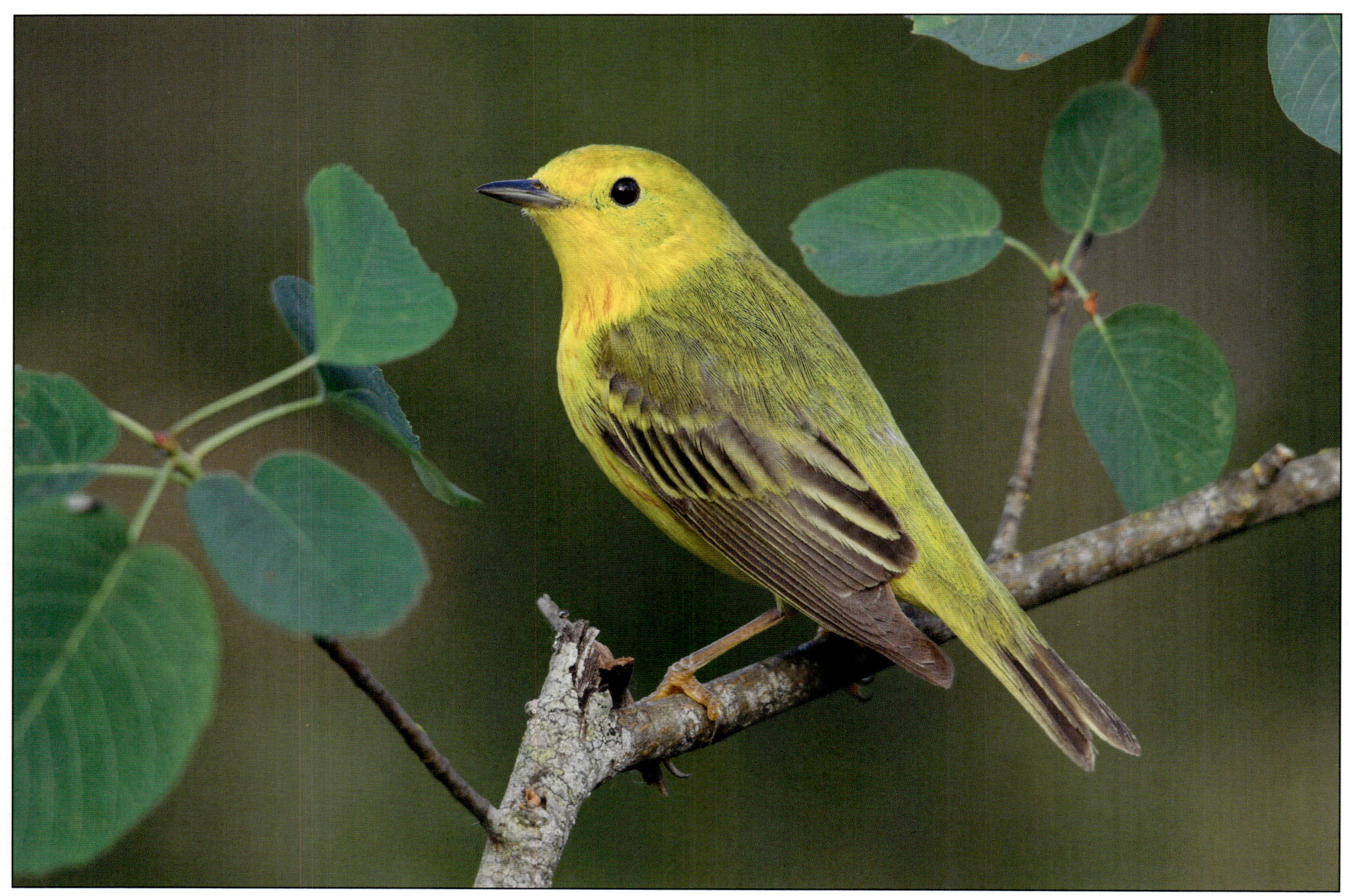

Most likely to be found in riparian areas, the Yellow Warbler is among the most widespread warblers in Canada.

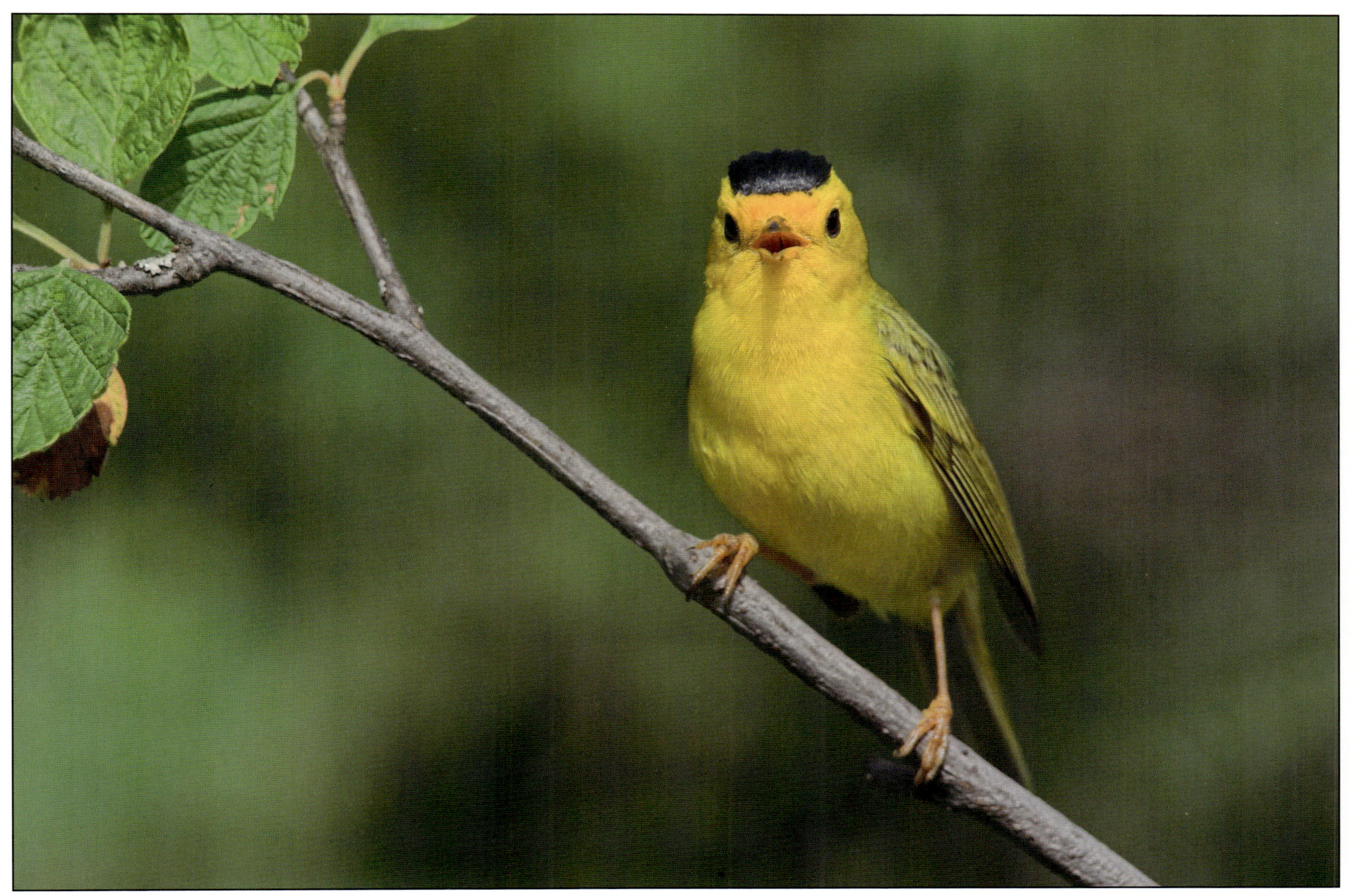

A Wilson's Warbler sings from a snowberry bush displaying its sleek black head feathers.

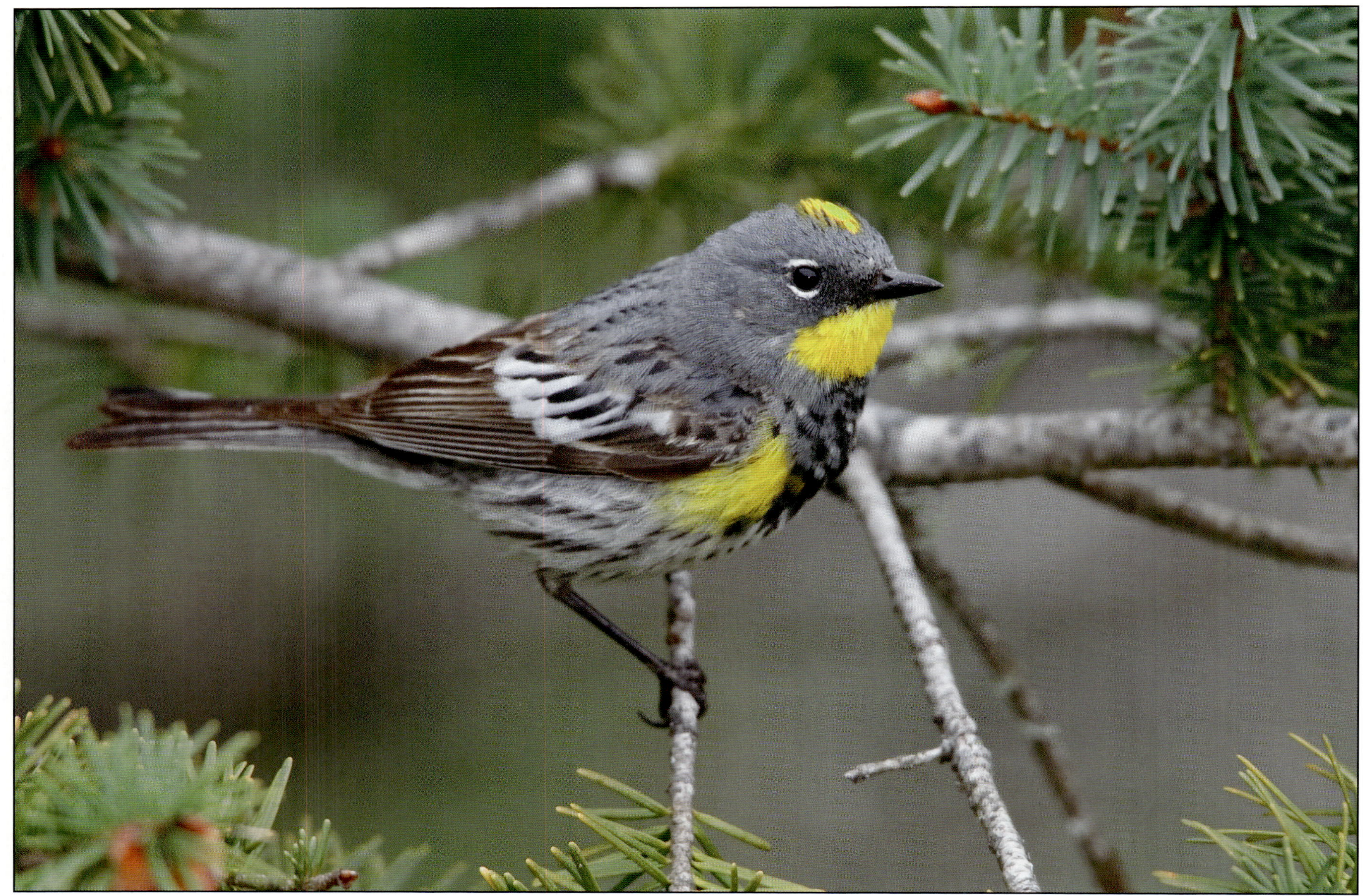

The western Yellow-rumped Warbler is also known as the "Audubon's Warbler". It differs from eastern birds in that it lacks a white eyebrow and its throat is yellow instead of white.

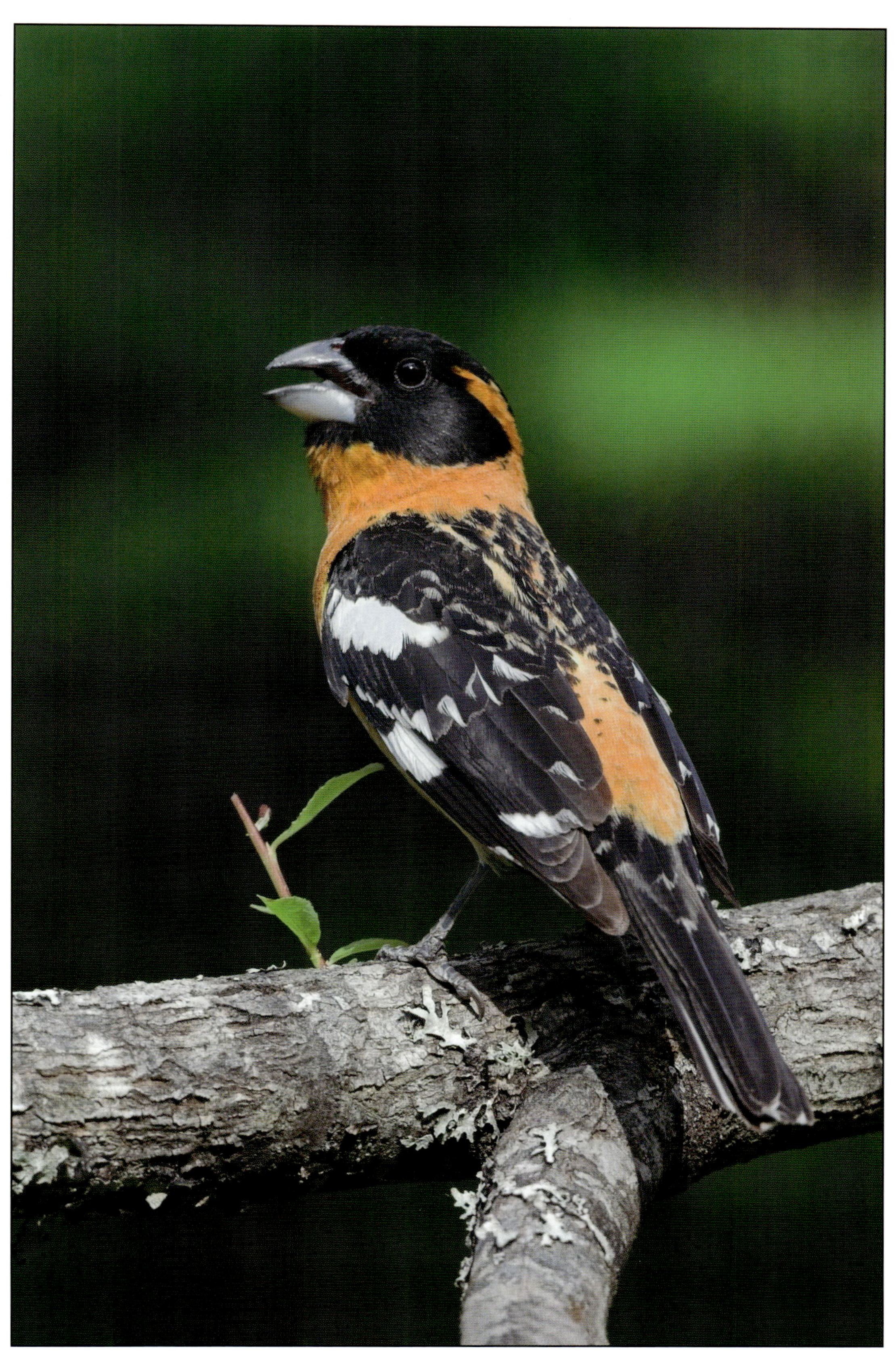

The powerful bill of the Black-headed Grosbeak is well suited for eating seeds that are impenetrable to other birds.

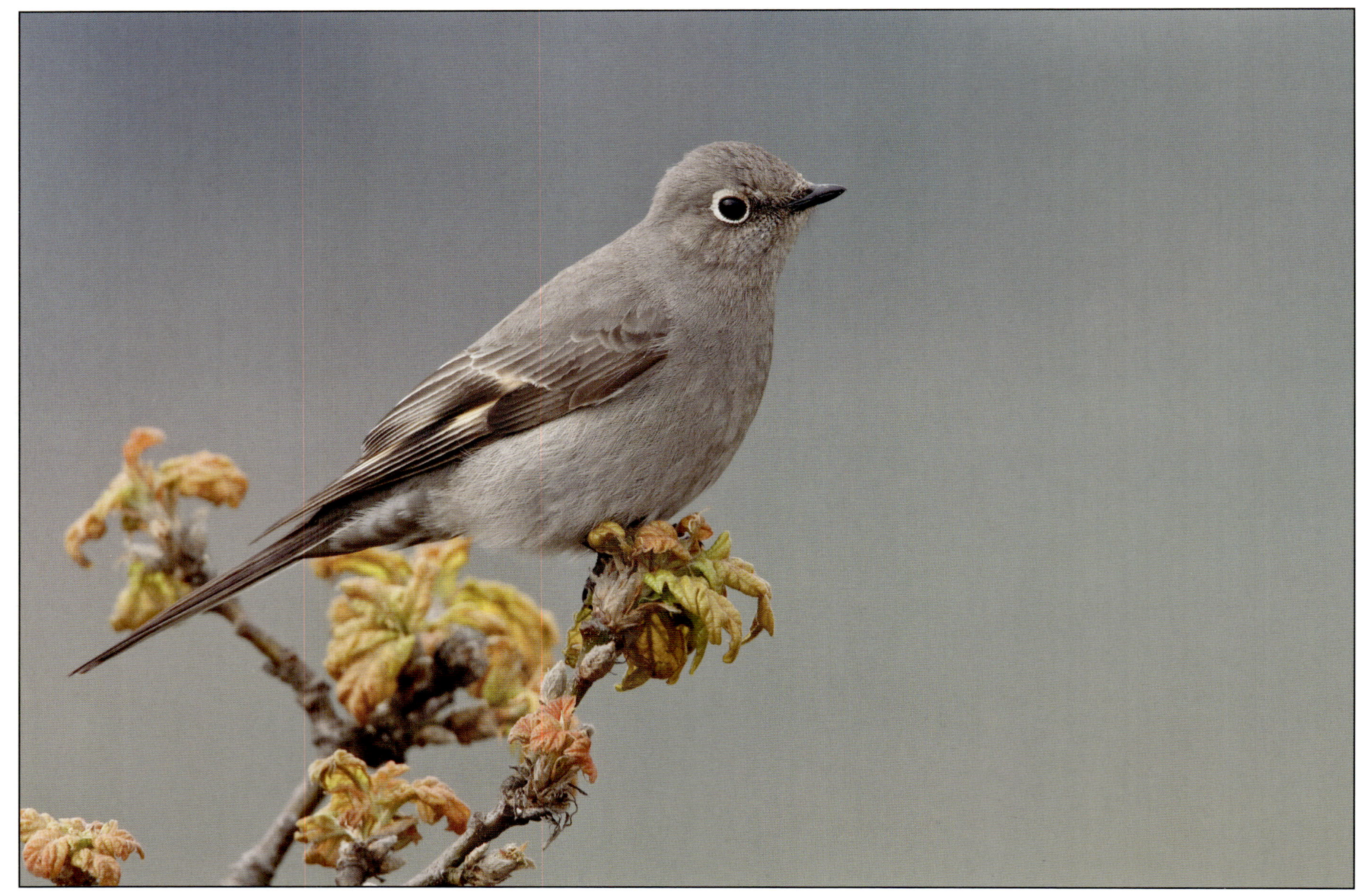

Townsend's Solitaires are most often seen during spring migration when they pass through the southern part of the Island on their way towards their higher elevation breeding grounds.

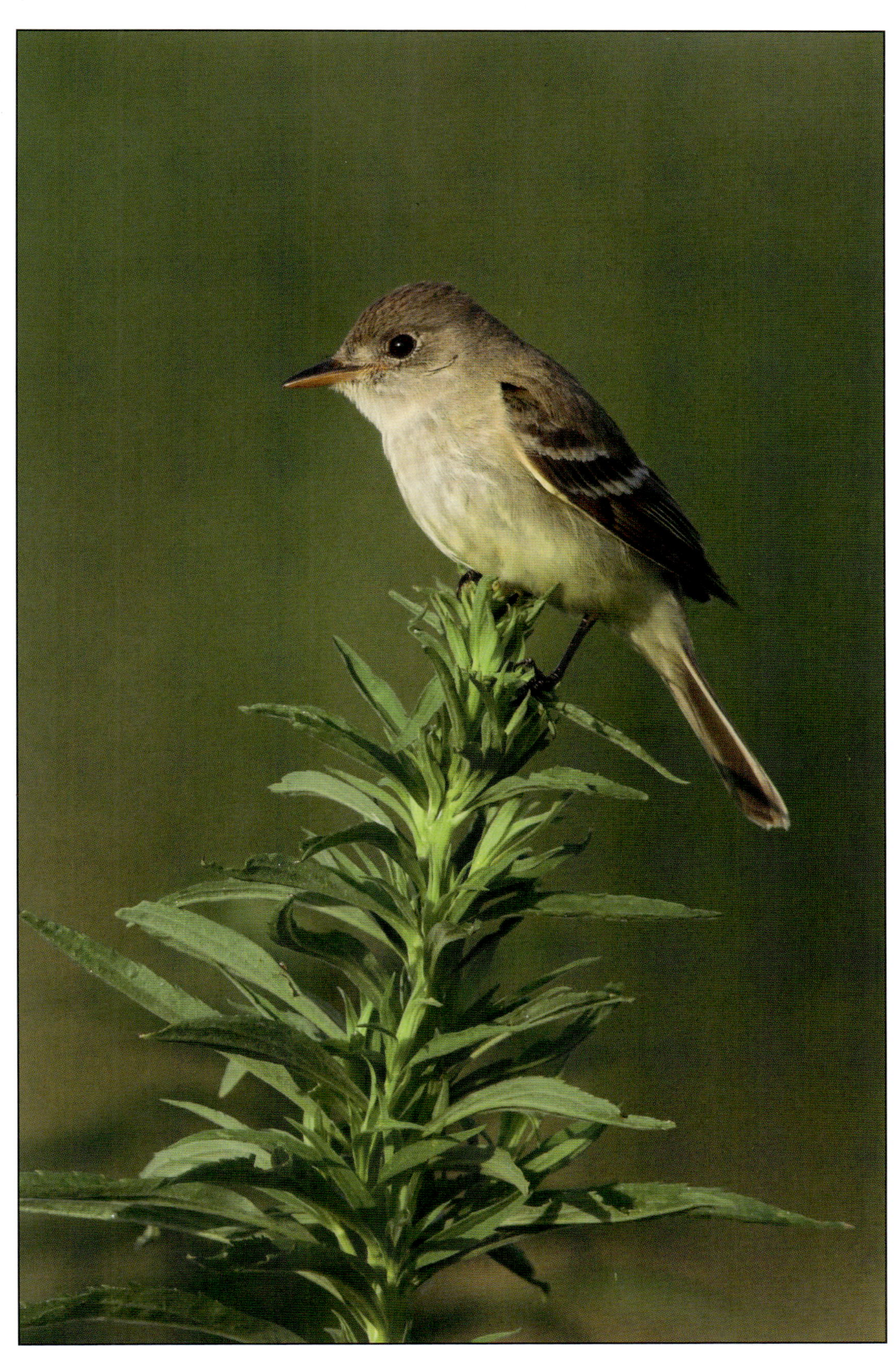

Belonging to the difficult to ID group of Empidonax flycatchers, the Willow Flycatcher is best identified by voice.

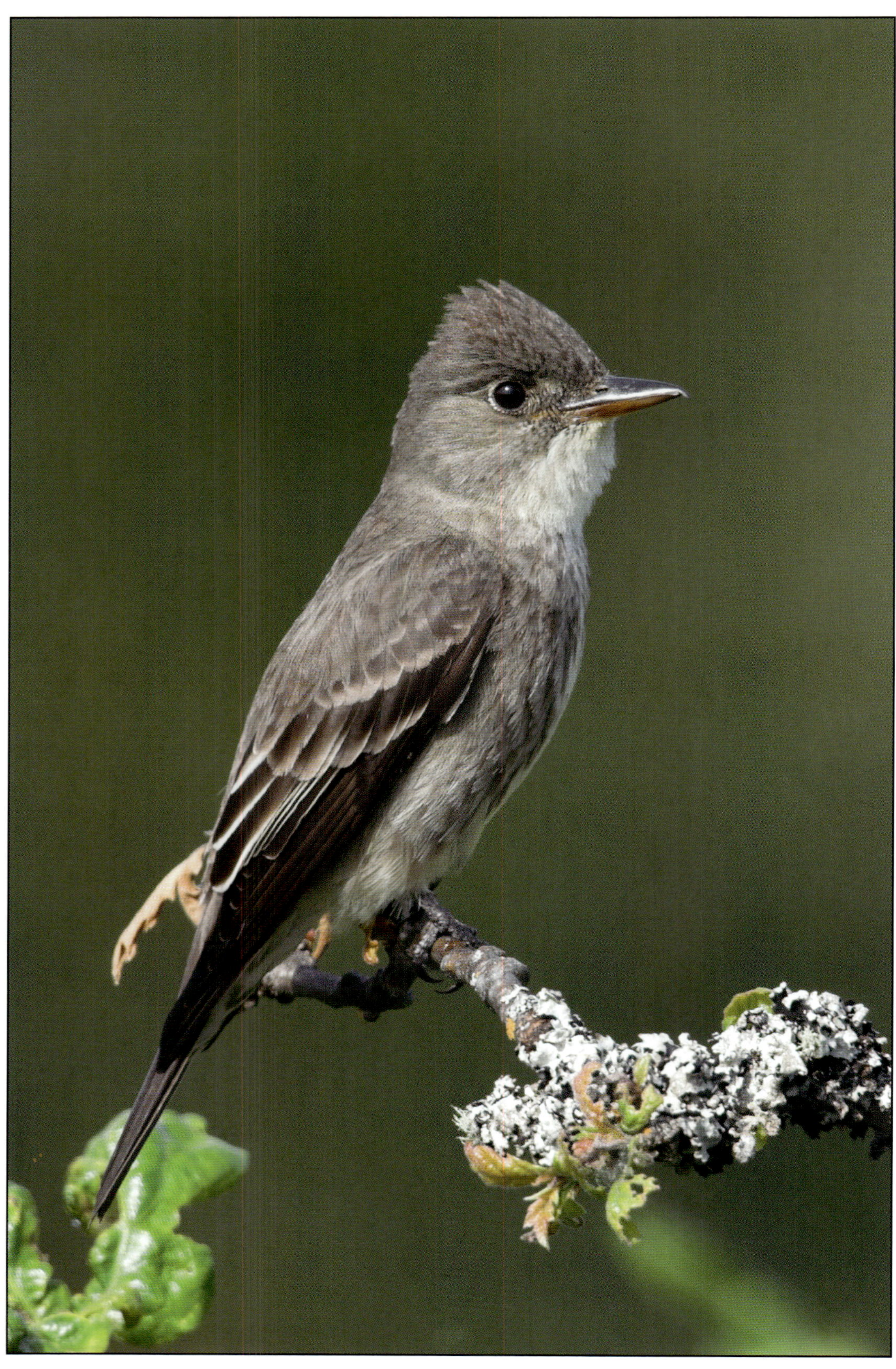

An Olive-sided Flycatcher returns to its perch on top of a Garry Oak tree in between short flights to snatch insects from the air.

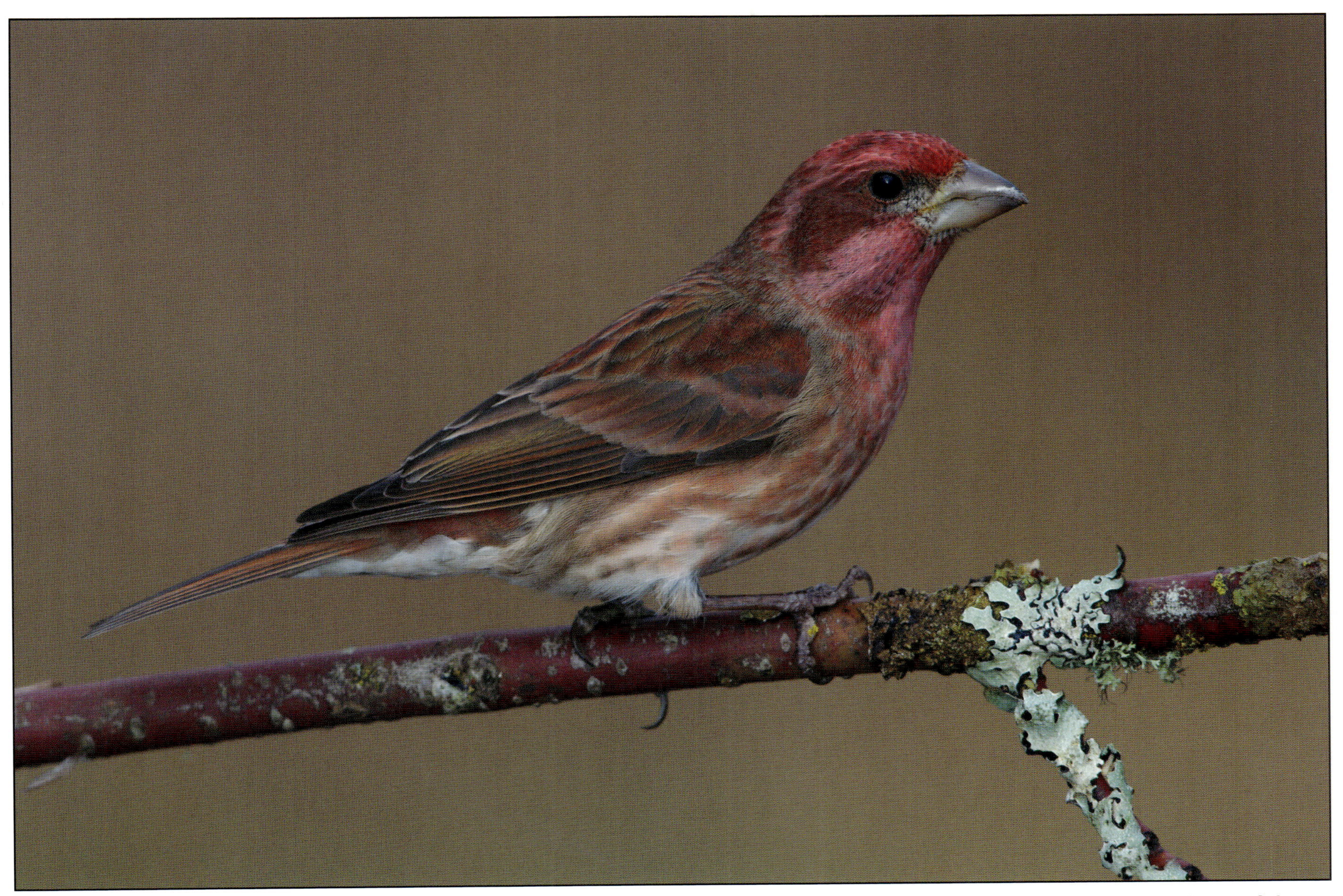

The male Purple Finch is a beautiful shade of red – almost matching the colour of this Red Osier Dogwood.

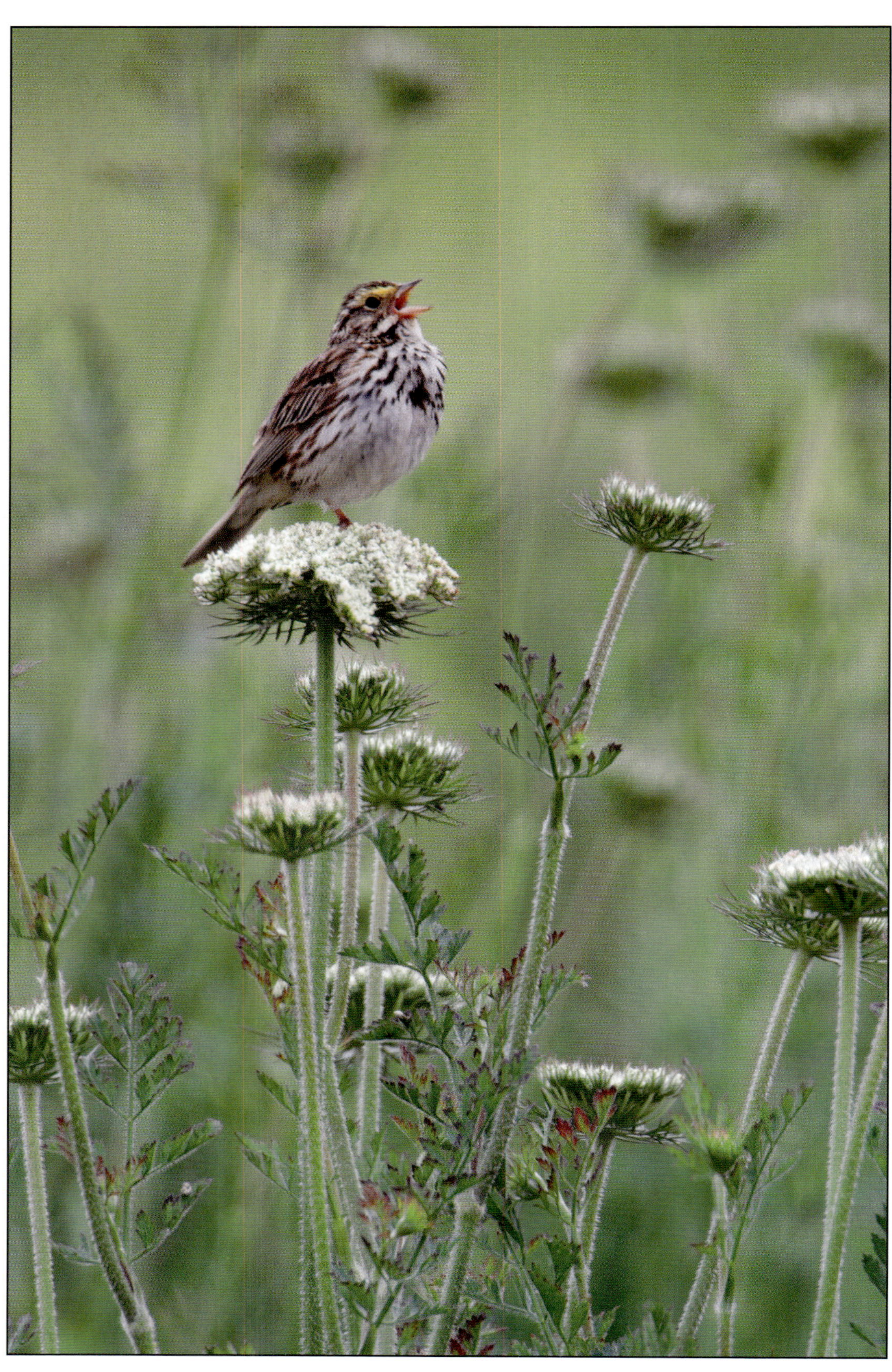

A Savannah Sparrow sings from the top of a Yarrow flower in an open meadow.

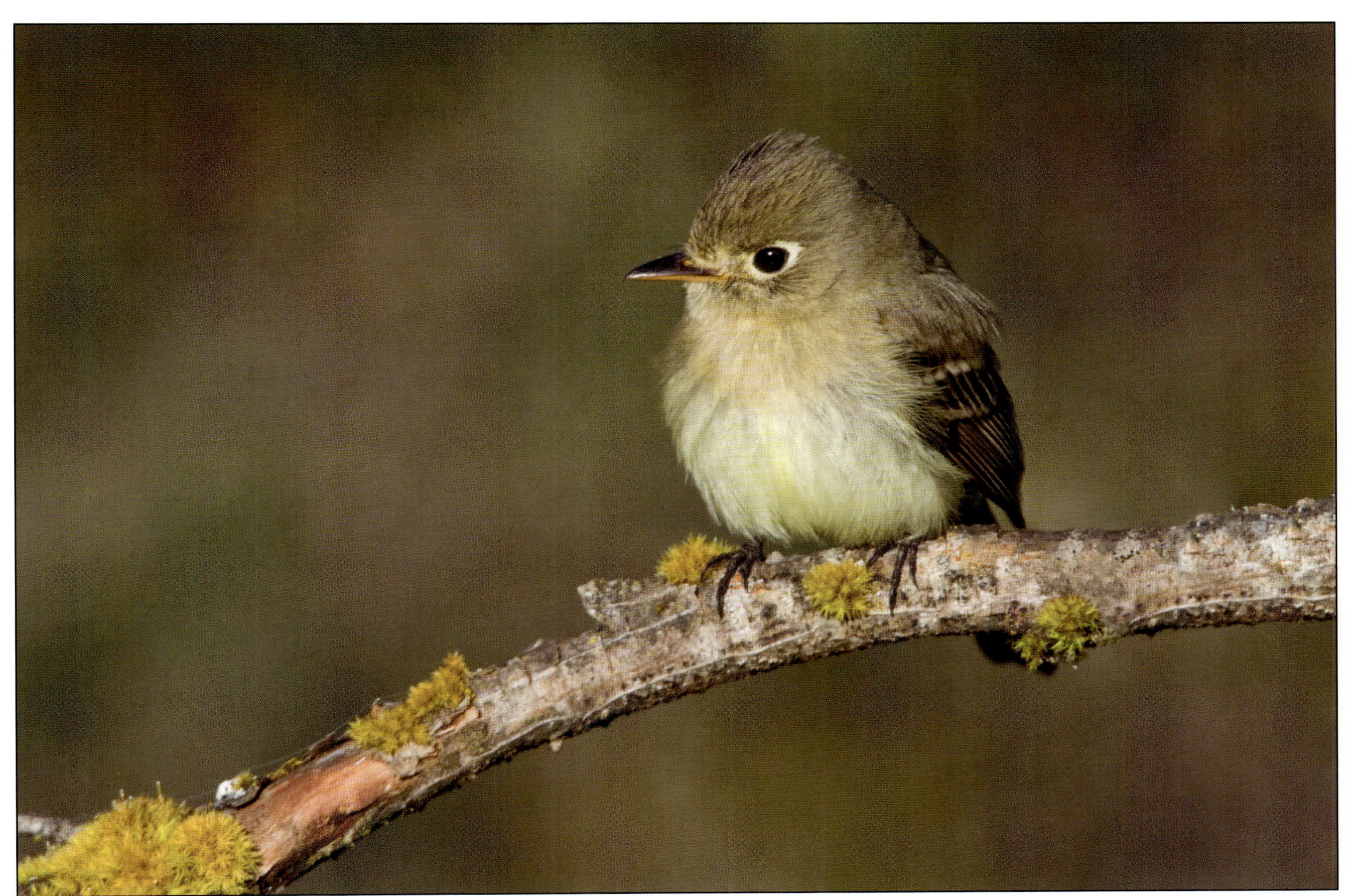

Pacific-slope Flycatchers breed in moist forests on Vancouver Island where their distinct call makes them easily identifiable.

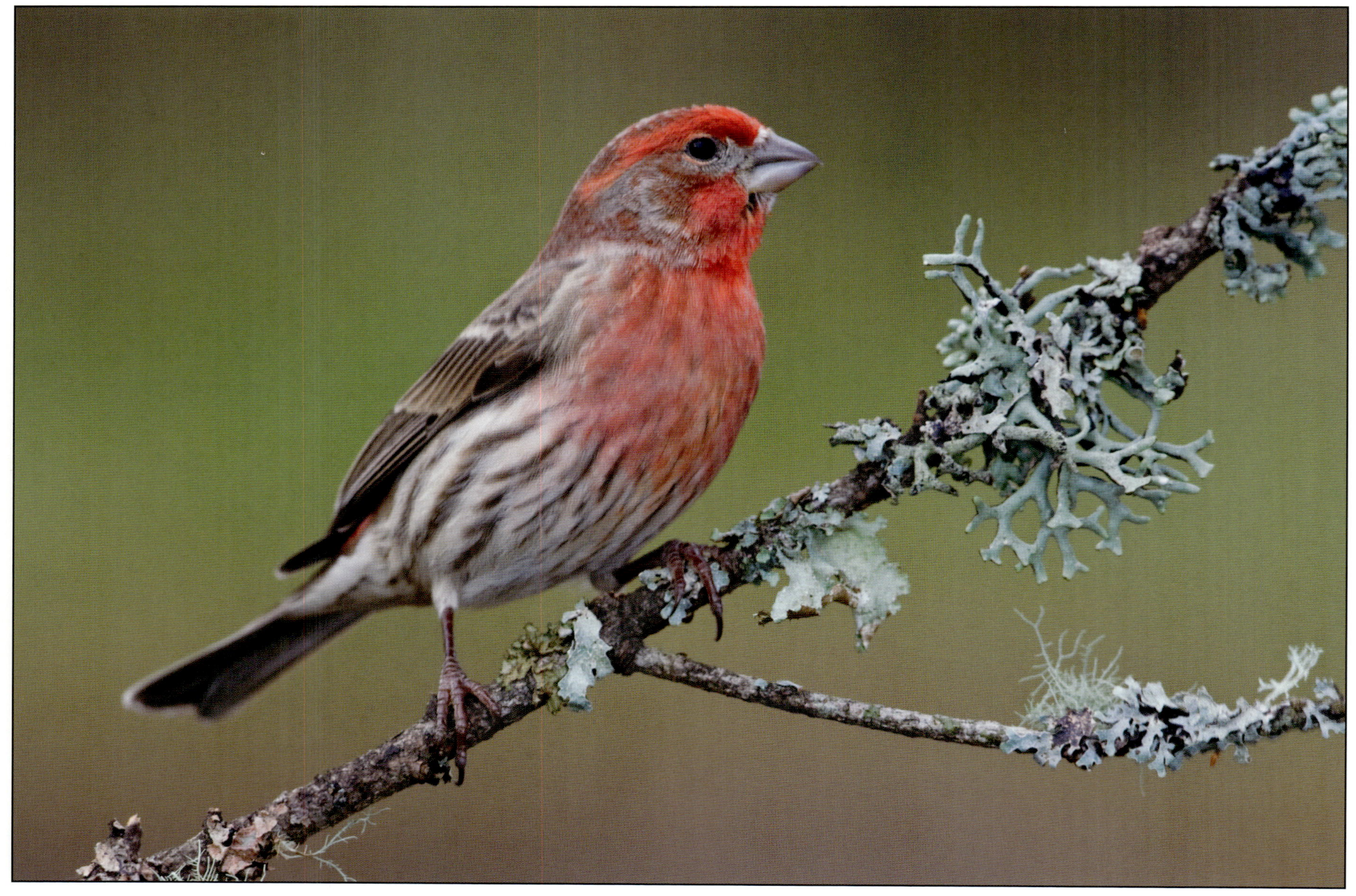

The House Finch is an abundant and widespread bird throughout Canada.

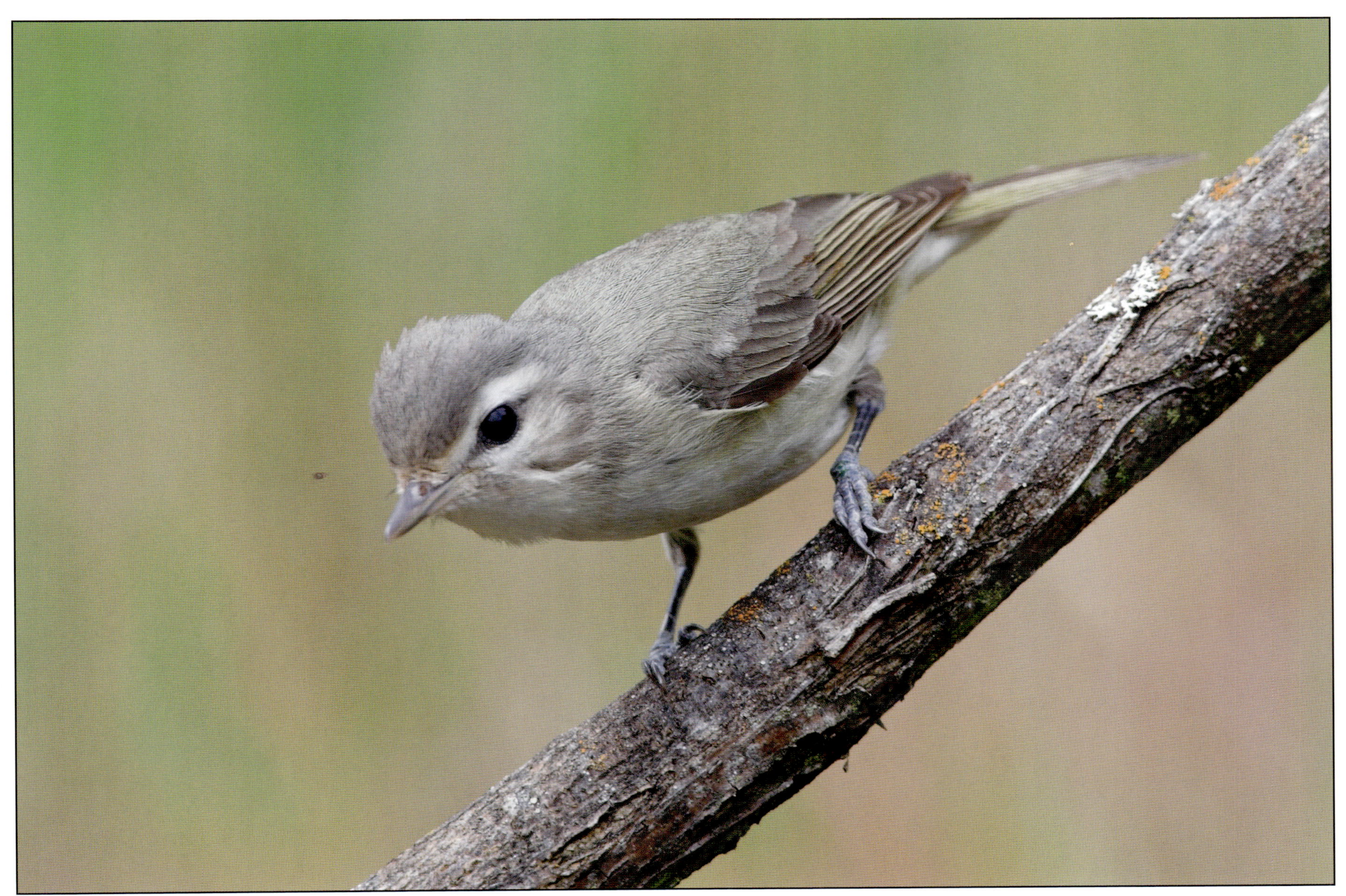

The Warbling Vireo is a common bird of deciduous forests throughout North America.

WATERFOWL

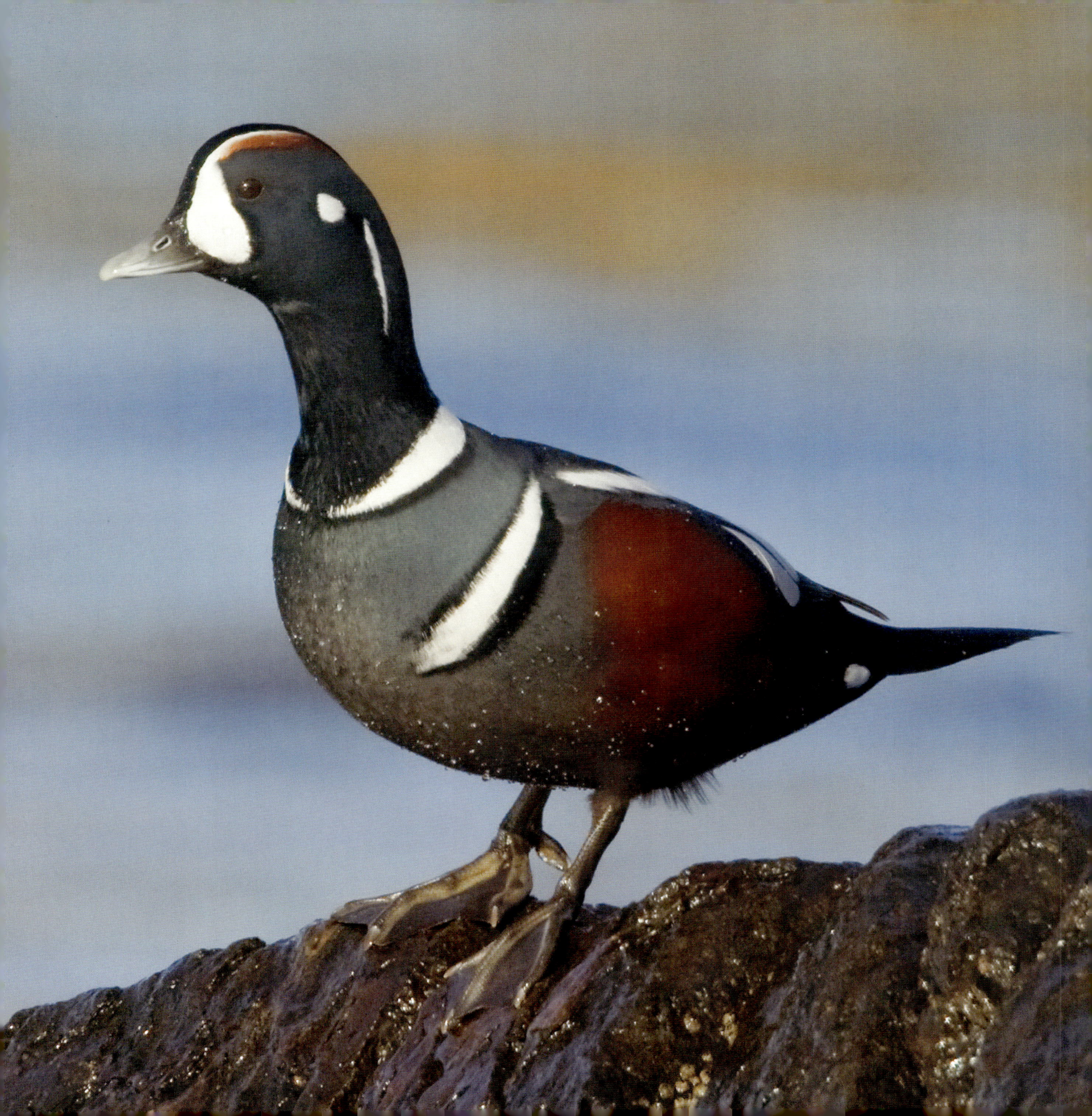

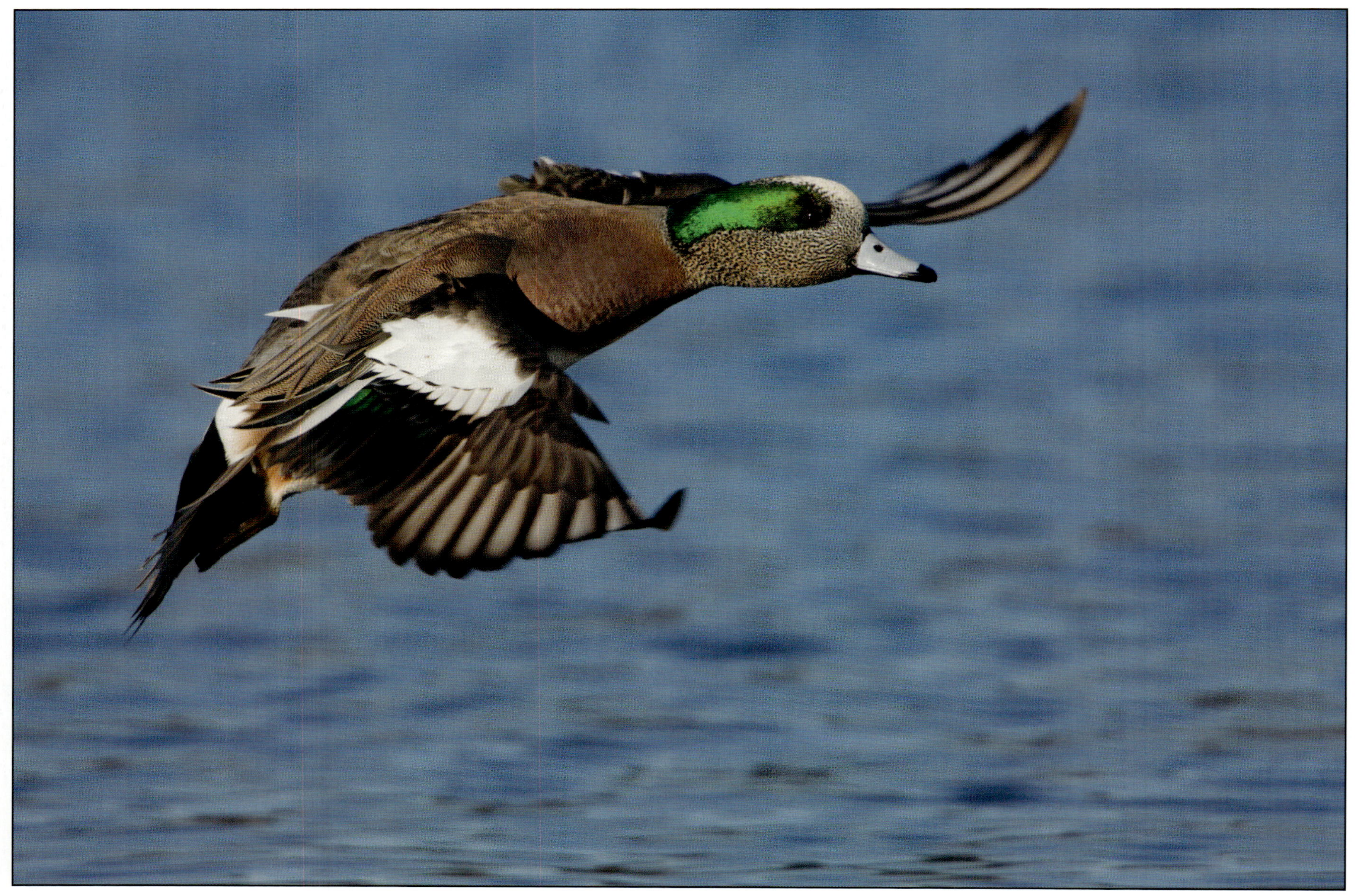

An American Wigeon takes flight from a lagoon off the coast of Vancouver Island – its striking colours shimmering in the sunlight.

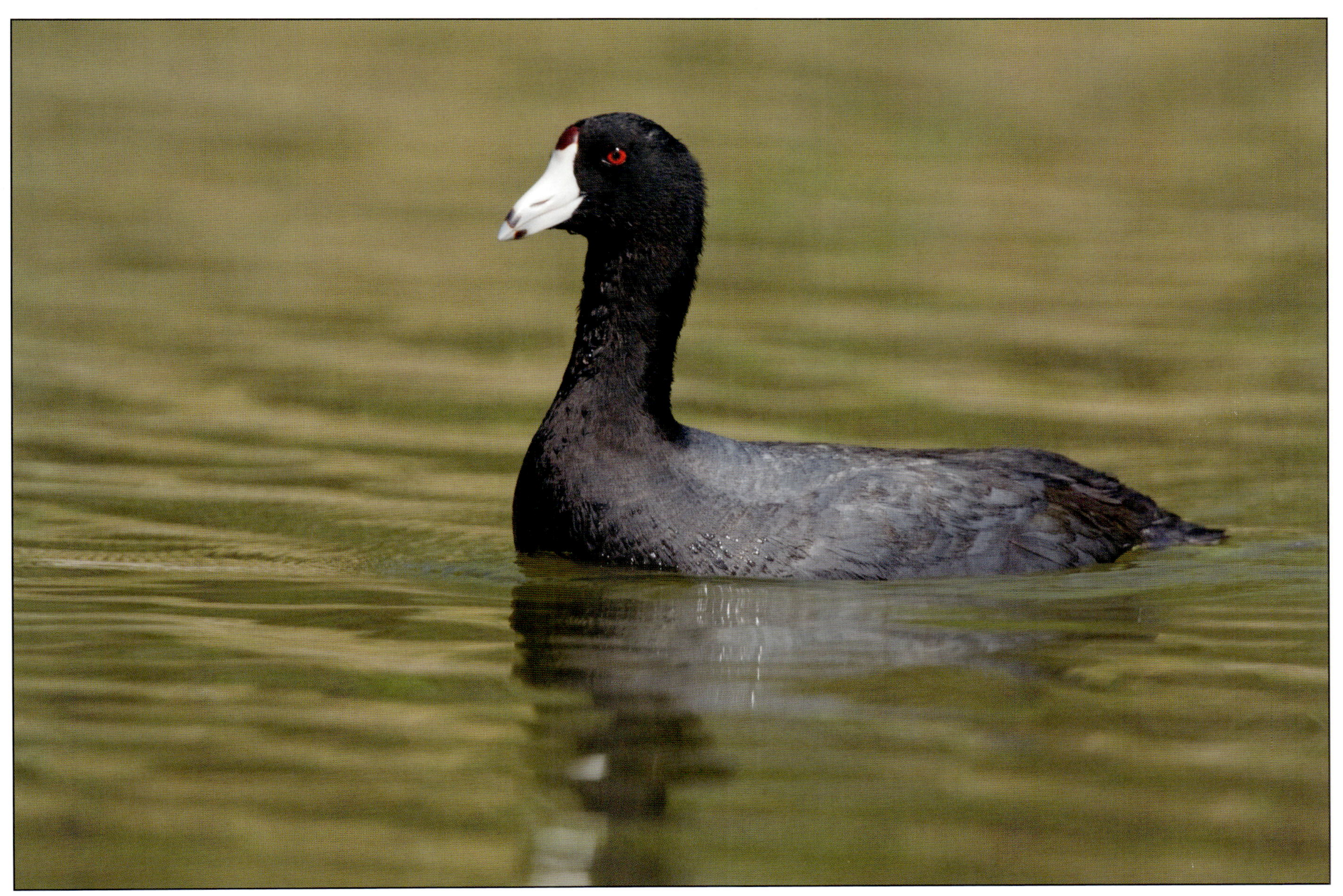

The strange looking American Coot is often found exploring the shallow waters at the margins of lakes.

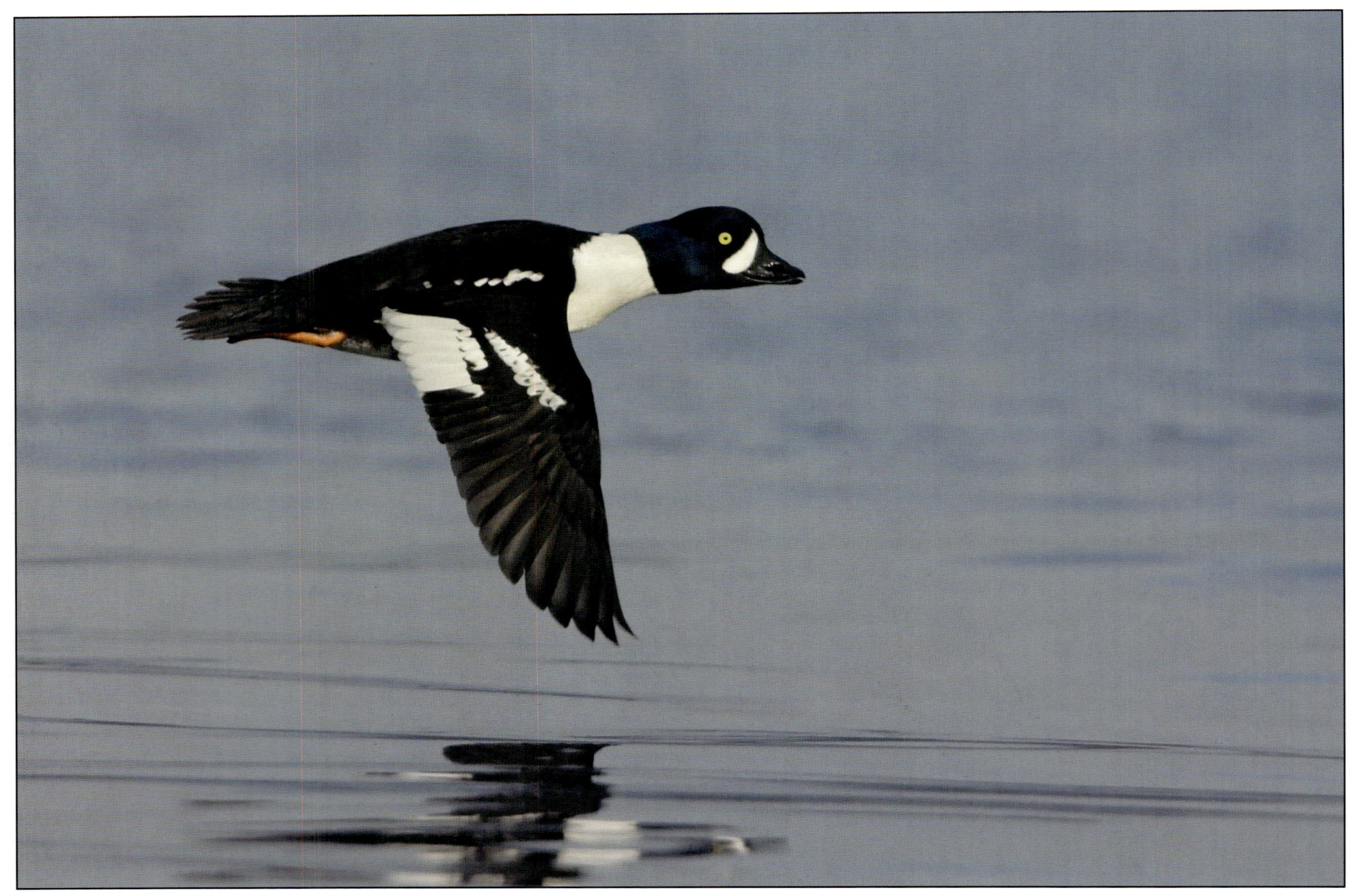

Much rarer than its common relative, the Barrow's Goldeneye is differentiated by a crescent-shaped white facial patch.

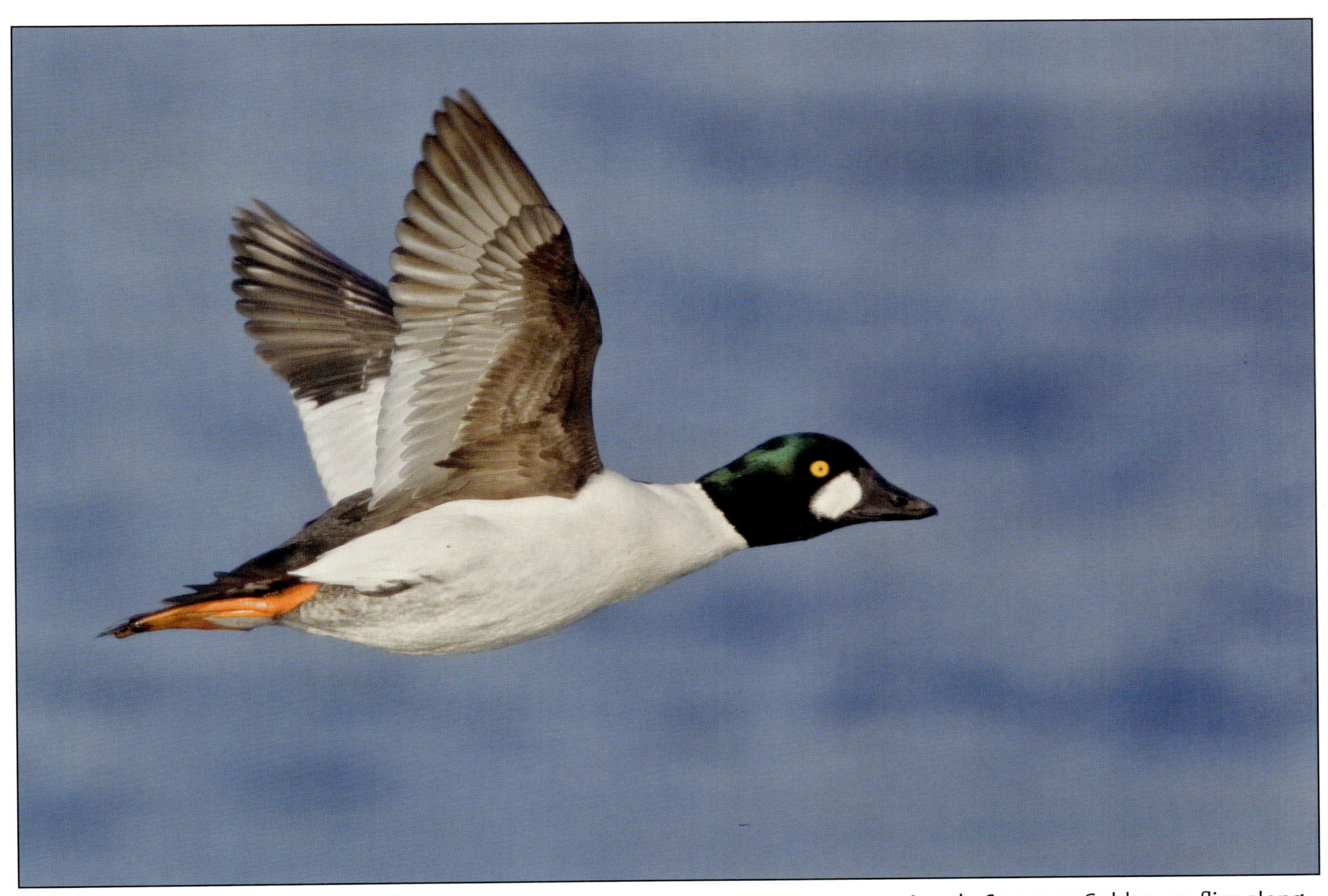

A male Common Goldeneye flies along the oceanfront illuminated by the early morning sunlight.

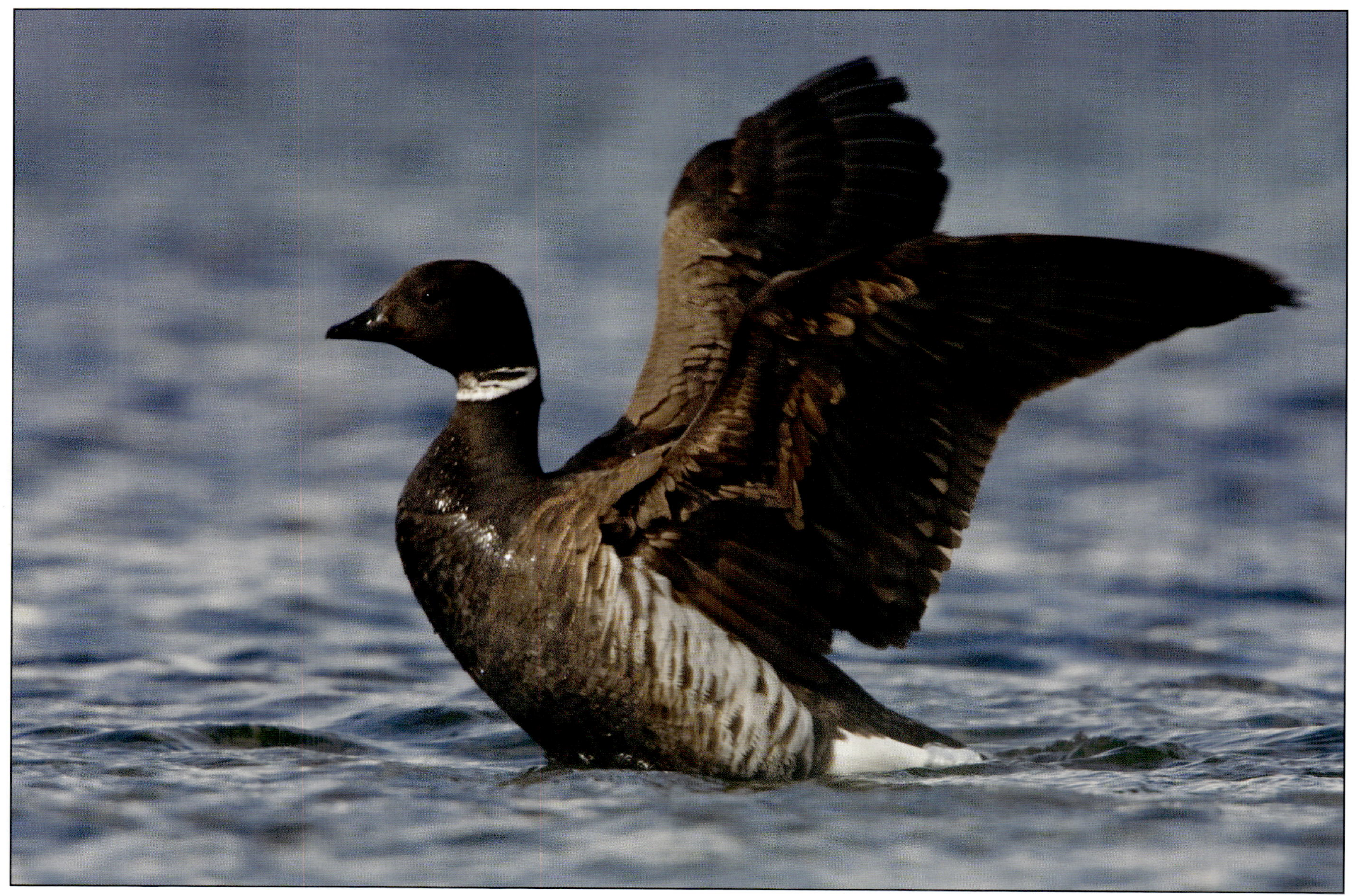

Thousands of Brant migrate along the coast of Vancouver Island each spring on their way north to breed.

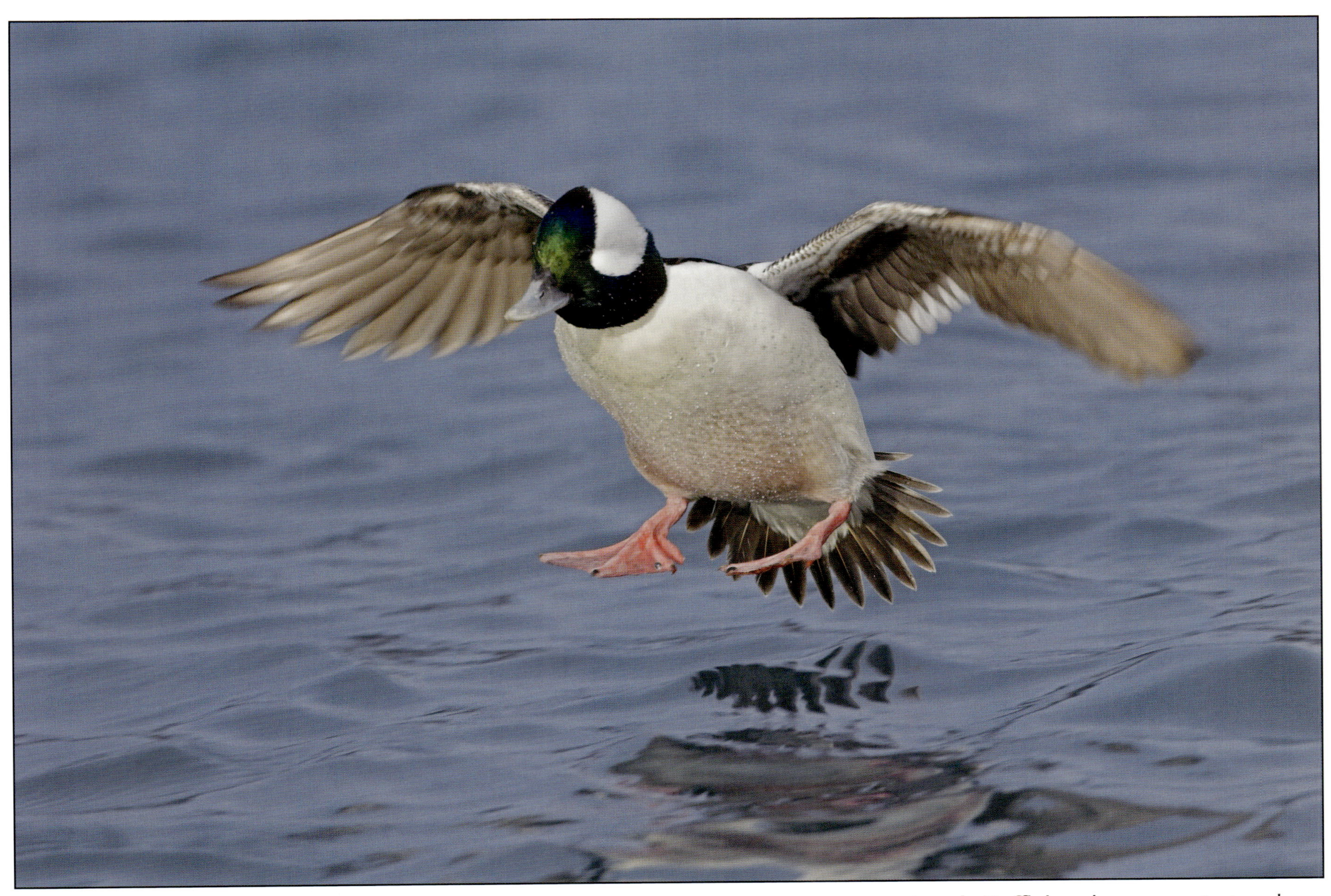

A male Bufflehead prepares to touch down for landing on a coastal lagoon.

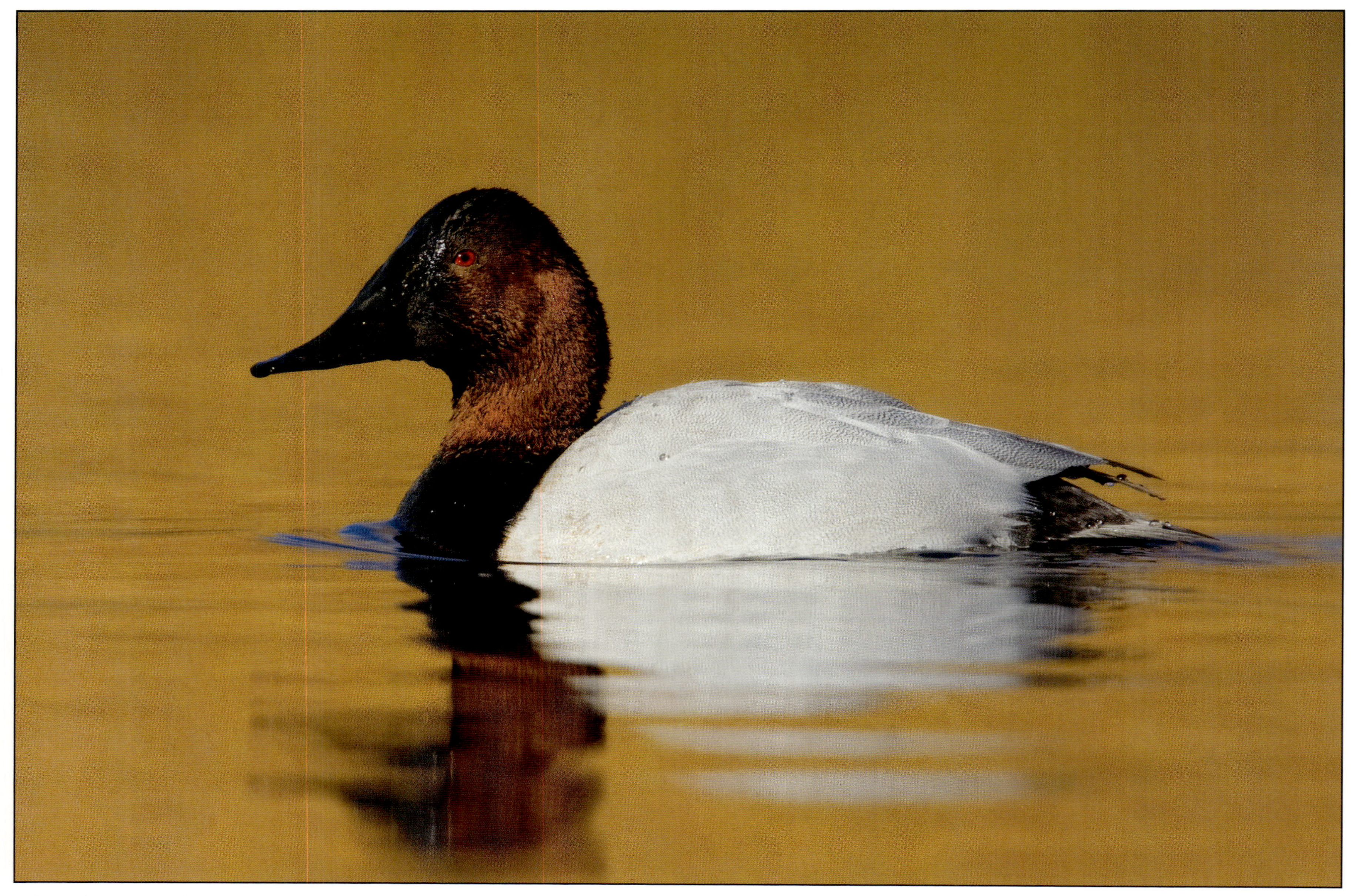

A handsome male Canvasback cruises through the calm water on this golden pond. These ducks dive for food buried in the sediment as is evident from this bird's muddy face.

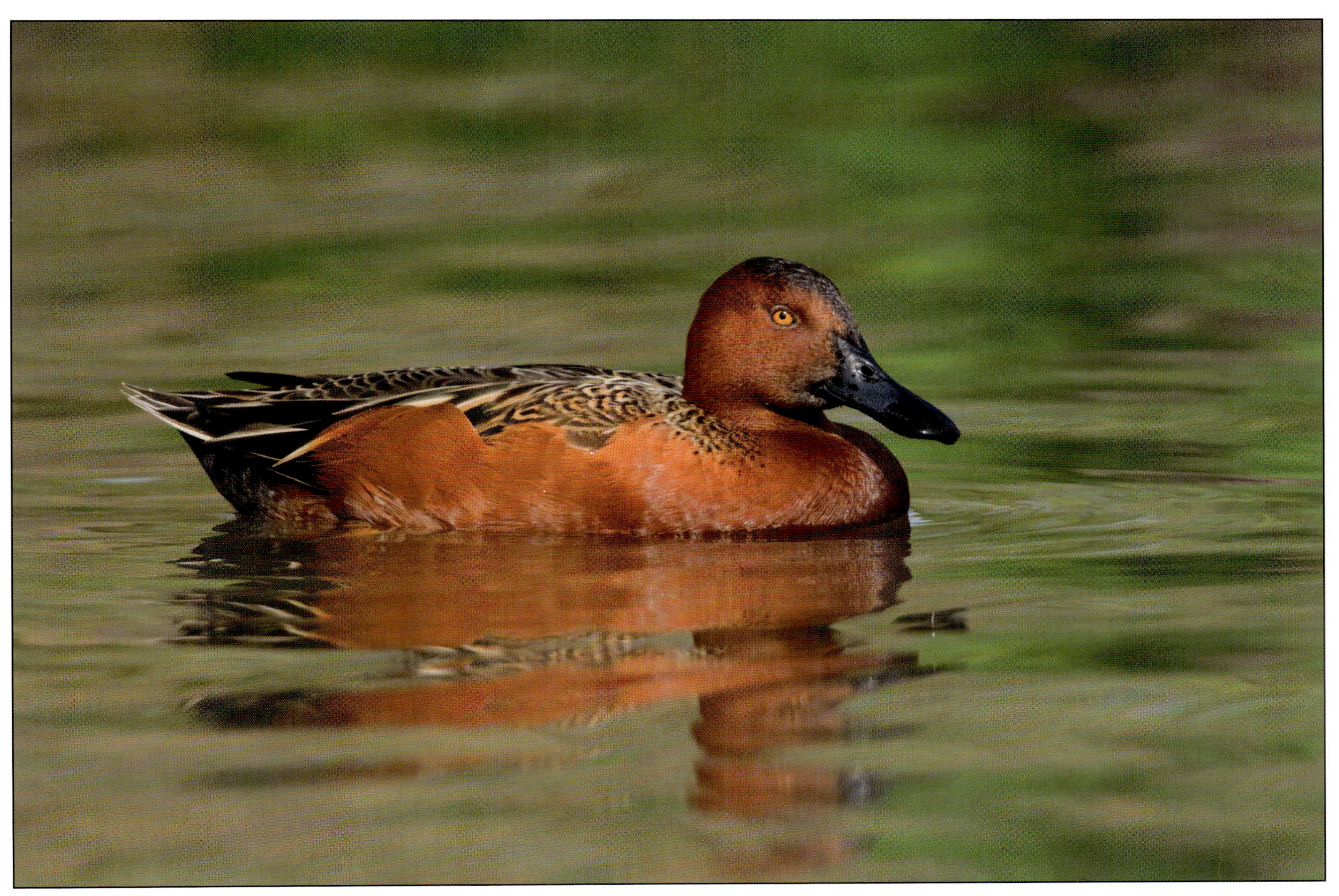

Found on southern Vancouver Island in marshes and small ponds, Cinnamon Teals are among Vancouver Island's most striking species of waterfowl.

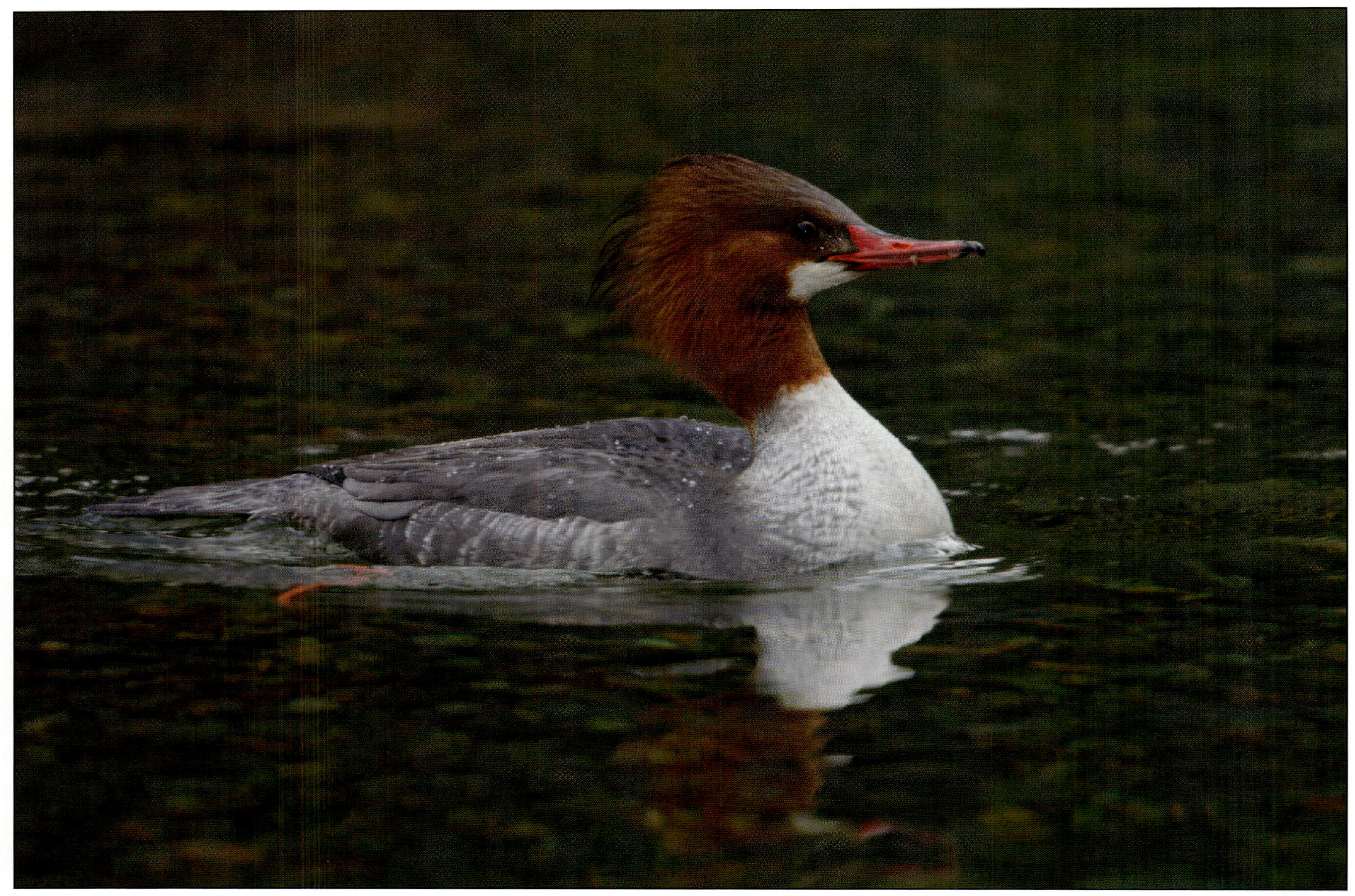

A female Common Merganser swims along a small stream during the fall salmon spawn hoping to take advantage of this seasonal abundance of food.

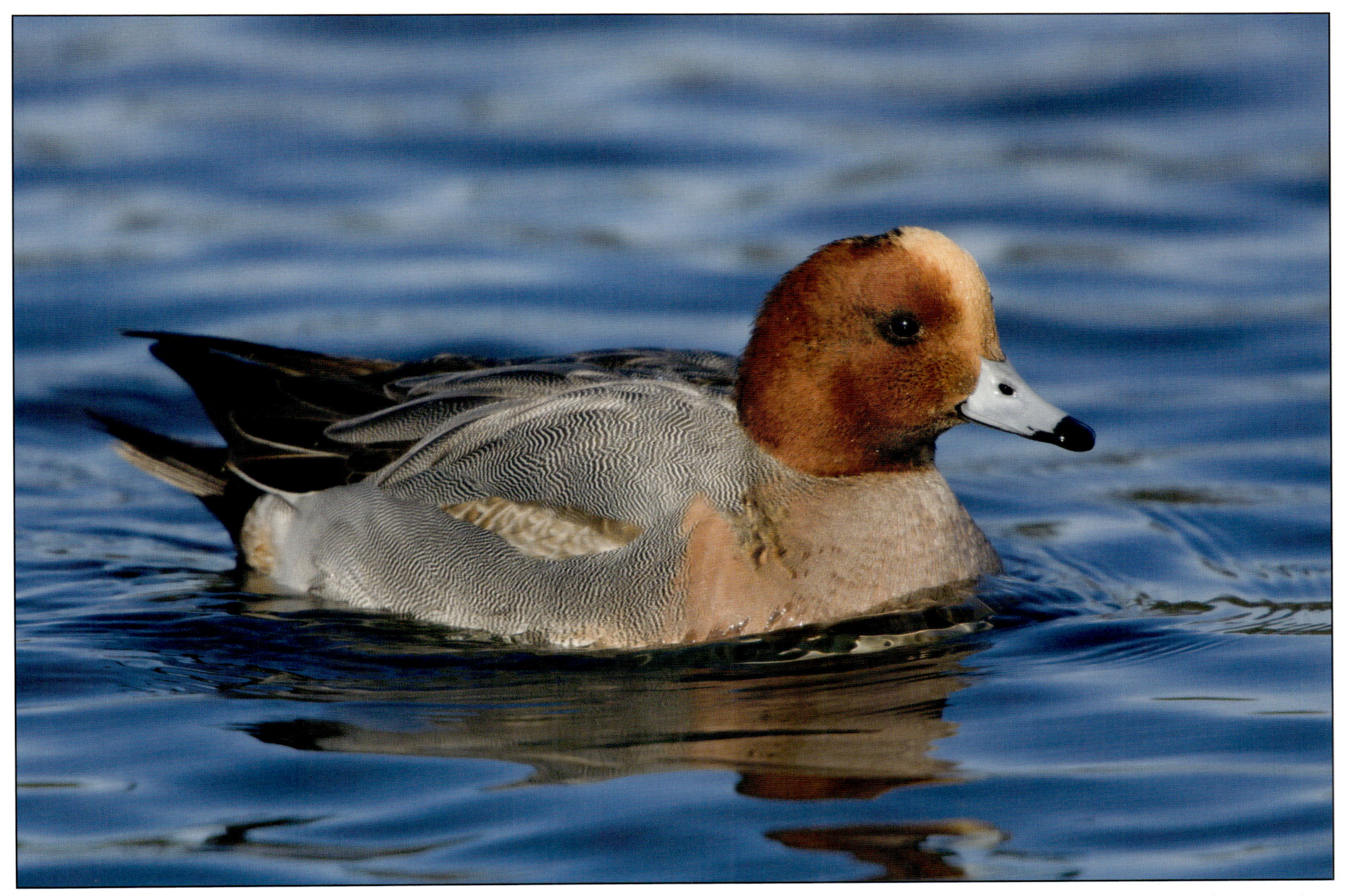

Unlike its American cousin, the Eurasian Wigeon has a rusty-red head. A few lost birds usually turn up in the winter amongst the flocks of other wigeons.

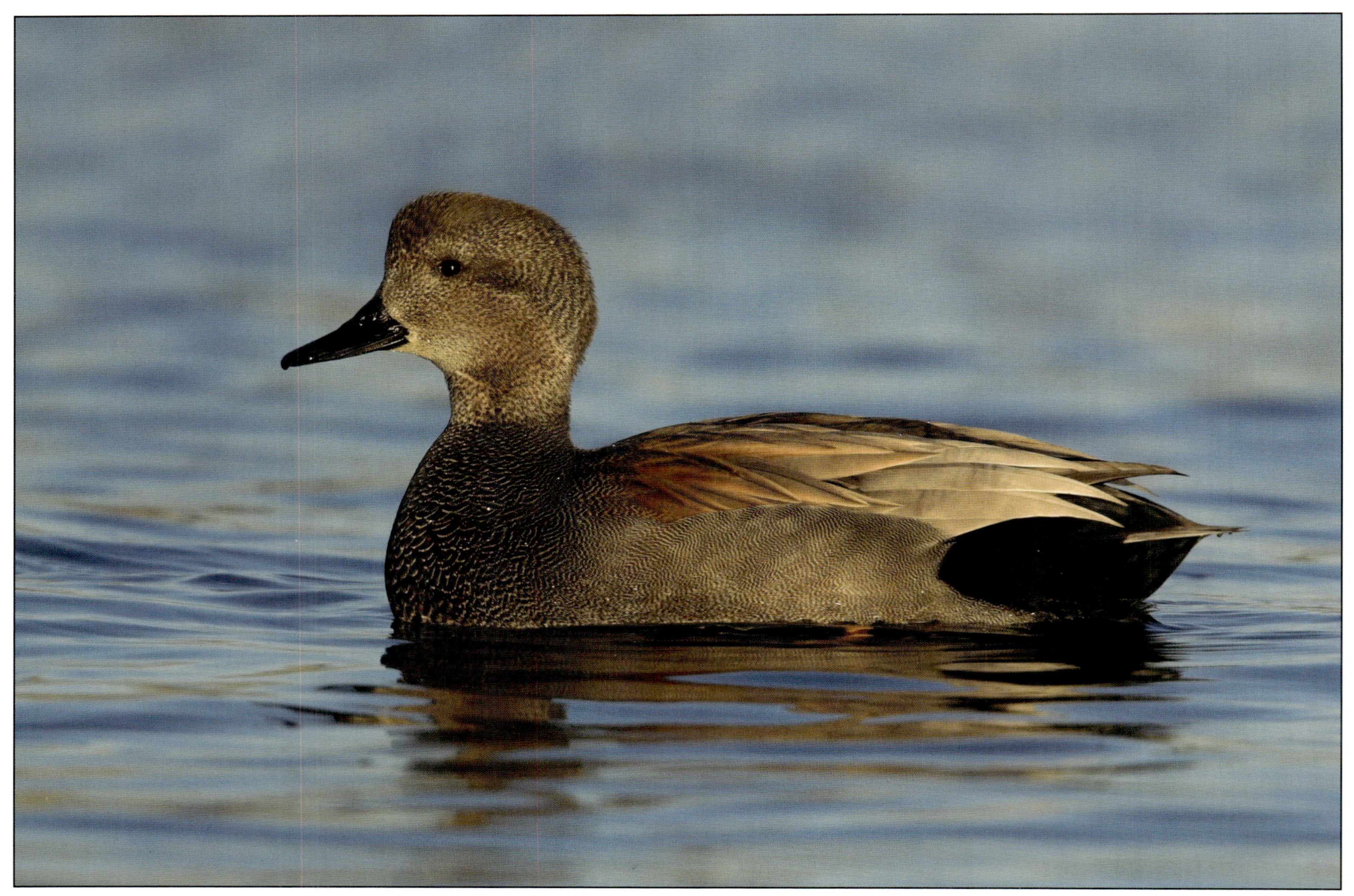

A sleek looking Gadwall basks in the late afternoon sunlight on a calm pond.

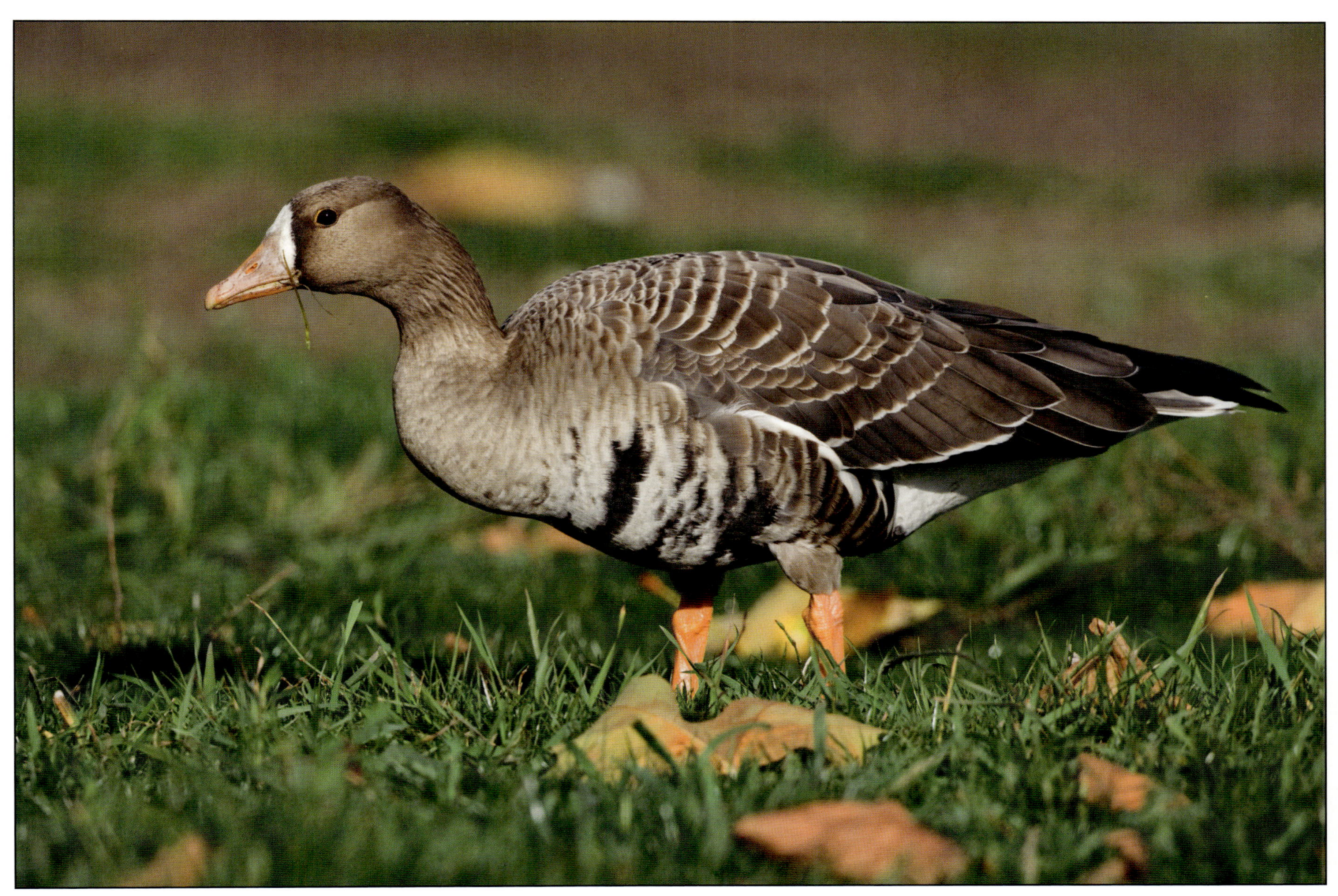

A Greater White-fronted Goose feeds on grass to fuel up for its long migratory journey south during the fall.

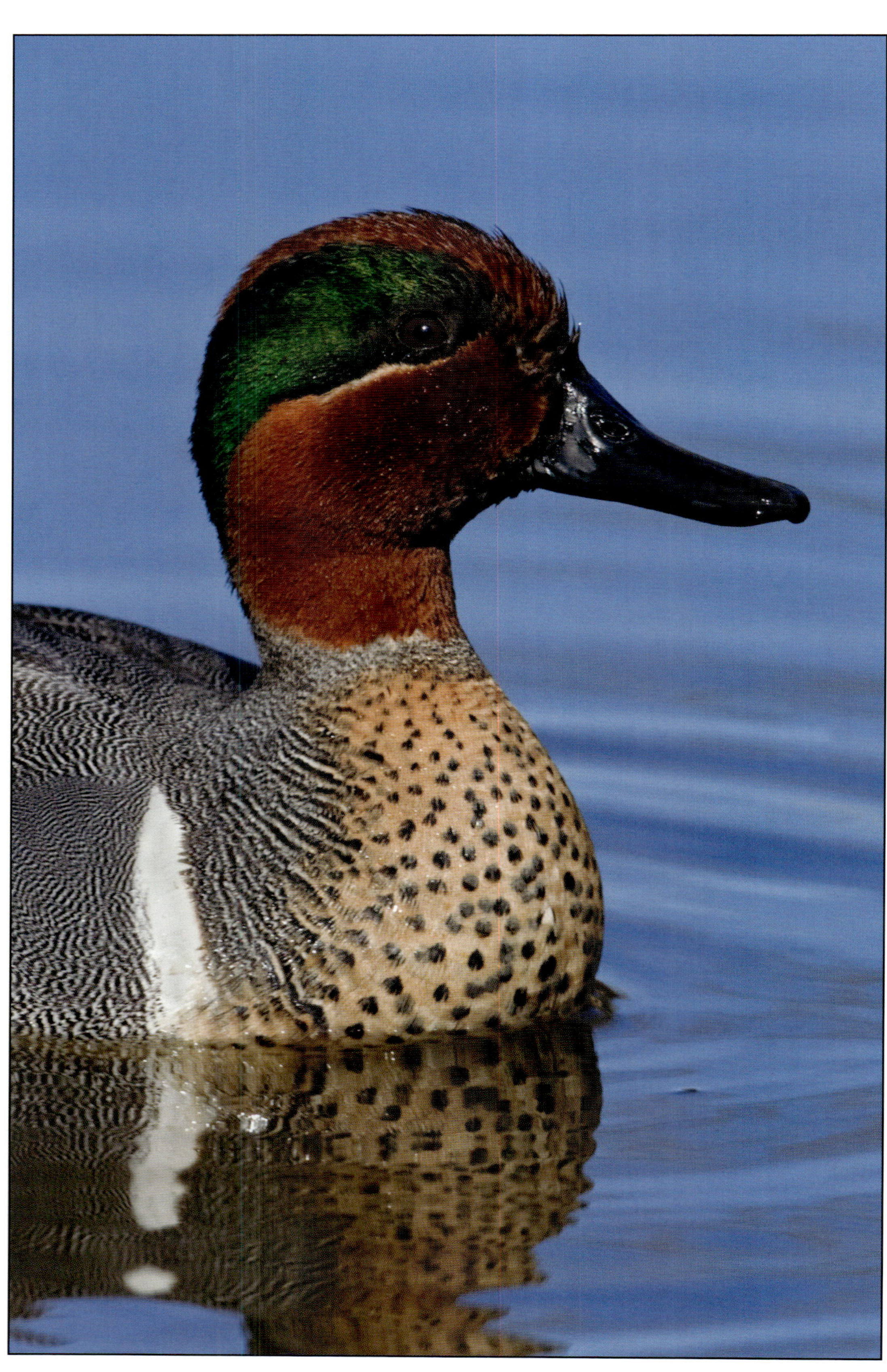

A male Green-winged Teal cautiously patrols a small pond near Victoria. These birds often winter on Vancouver Island before returning inland to breed.

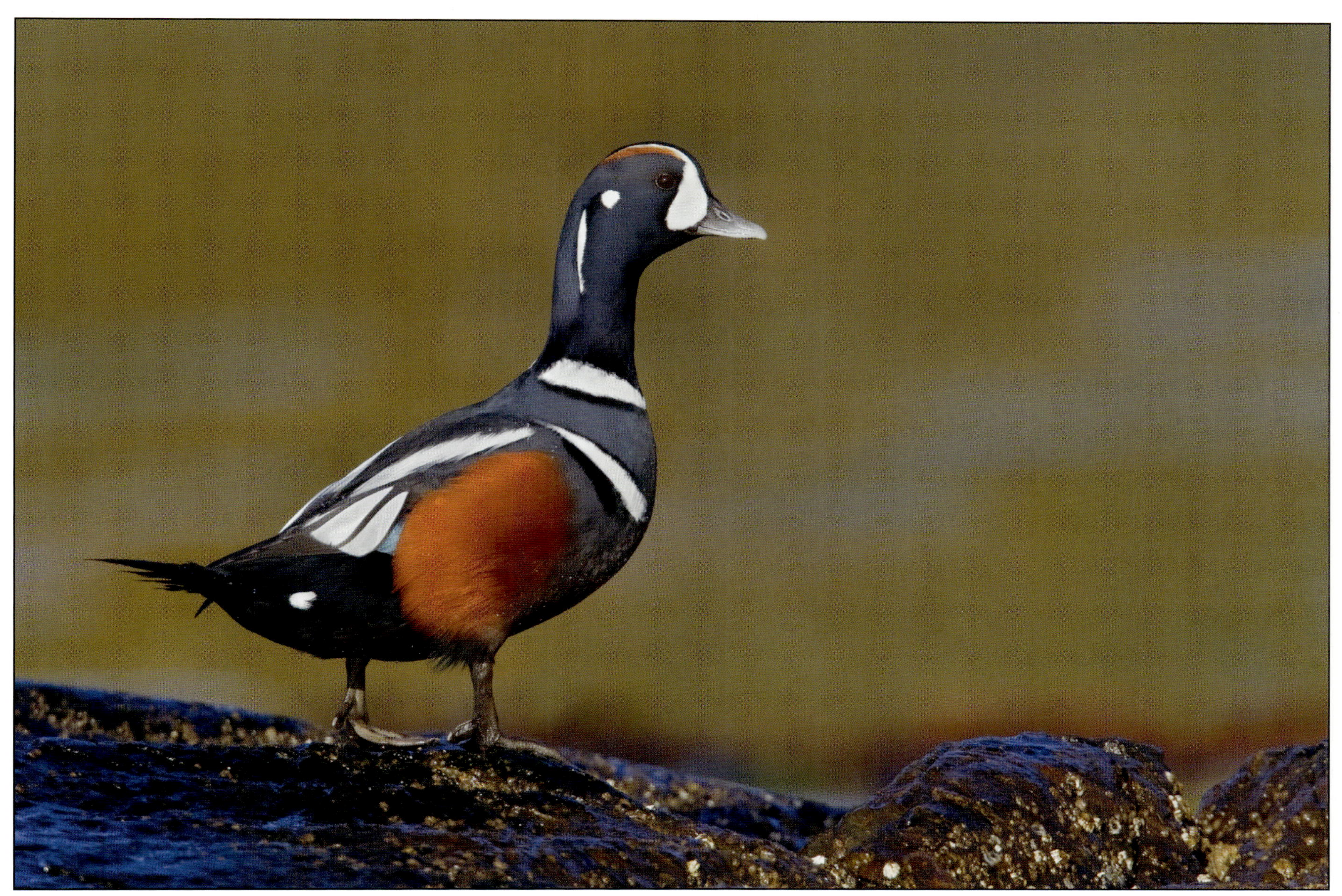

A gorgeous male Harlequin Duck poses along the coastline before diving back into the turbulent waters to search for a meal.

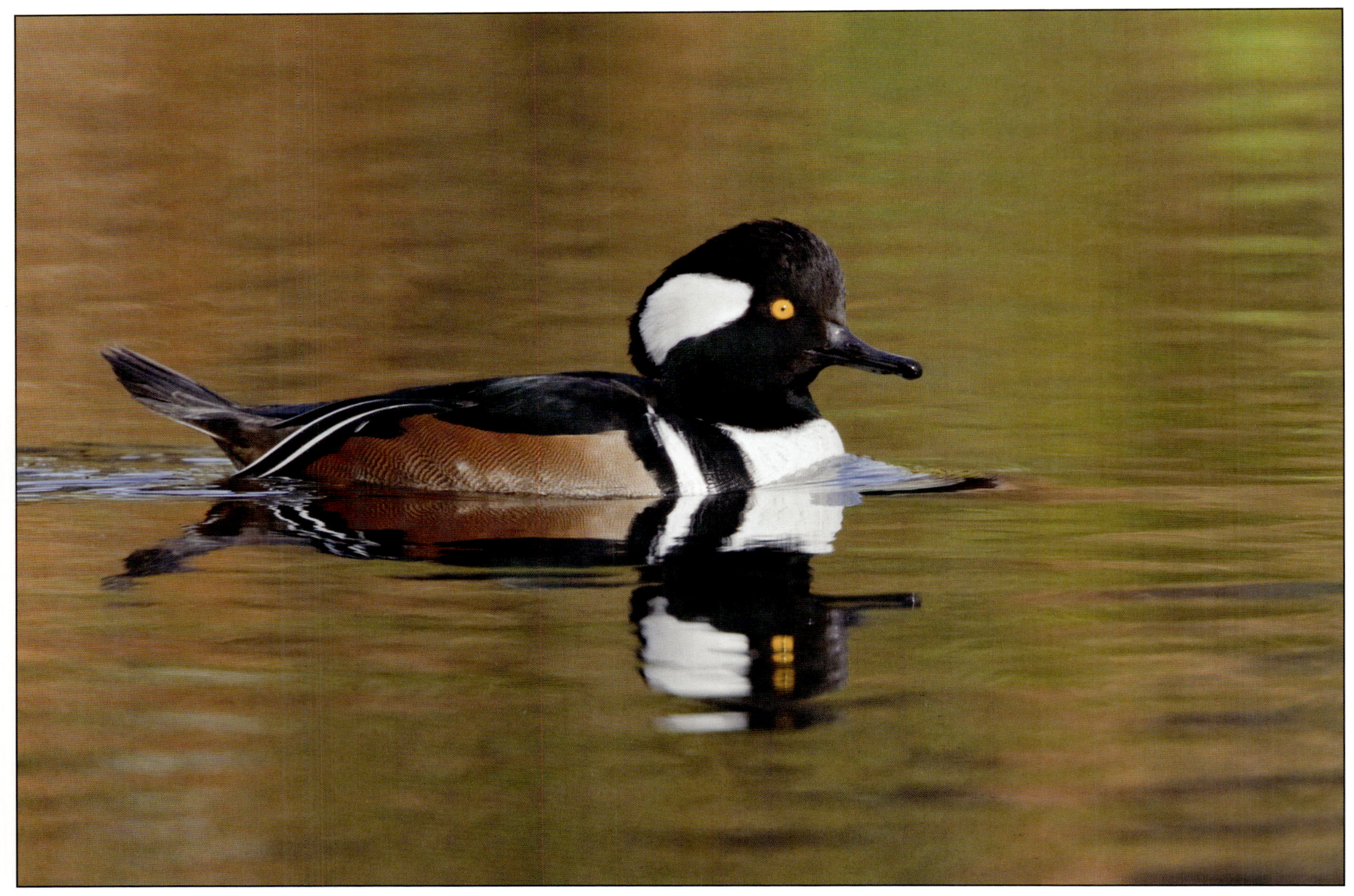

The male Hooded Merganser is unmistakable with its black and white crest and long serrated bill.

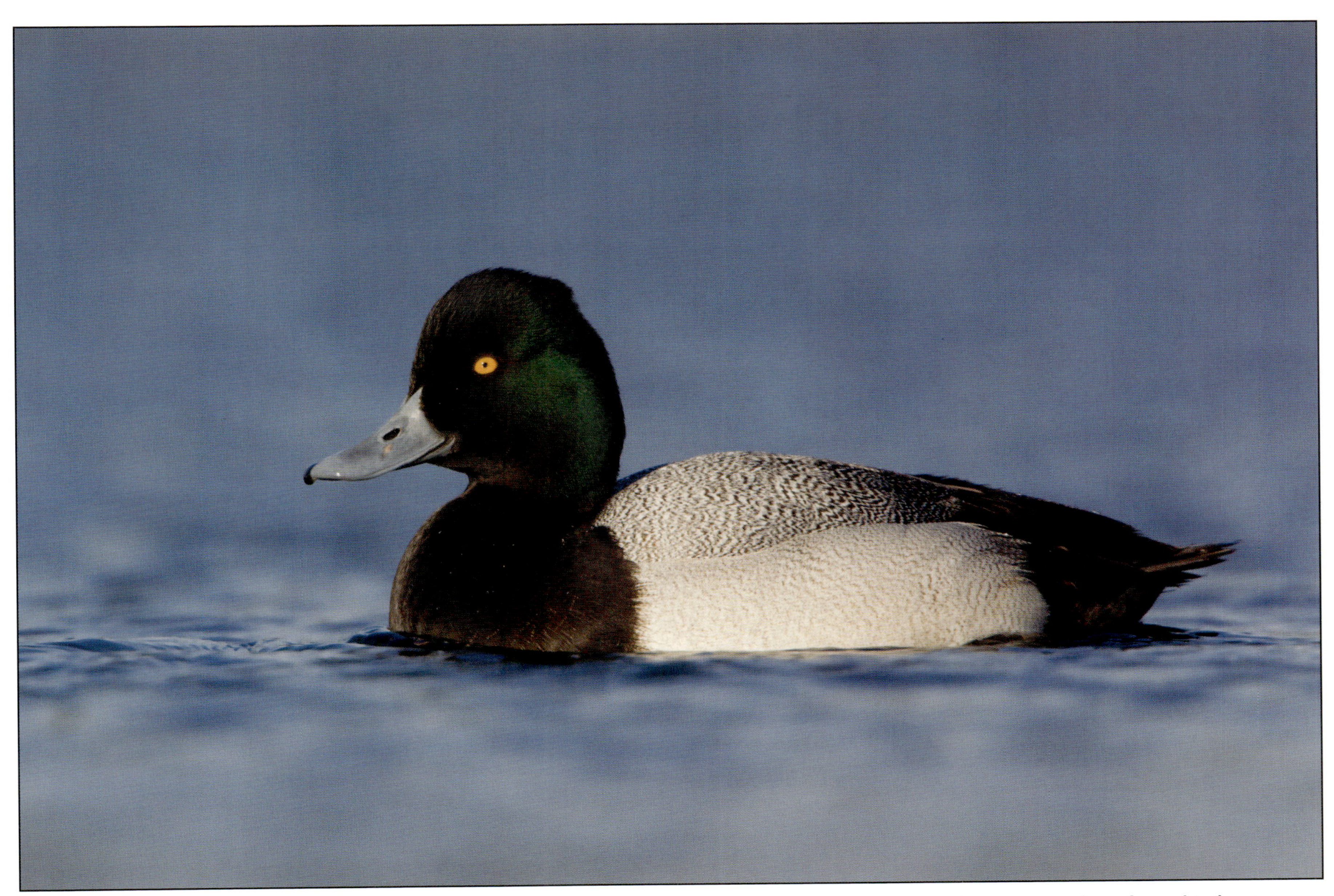

Lesser Scaup are often found in large flocks during the winter months on Vancouver Island where they seek food and shelter on protected bodies of water.

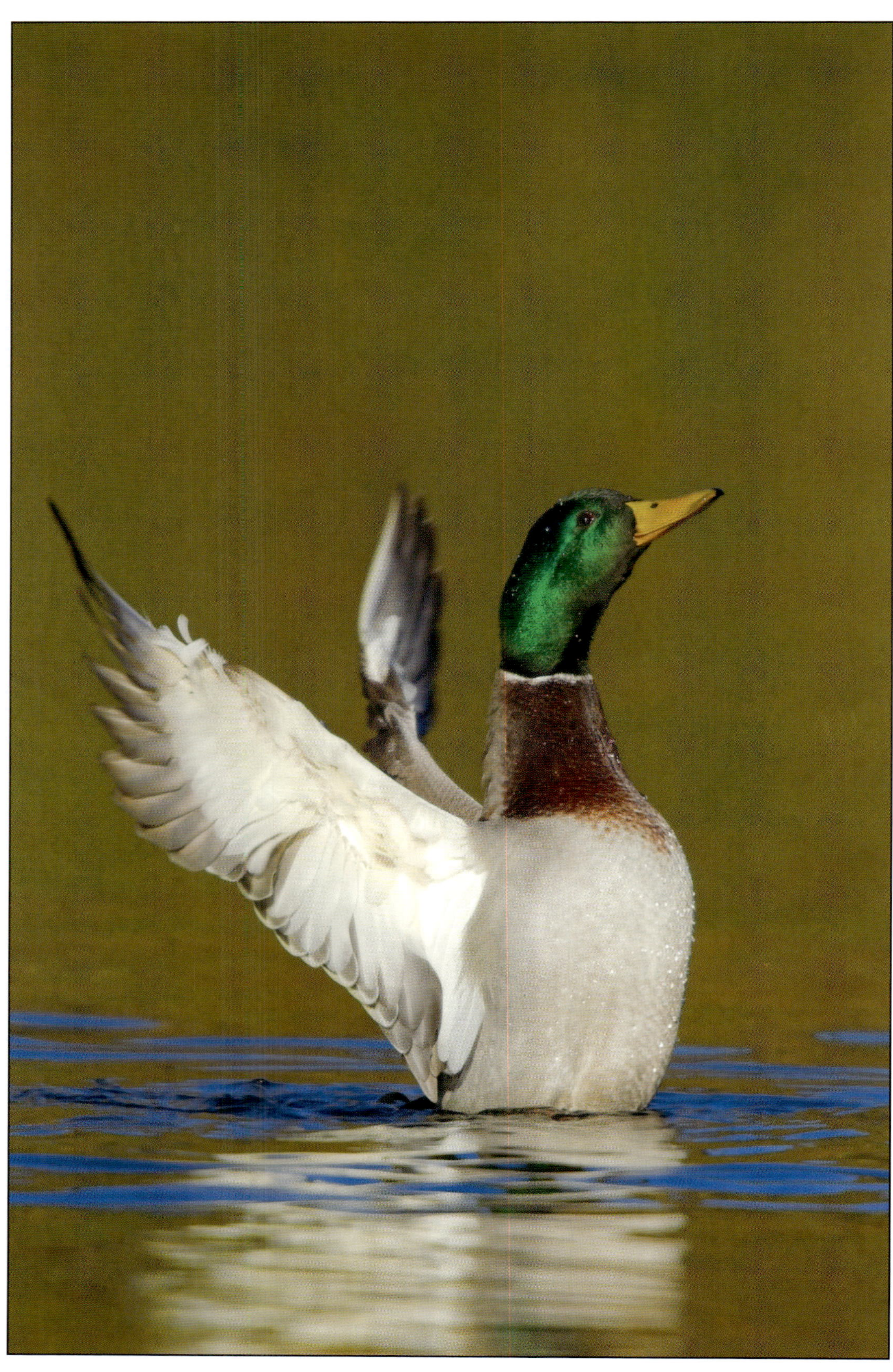

Common throughout North America, it is easy to forget how stunning Mallard ducks really are.

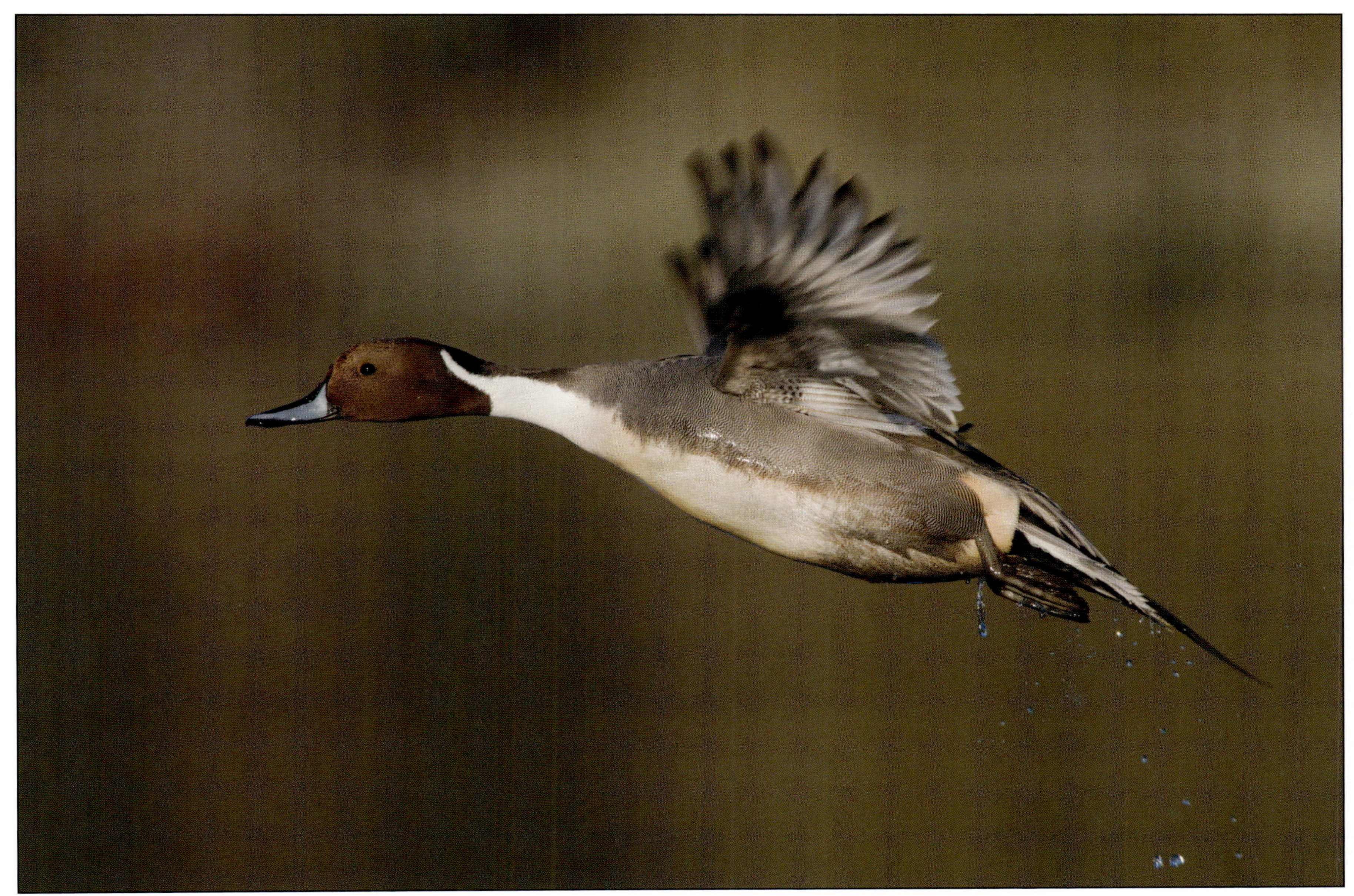

A male Northern Pintail launches off from a coastal lagoon. Like many waterfowl, this species winters on Vancouver Island where food and sheltered areas are abundant.

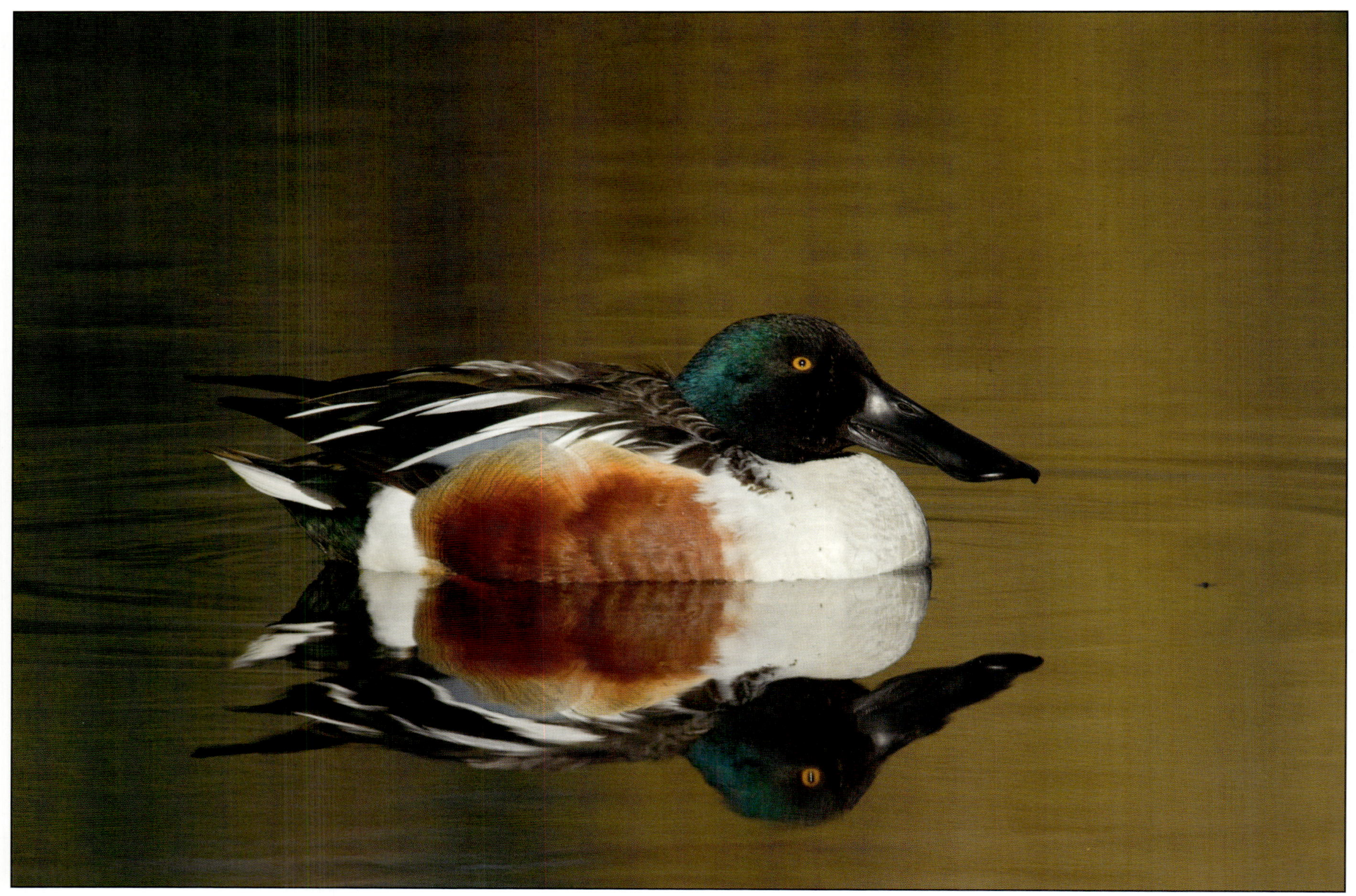

Northern Shovellers are easily identifiable by their massive bills. They use this impressive tool to filter water through comb-like bristles and strain out morsels of food.

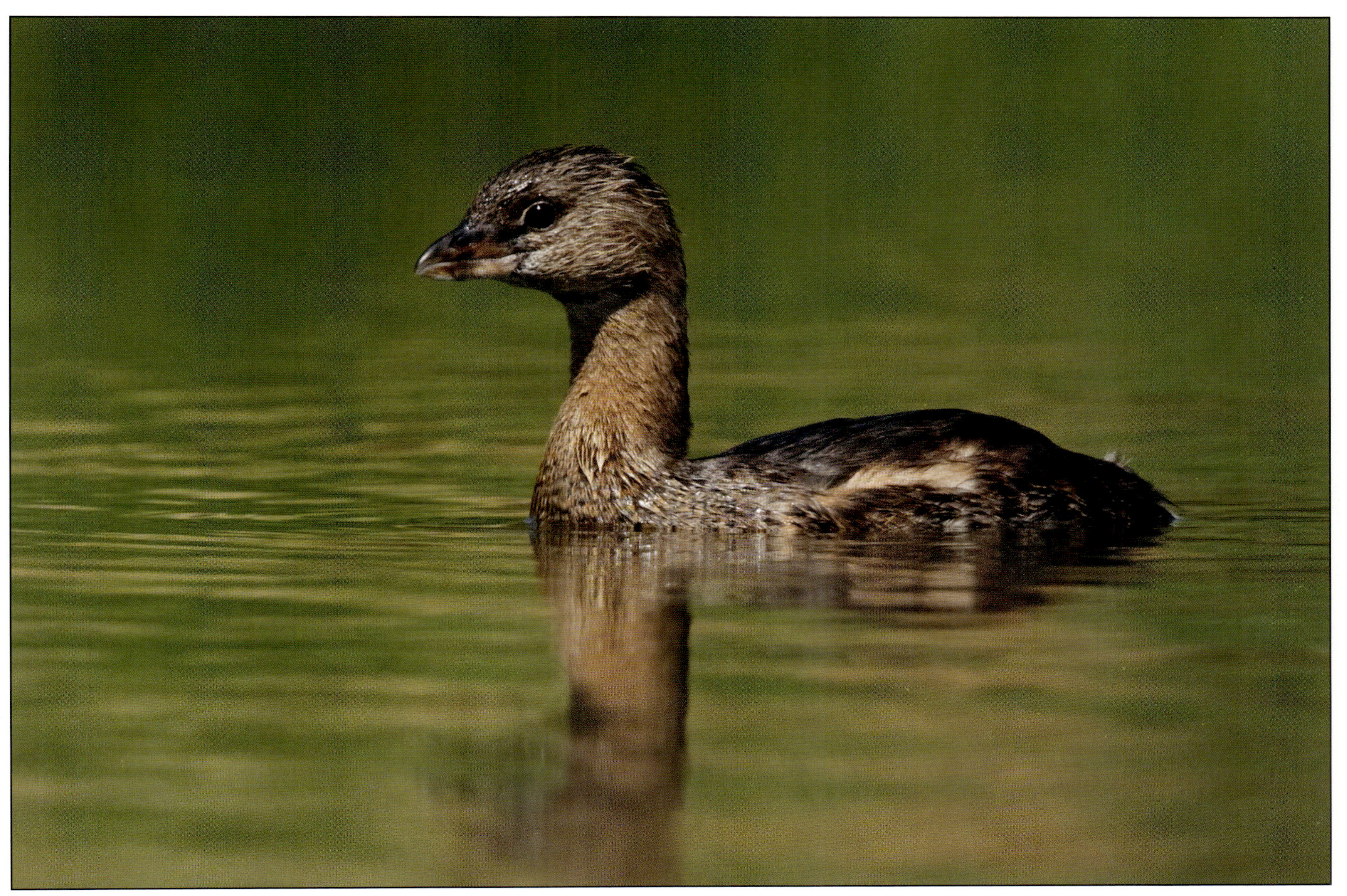

The small Pied-billed Grebe is almost entirely aquatic and uses its large feet as a rudder and propellers in search of small fish to feed upon.

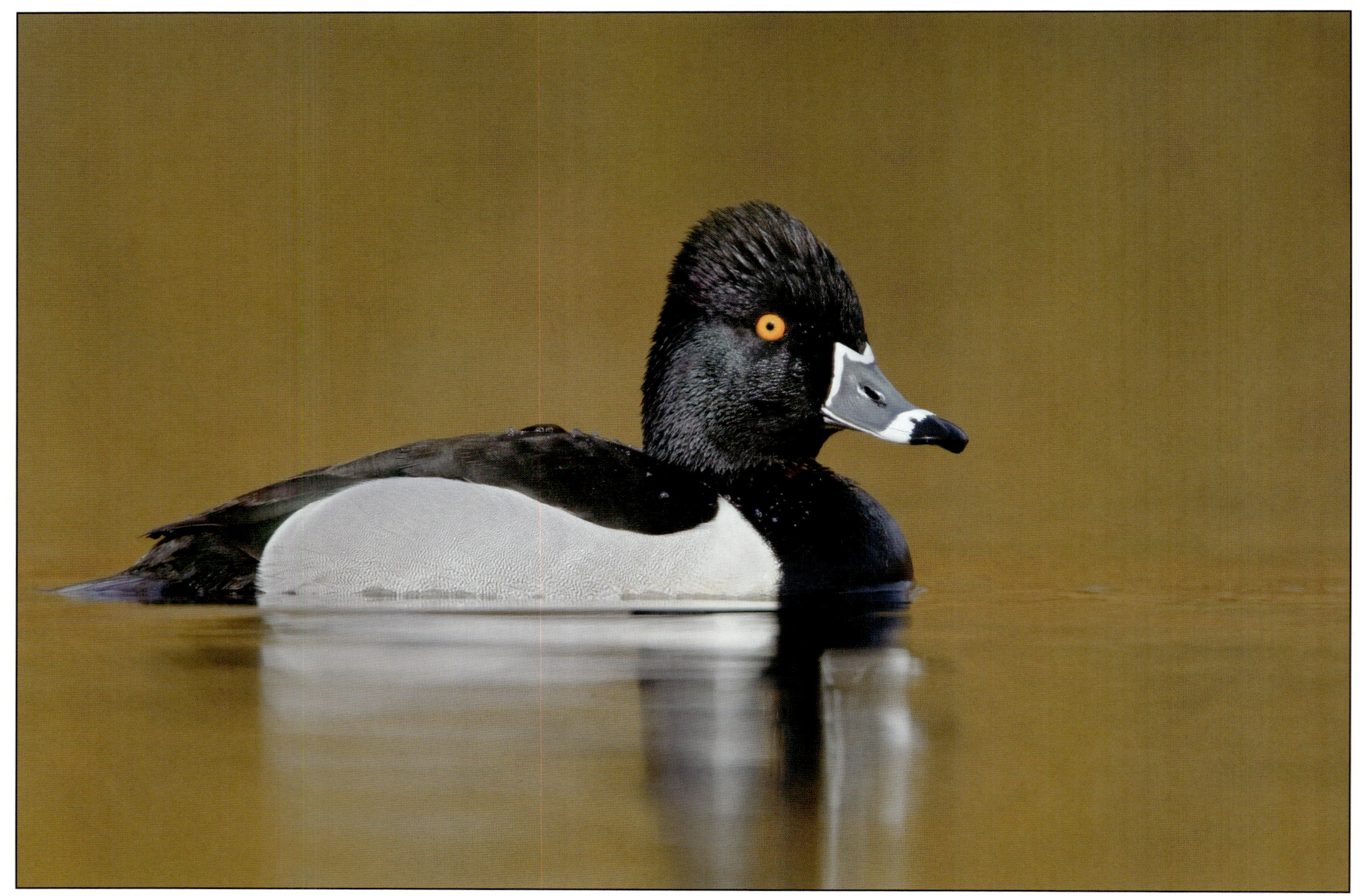

Although often difficult to see in the field, the Ring-necked Duck has a maroon coloured stripe at the base of its neck.

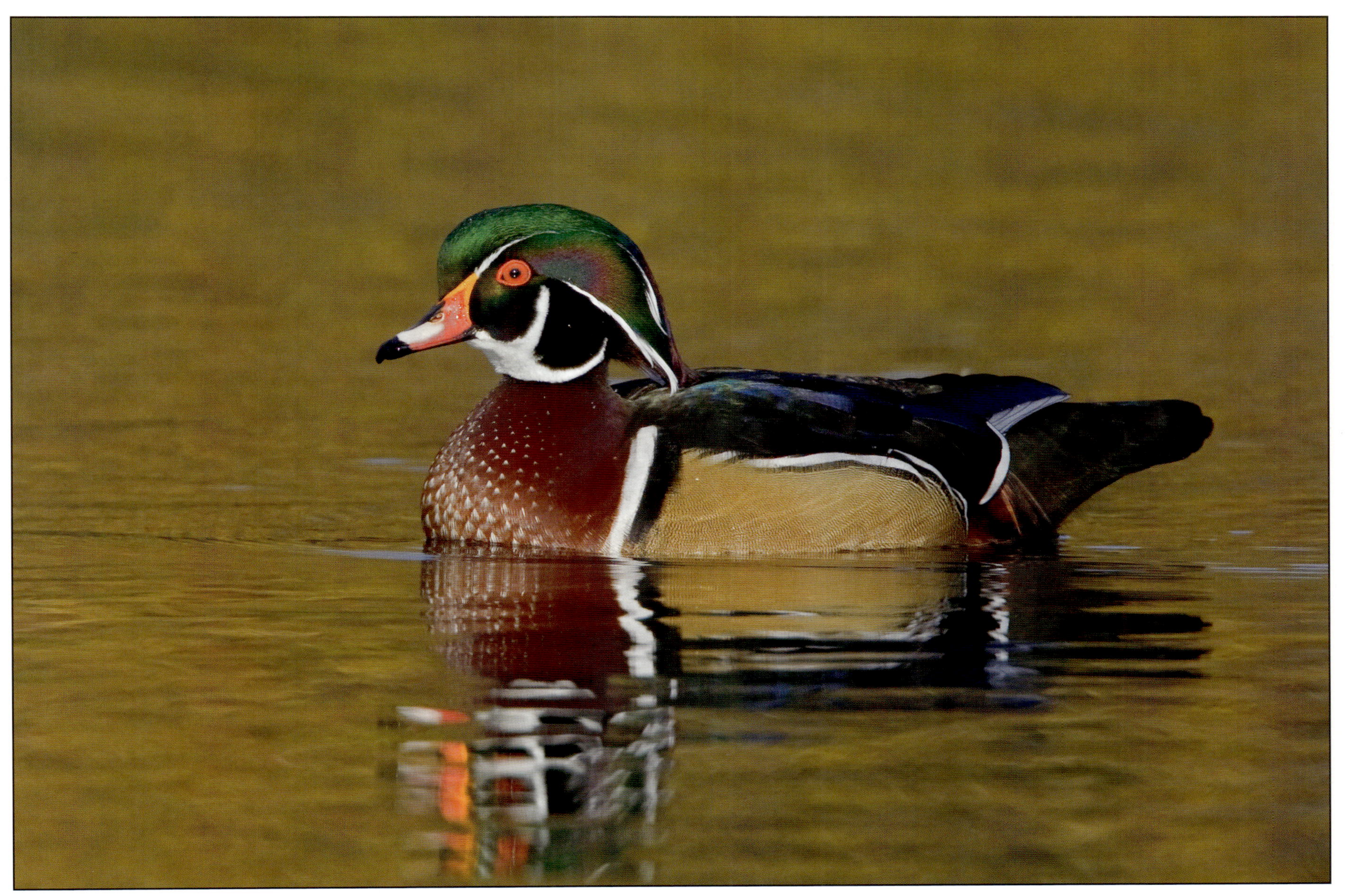

Even on a pond full of ducks the spectacular plumage of the male Wood Duck makes it stand out from the crowd.

SHOREBIRDS

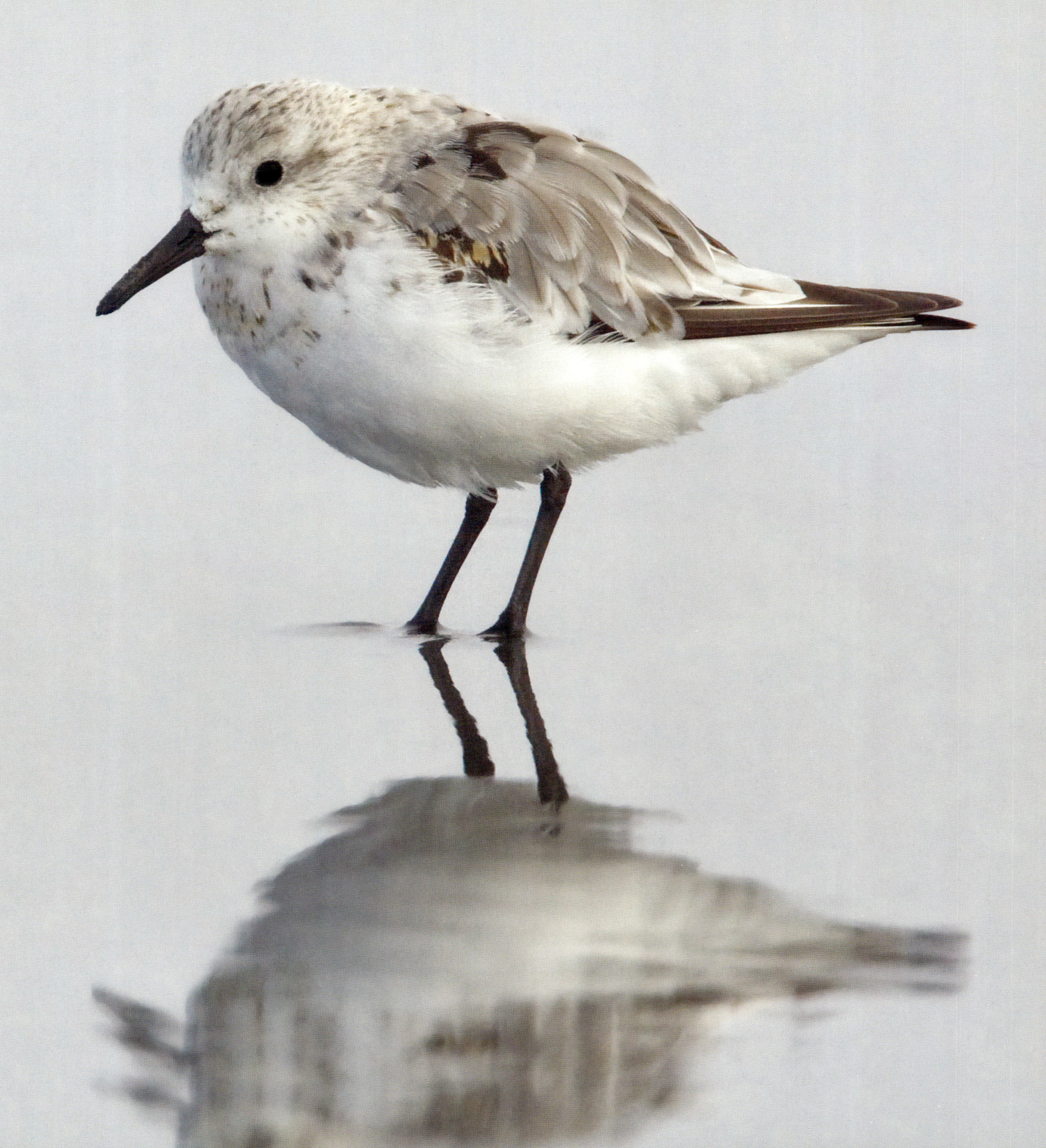

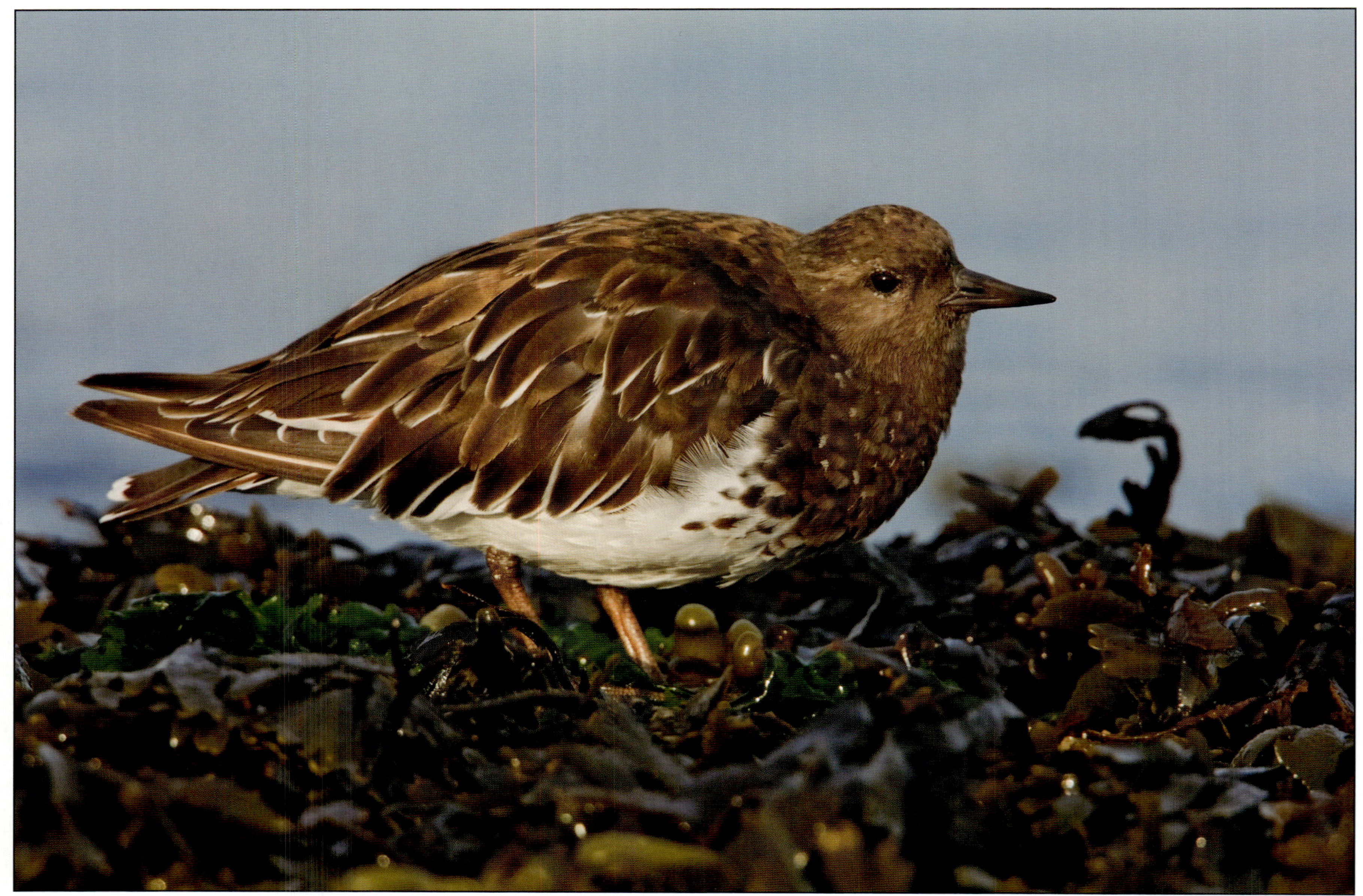

A Black Turnstone picks through the seaweed at low tide.

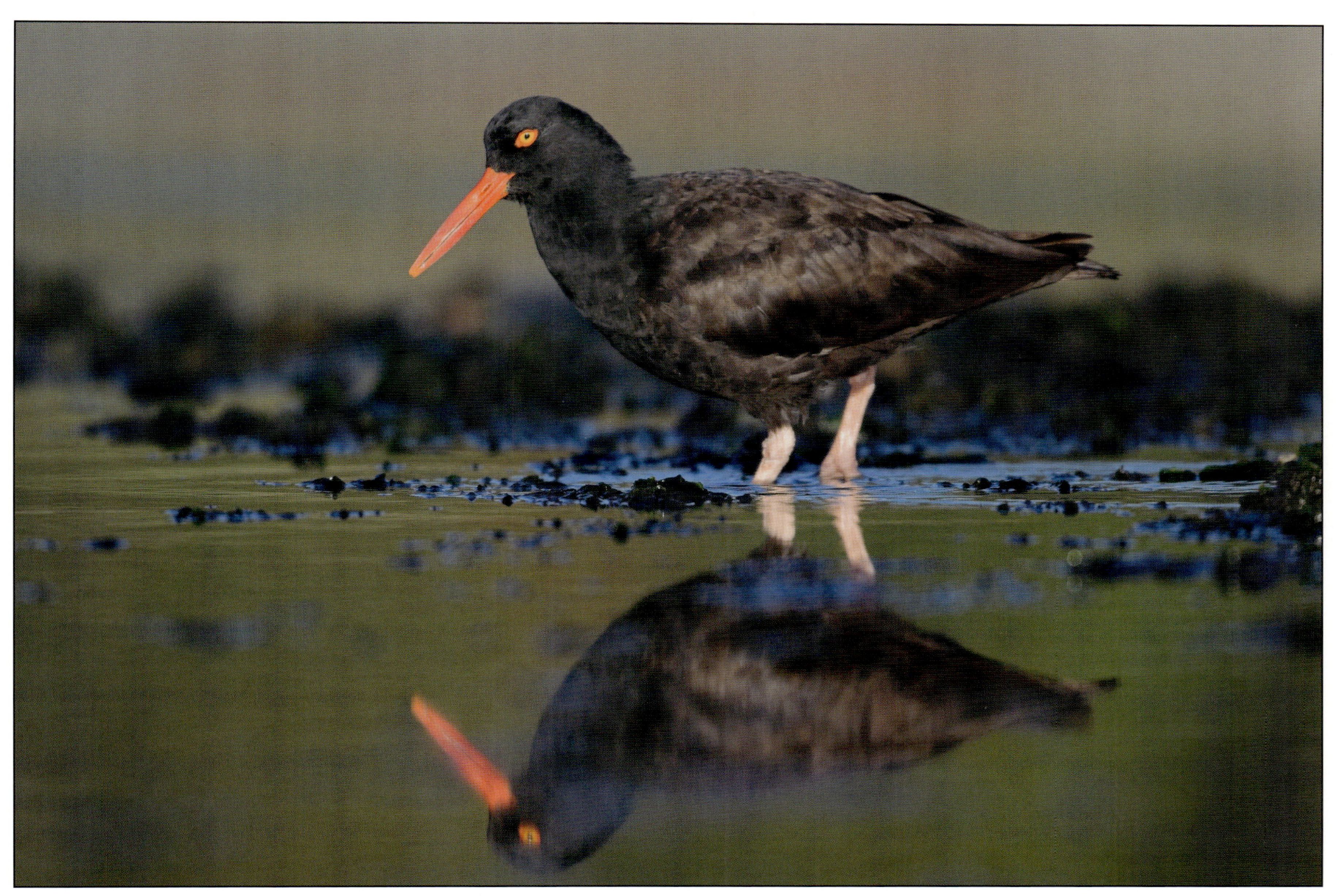

One of the shorebirds that resides on Vancouver Island year round, the Black Oystercatcher is a comical looking bird that scours the shoreline for snacks to pluck from the rocks and tide pools.

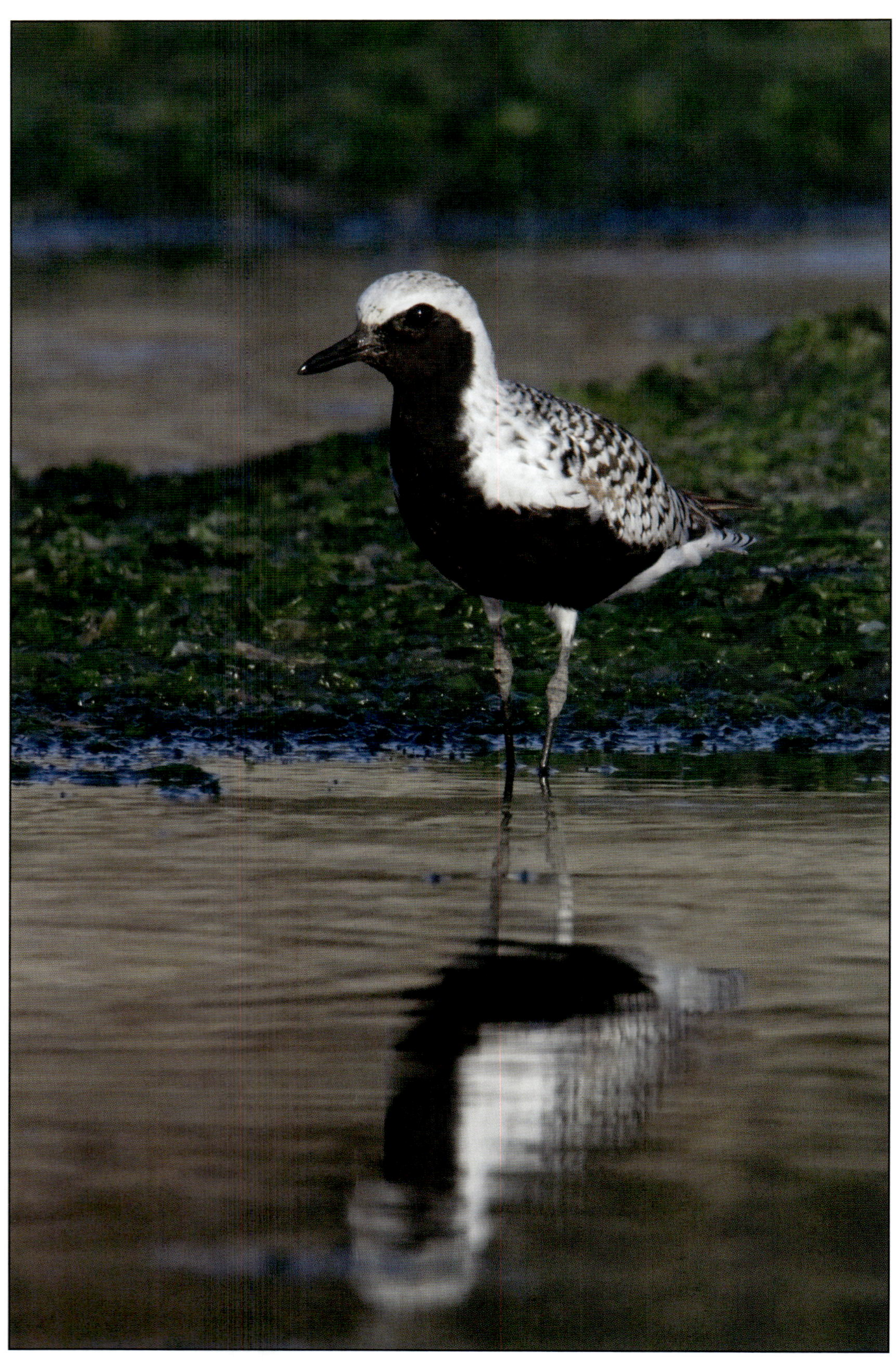

A Black-bellied Plover in late spring is one of the most stunning shorebirds that migrates along the coast of Vancouver Island.

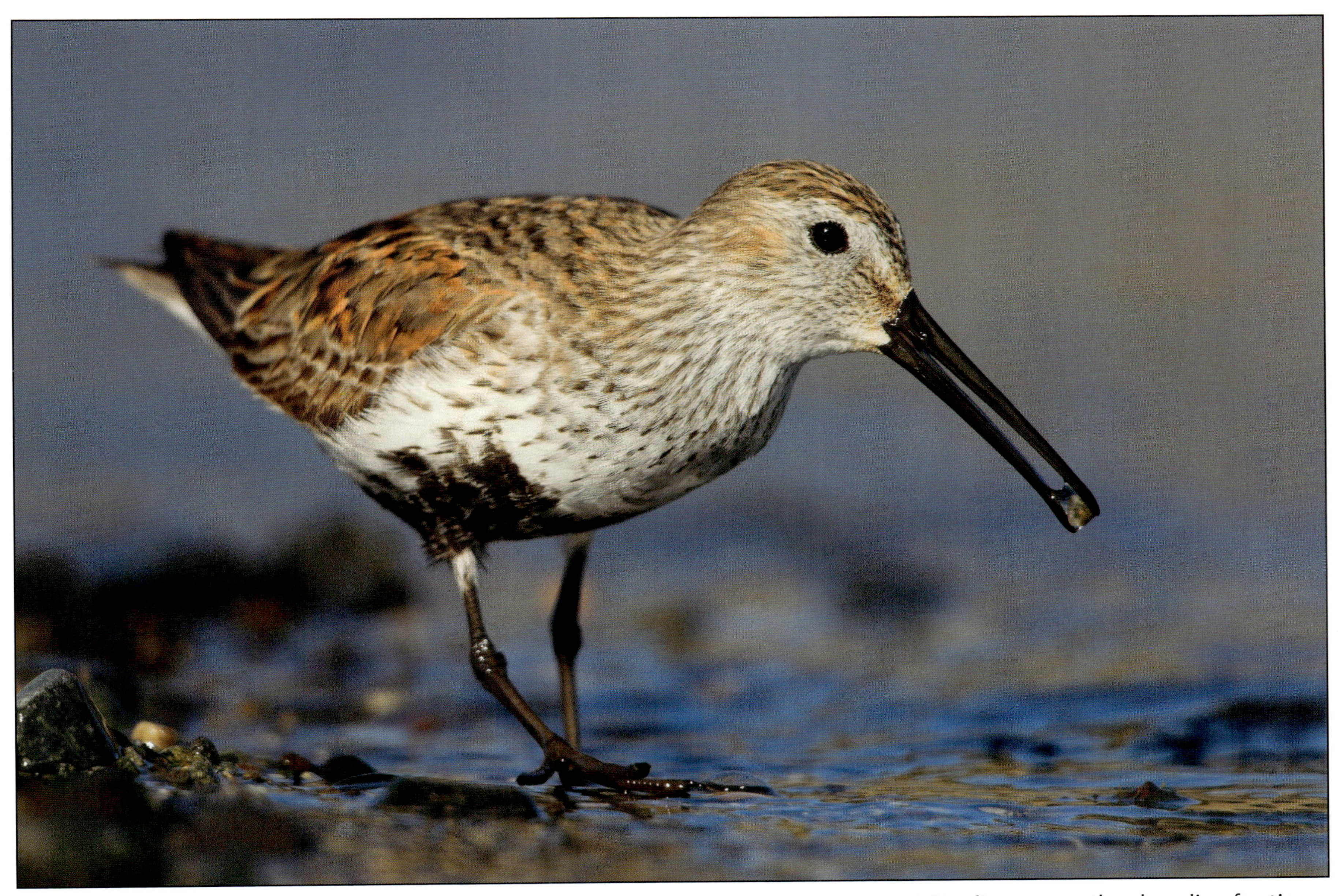

A Dunlin surveys the shoreline for tiny invertebrates to feed upon. Like many shorebirds these birds stop on the Island to fuel up during their lengthy migratory journeys.

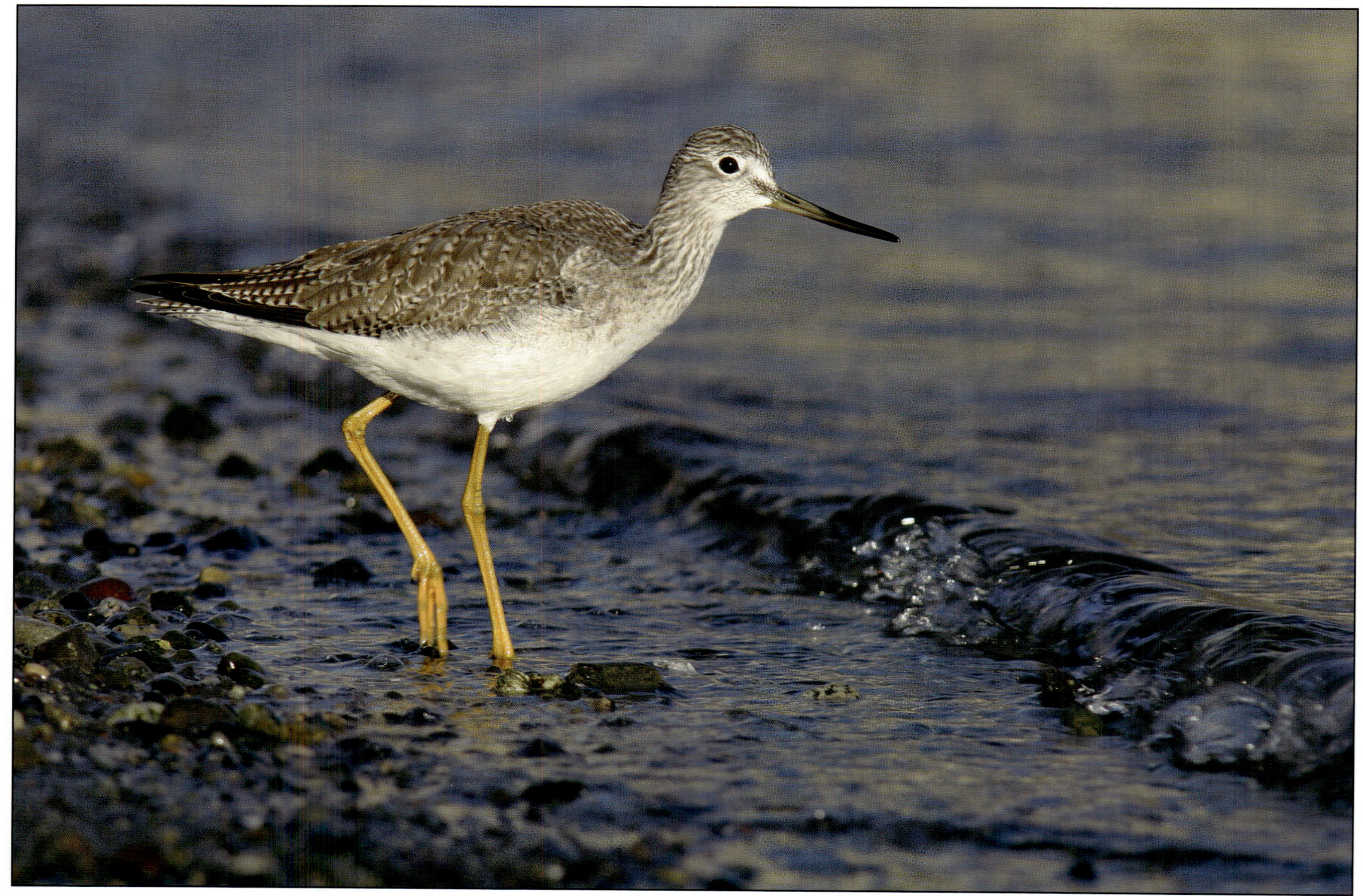

The Greater Yellowlegs is indeed larger than the Lesser Yellowlegs. The easiest way to identify them however is the much longer bill length on the greater (approximately twice the length of the head).

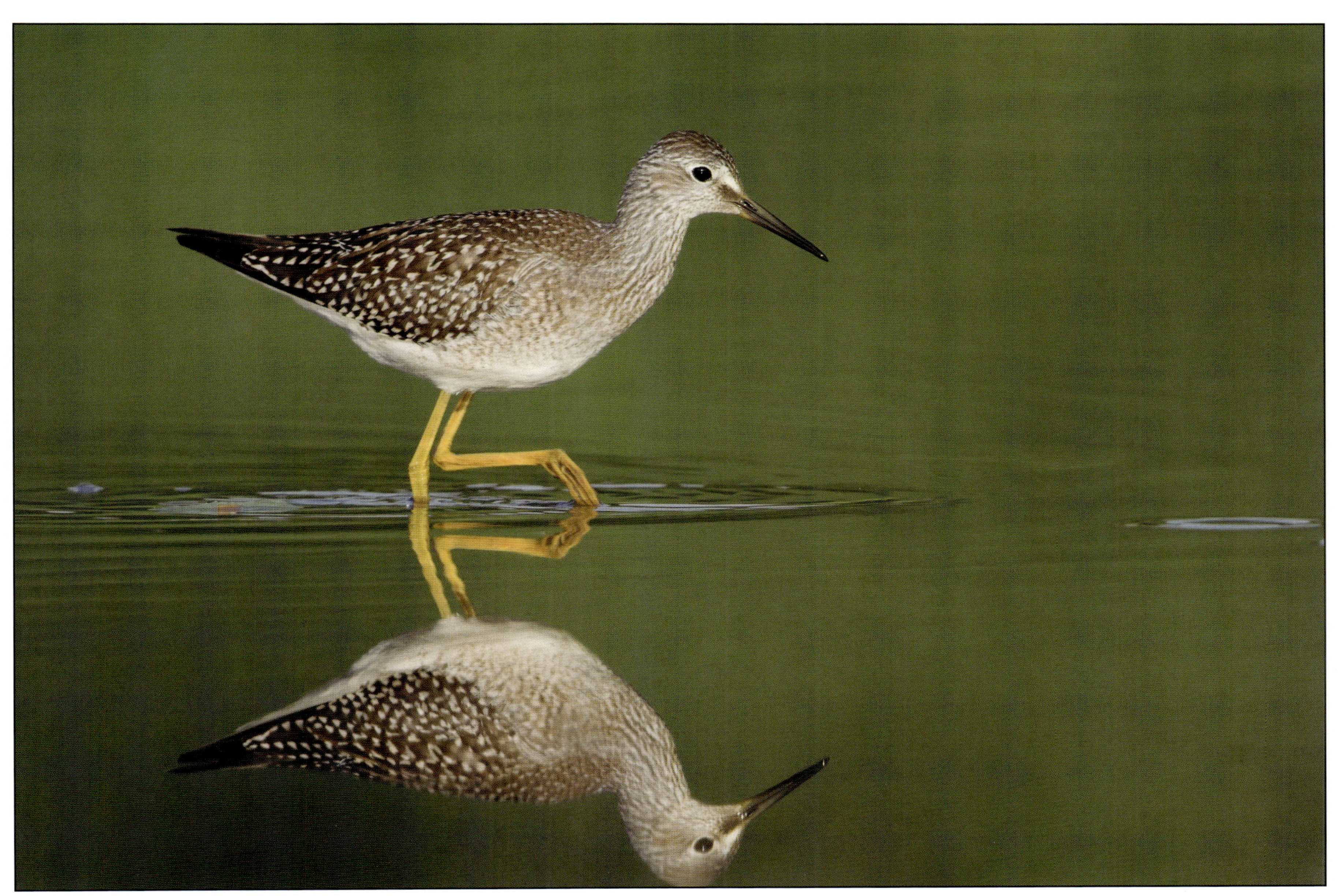

A Lesser Yellowlegs wades in the calm shallow water of a small pond.

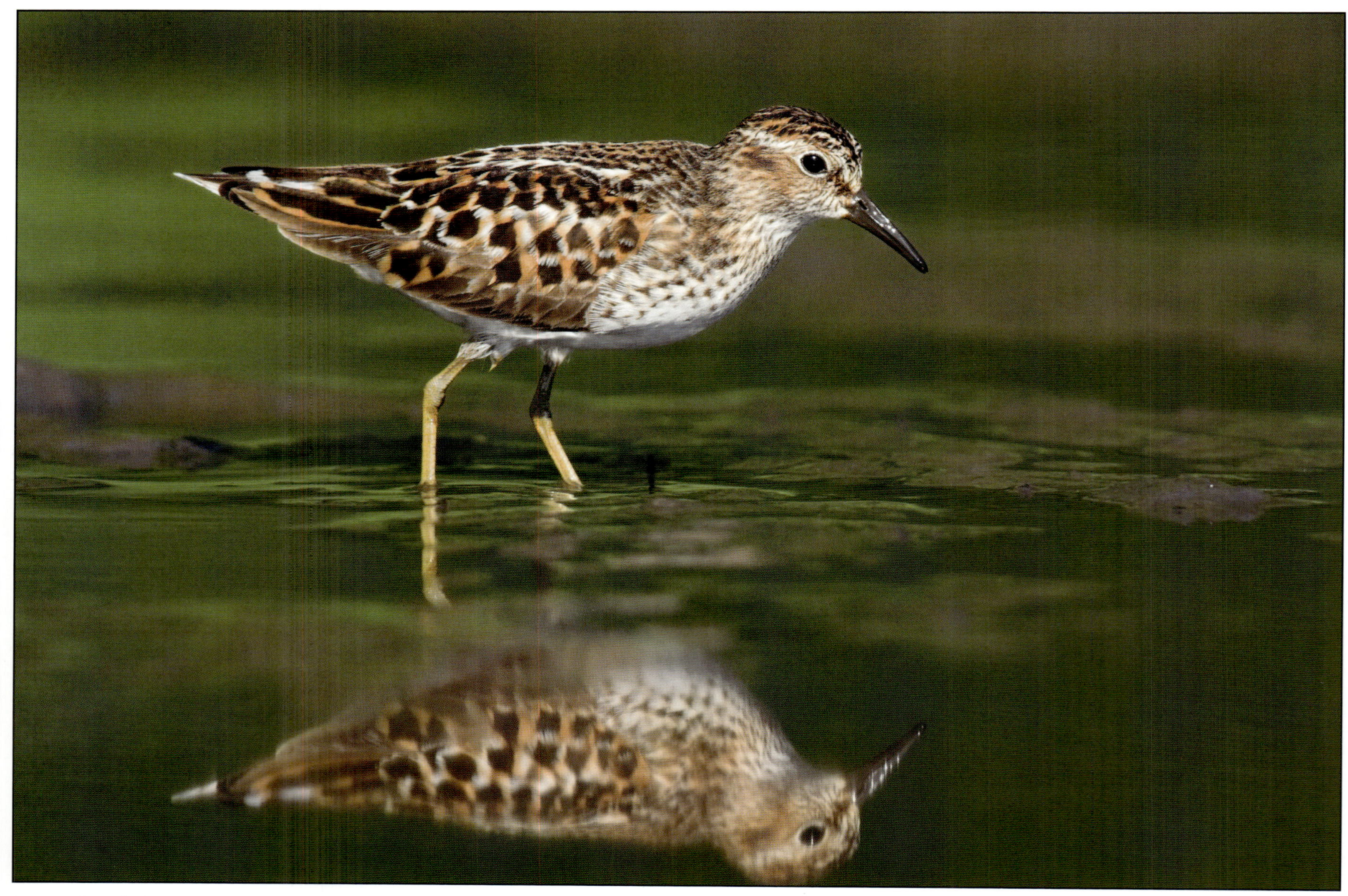

Least Sandpipers are common on Vancouver Island during both spring and fall migration.

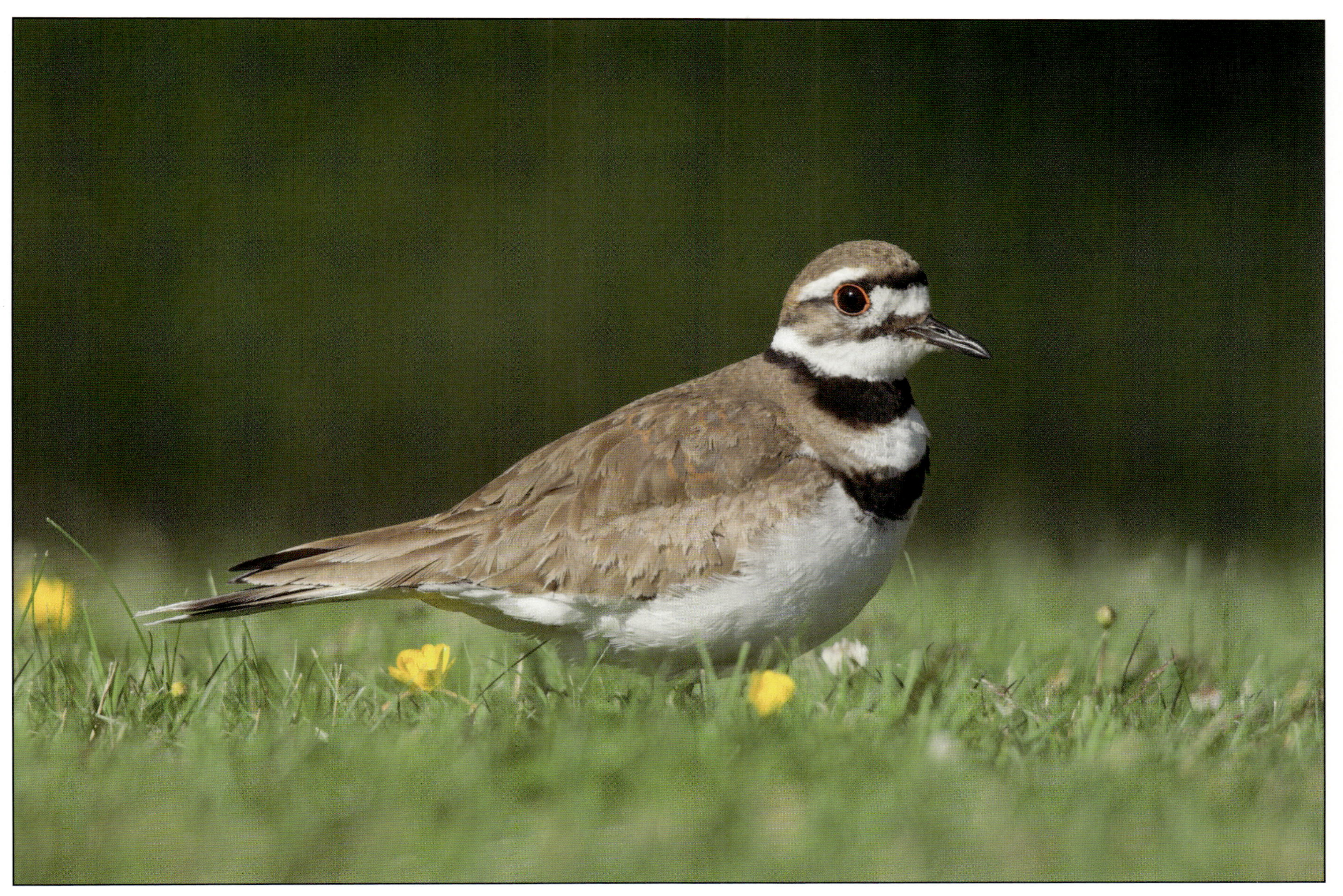

Killdeers are common breeding residents on Vancouver Island. They may even nest in public parks, backyards and on rooftops.

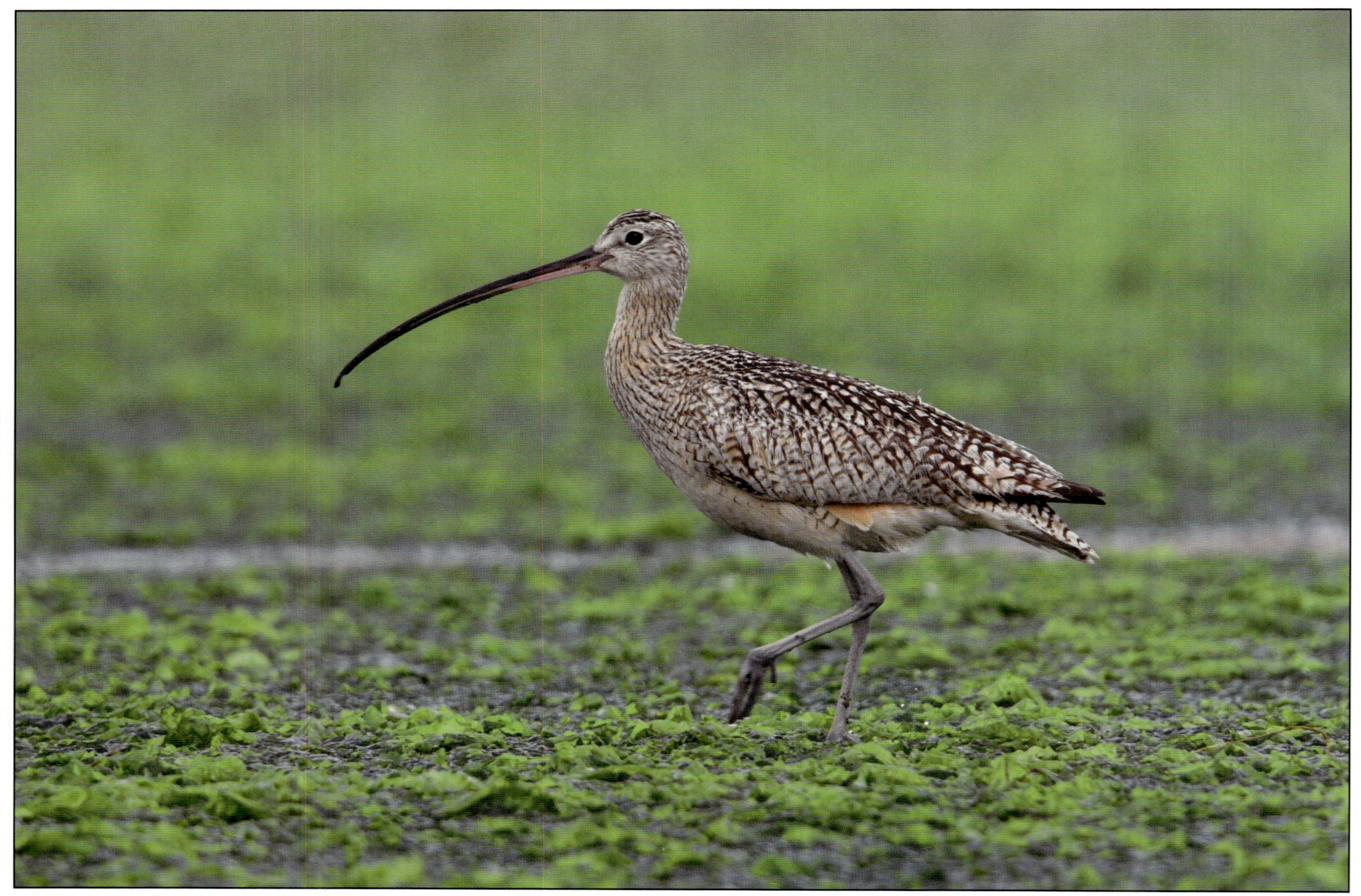

Equipped with an unquestionably impressive bill the Long-billed Curlew is also the largest shorebird in North America.

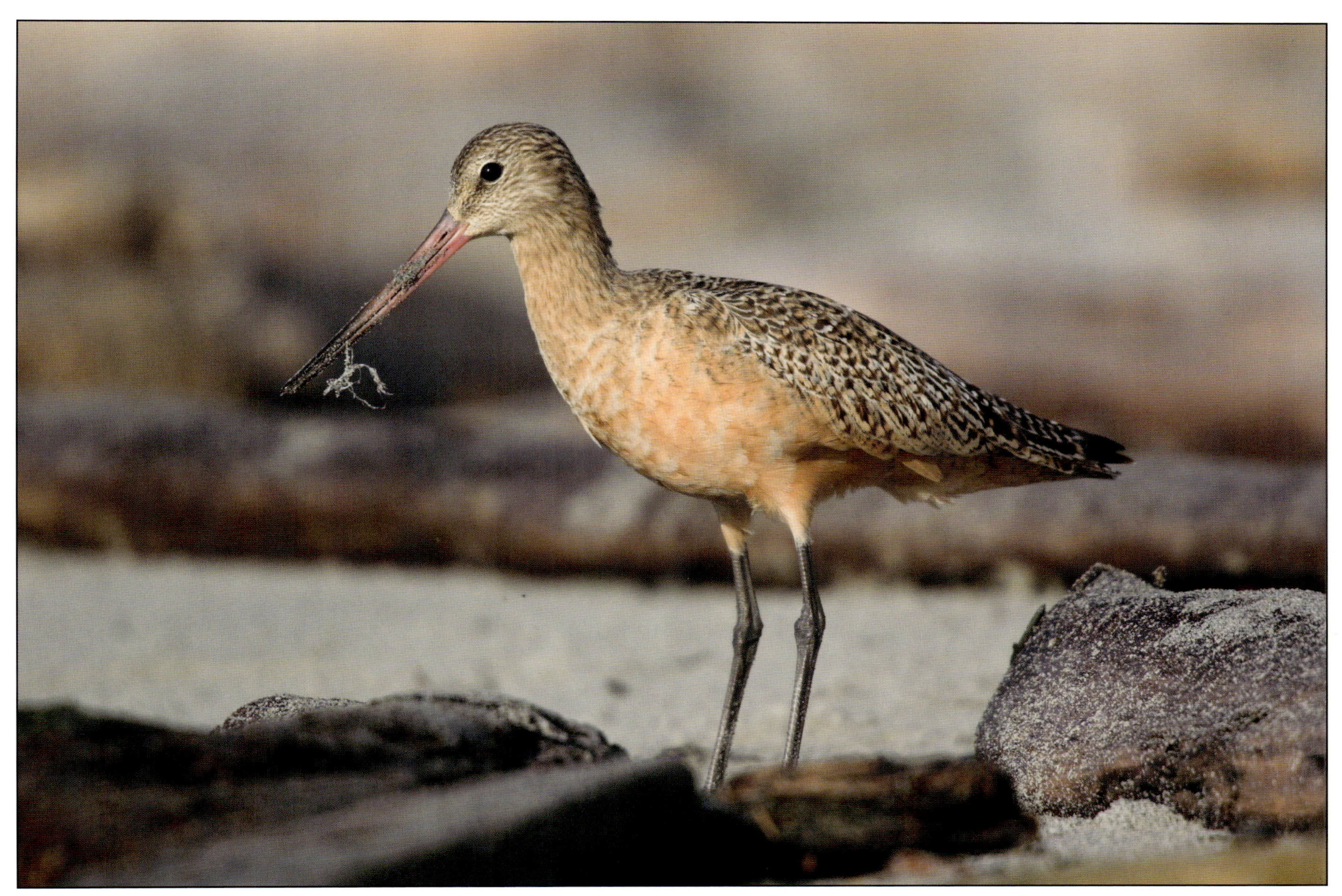

Another long-billed shorebird that migrates through Vancouver Island is the Marbled Godwit.

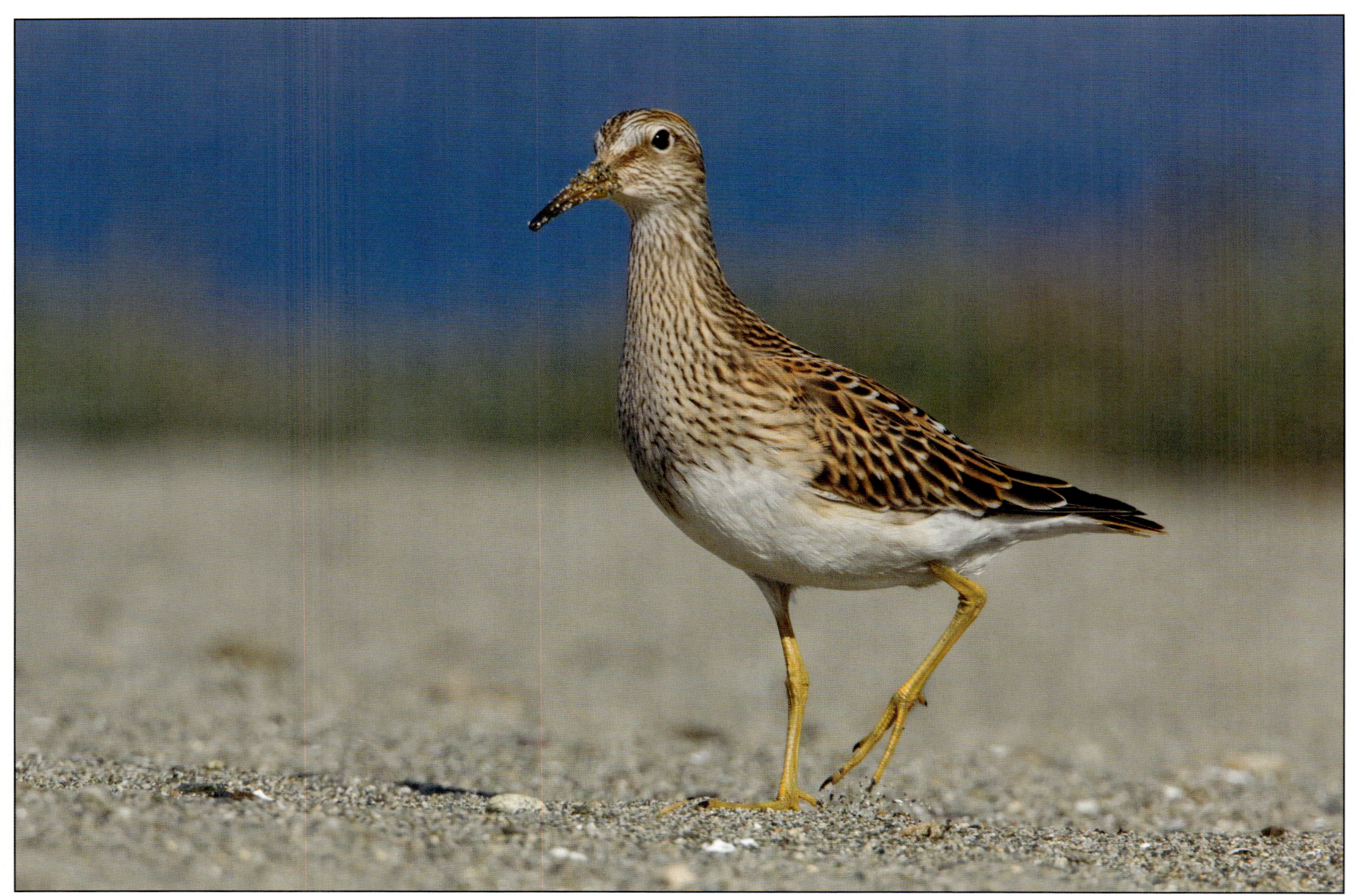

Pectoral Sandpipers have heavily streaked breast feathers which males use to attract mates during their courtship rituals on the high Arctic.

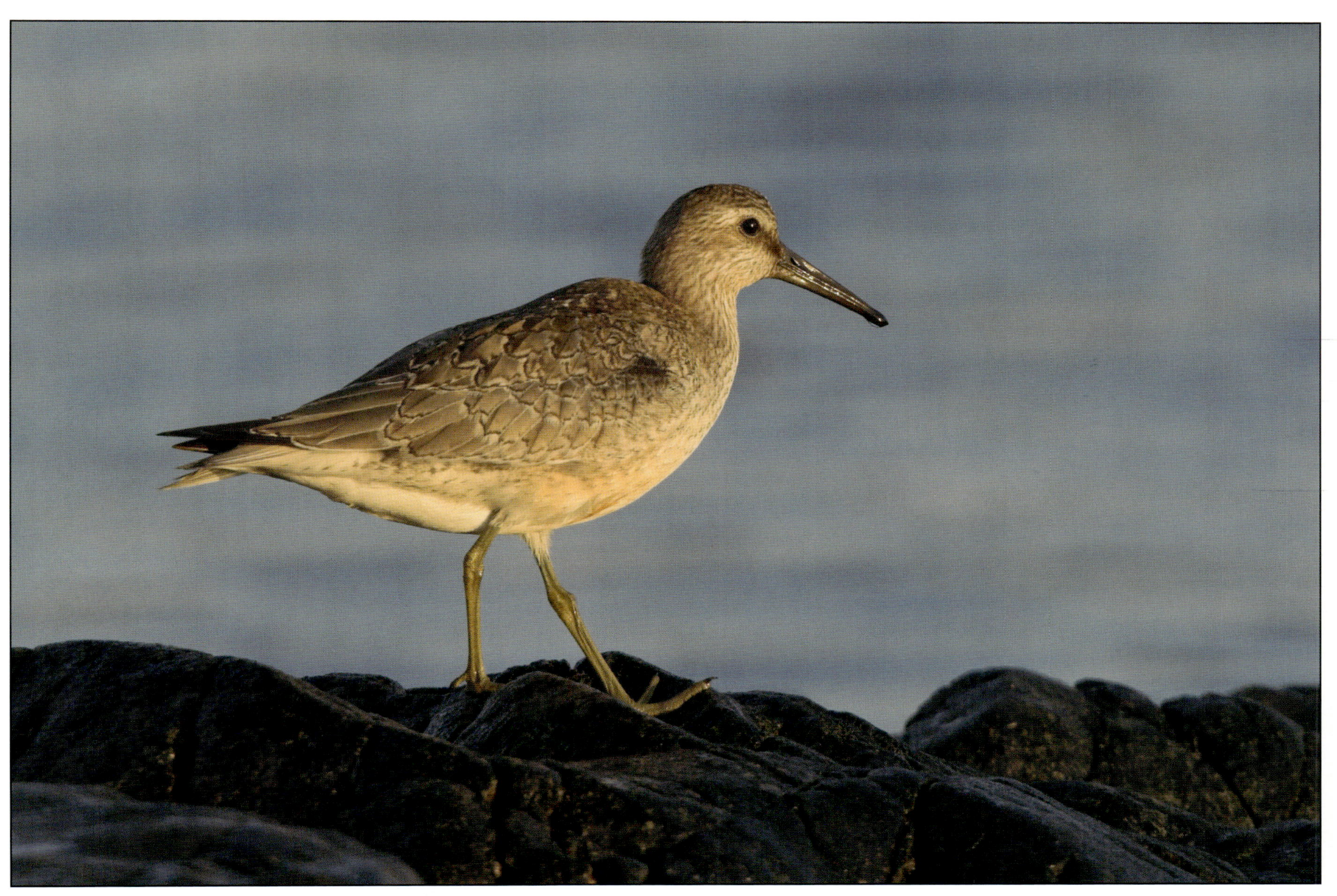

Seen here in winter plumage, the Red Knot is a rare visitor to Vancouver Island.

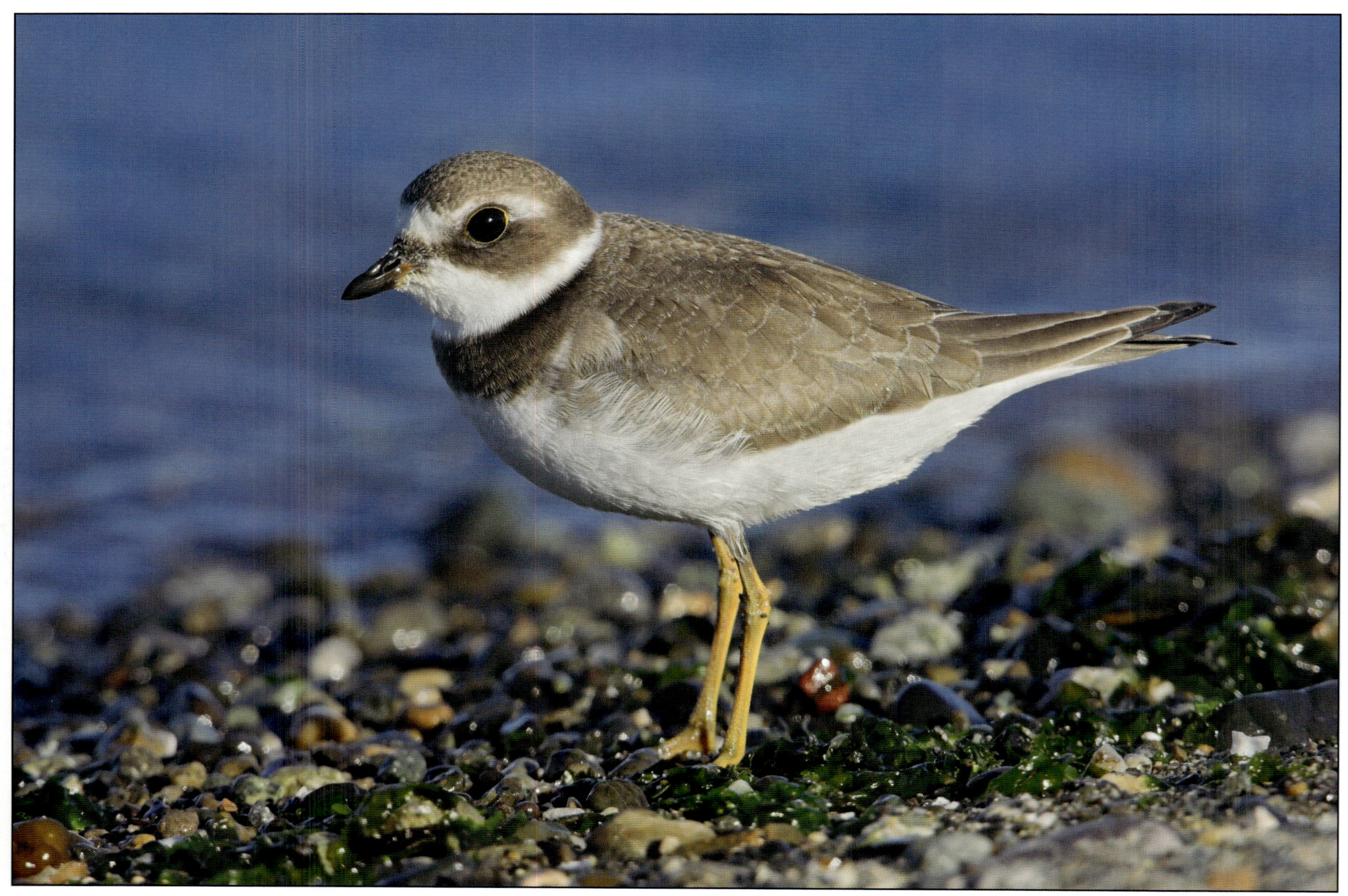

A Semipalmated Plover feeds along the tide-line - fueling up for the next leg of its lengthy migratory journey.

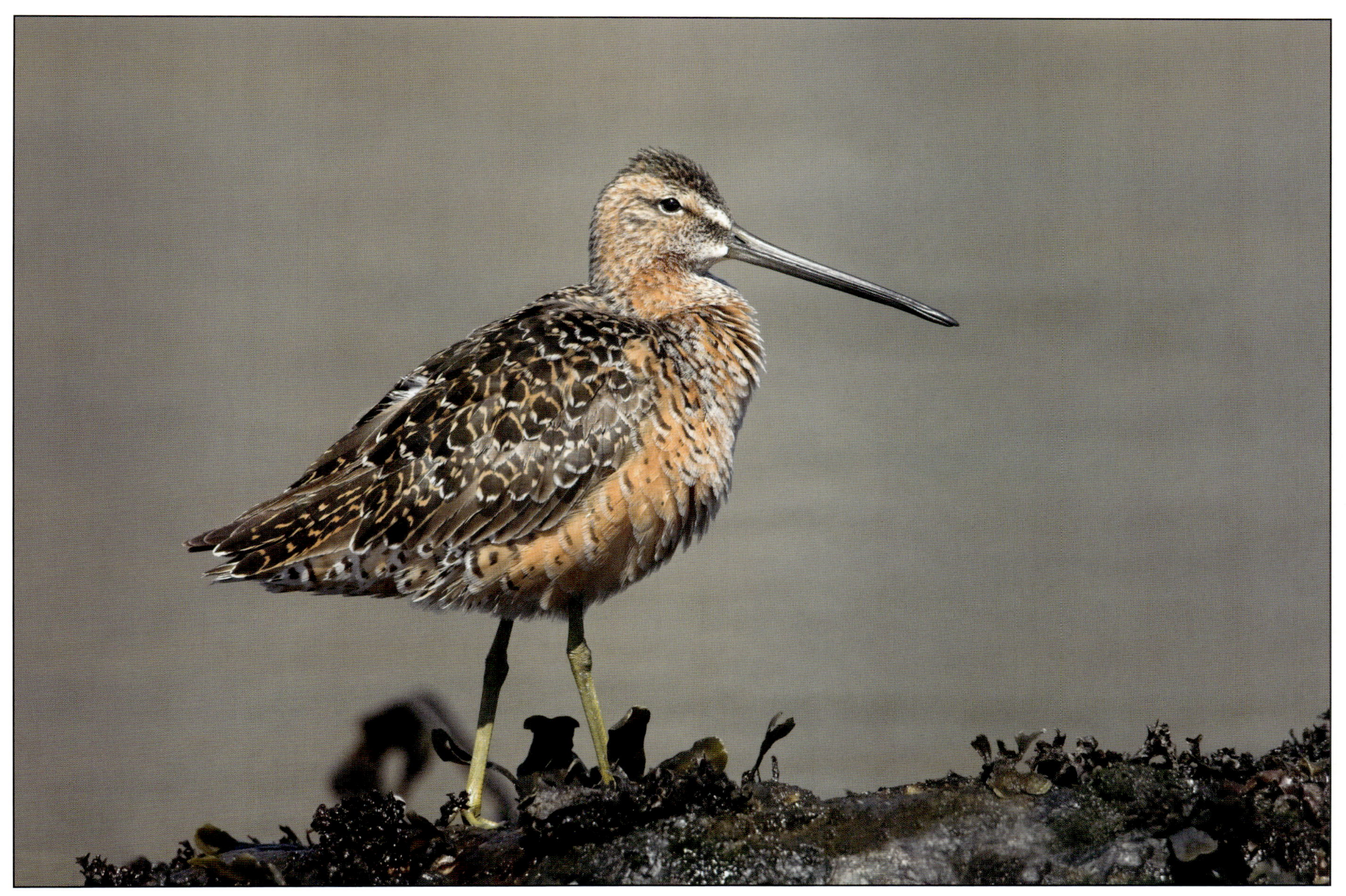

A Short-billed Dowitcher rests off the coast of Vancouver Island before flying farther north to breed

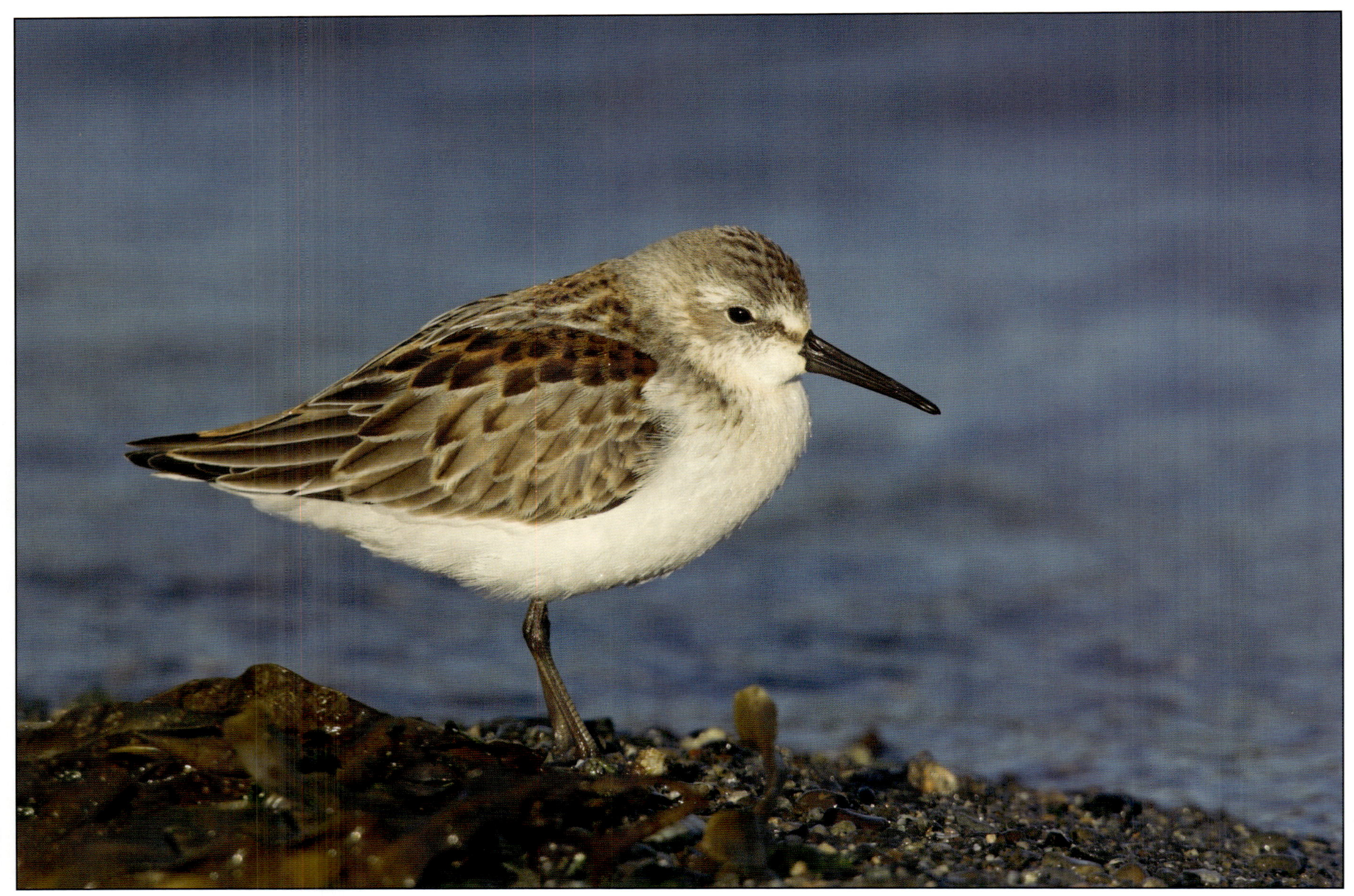

A member of the group of small shorebirds known as "peeps" the Western Sandpiper is a common fall visitor to Vancouver Island.

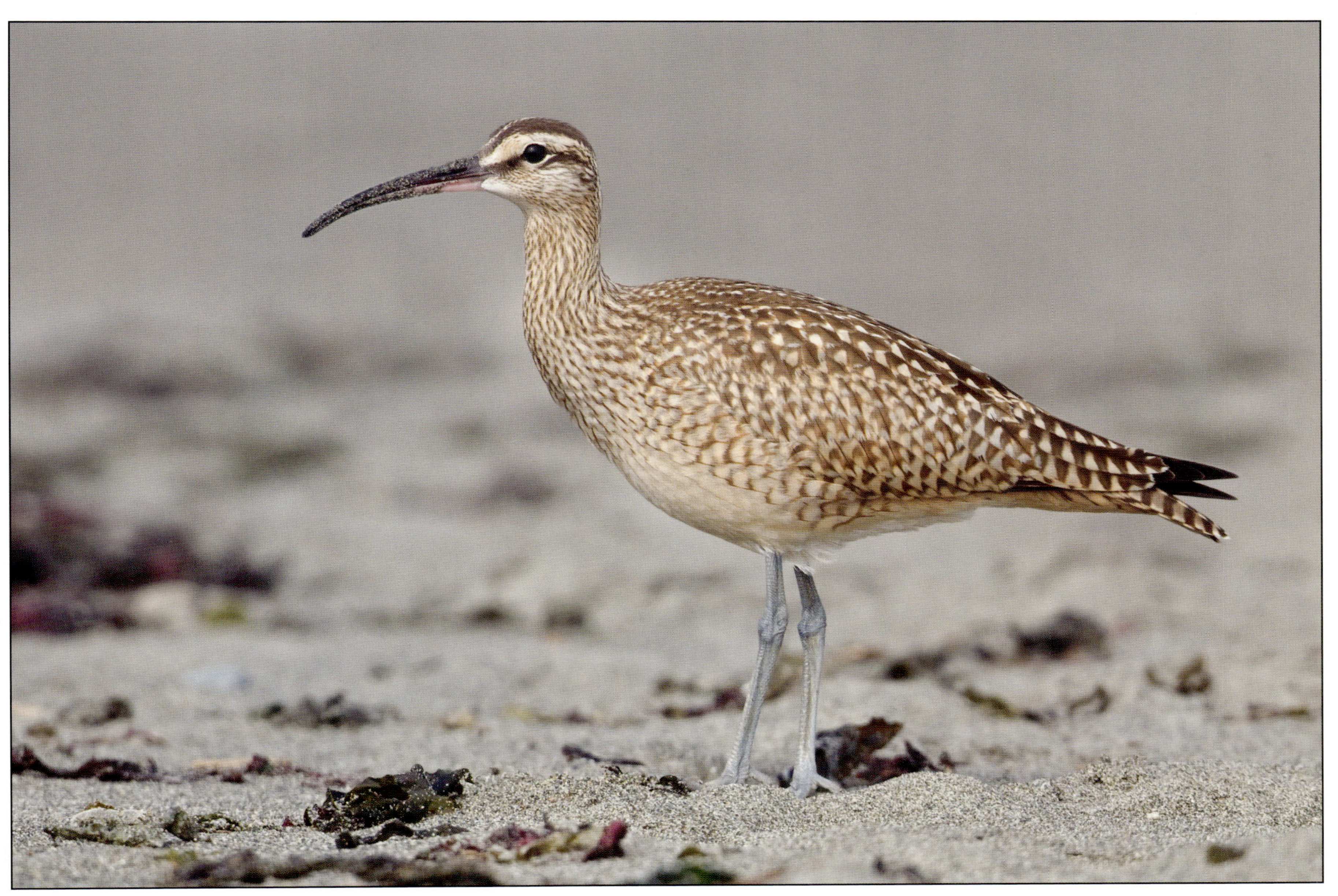

A Whimbrel feeds on invertebrates along a sandy beach to build up much needed energy supplies for its fall migration.

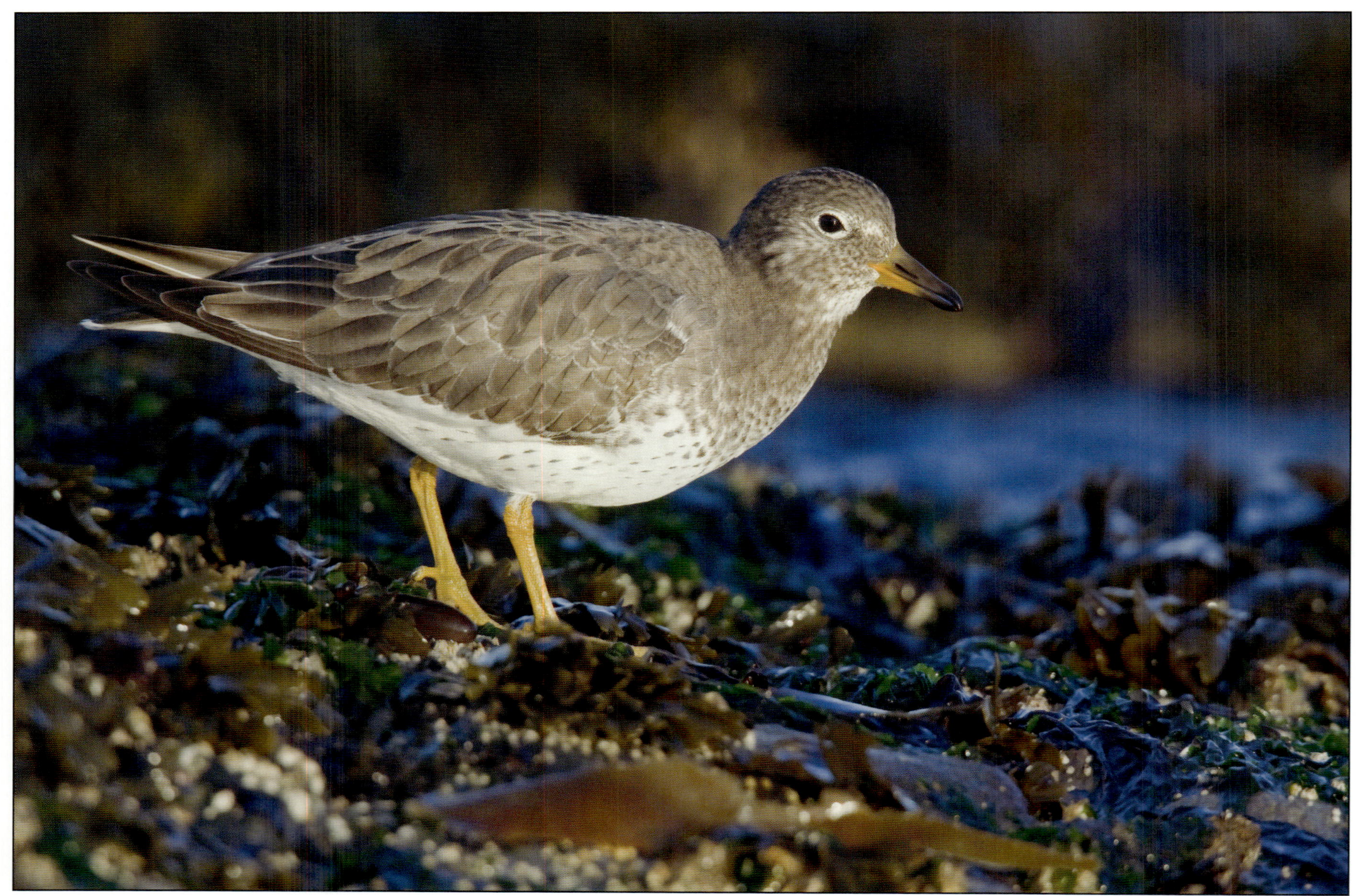

A Surfbird in winter plumage cautiously picks its way through the seaweed in hopes of finding sustenance.

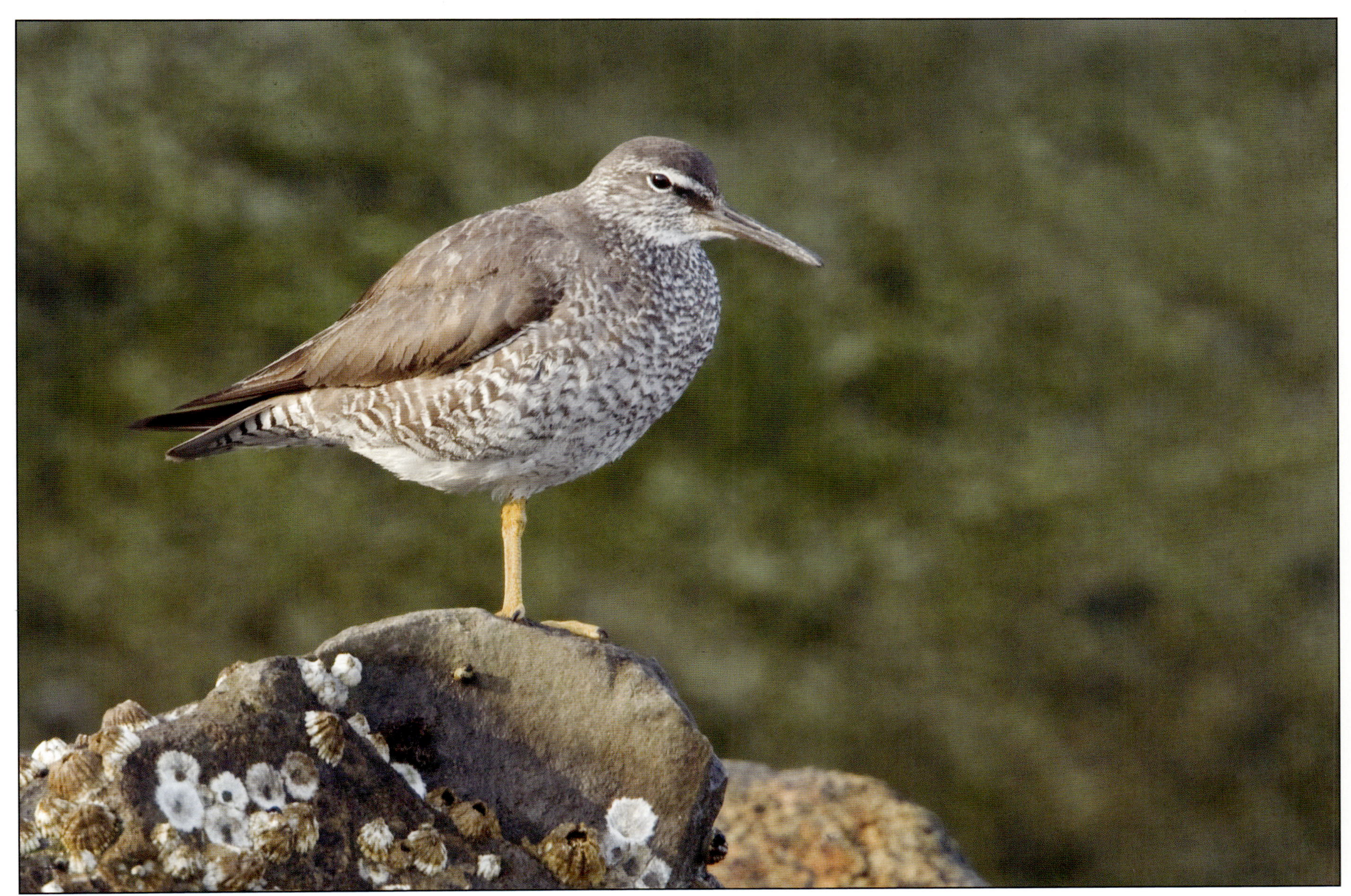

A Wandering Tattler gives one leg a rest while perched on a barnacle covered rock.

BIRDS OF PREY

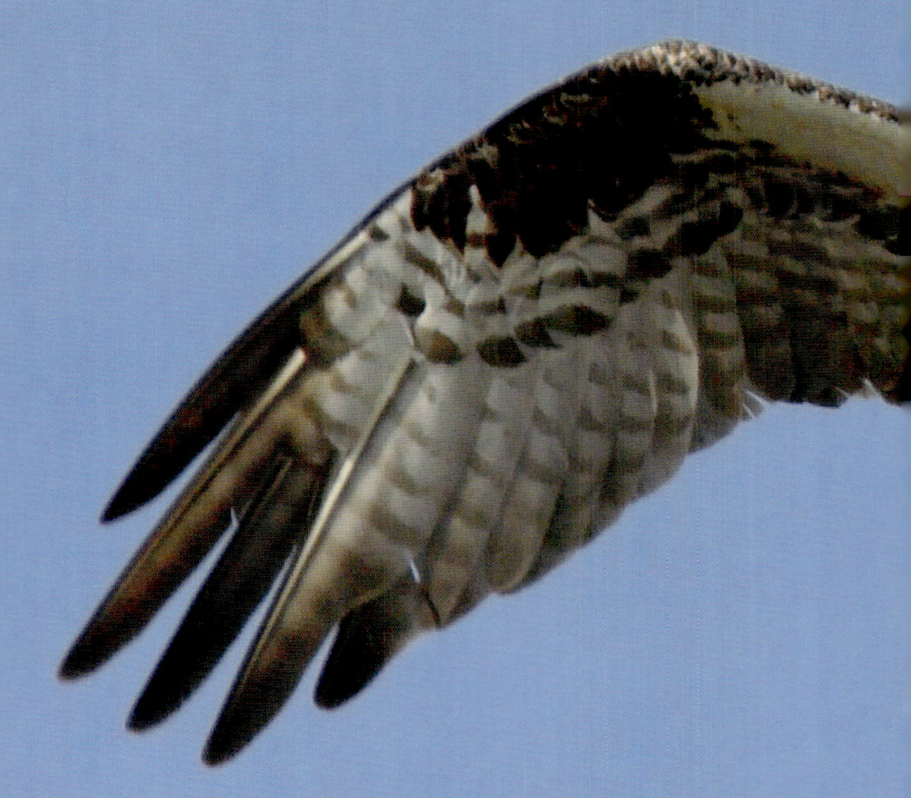

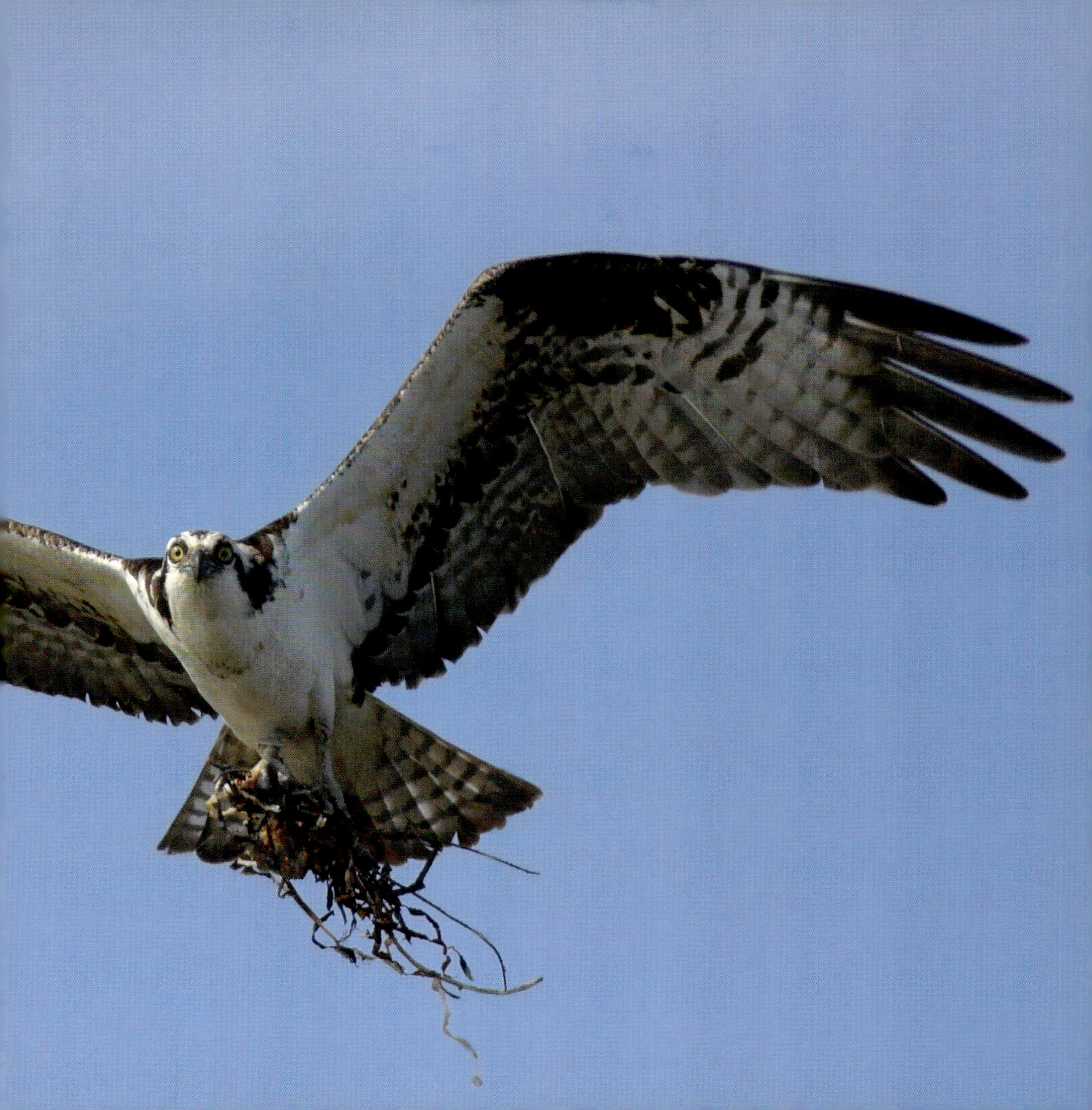

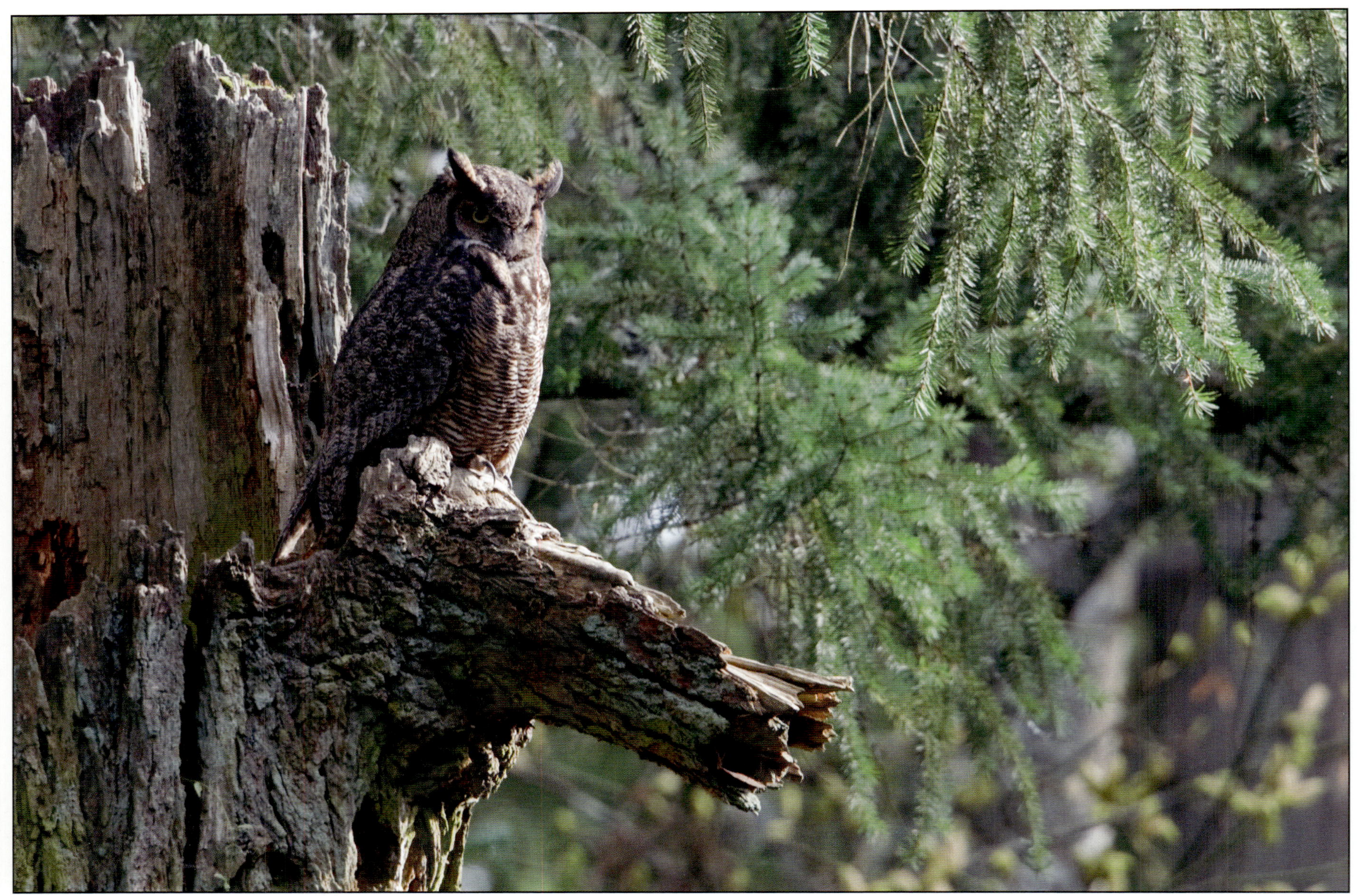

A Great-horned Owl perches beside its nest on a massive Douglas Fir snag.

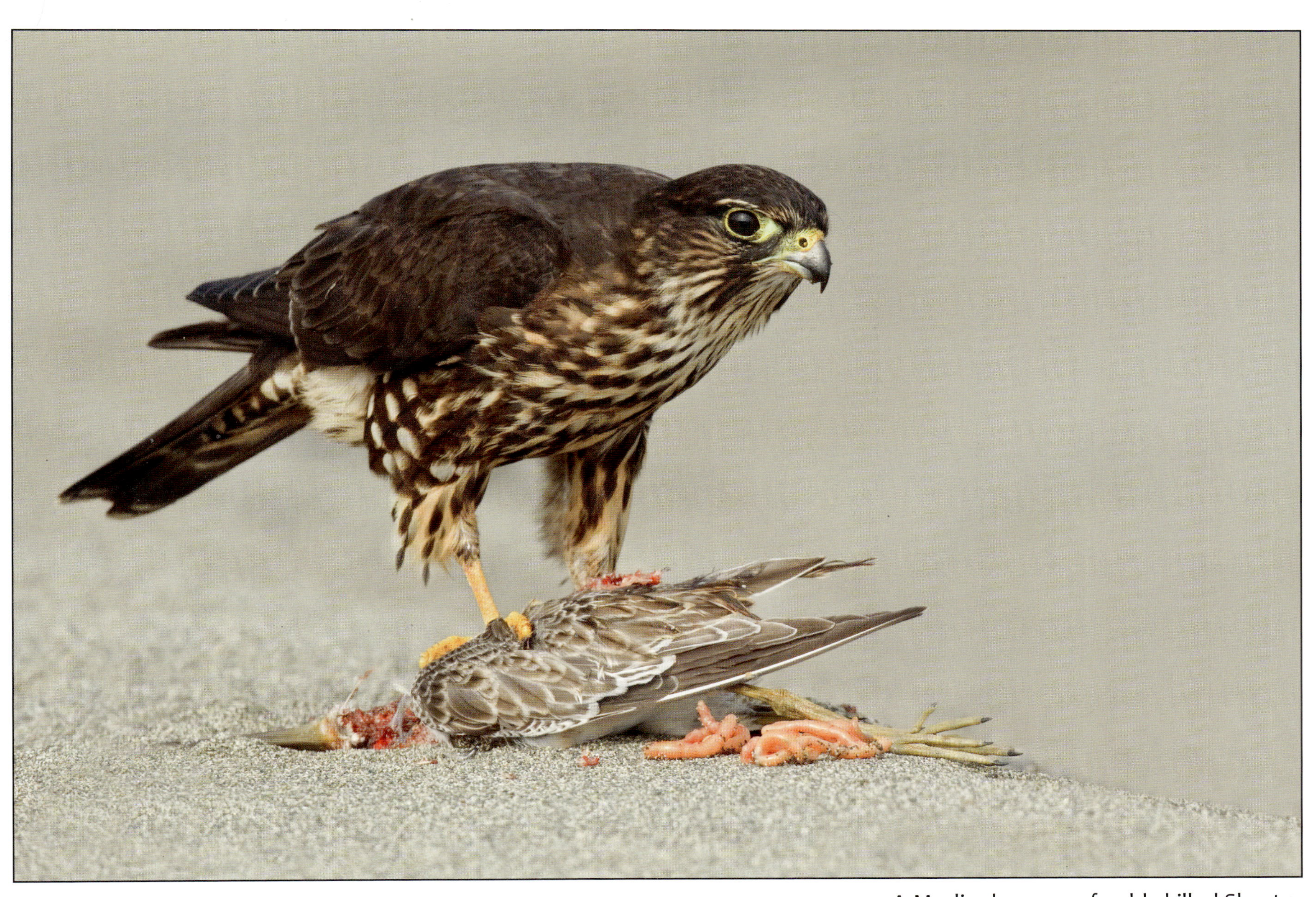

A Merlin devours a freshly killed Short-billed Dowitcher during fall migration.

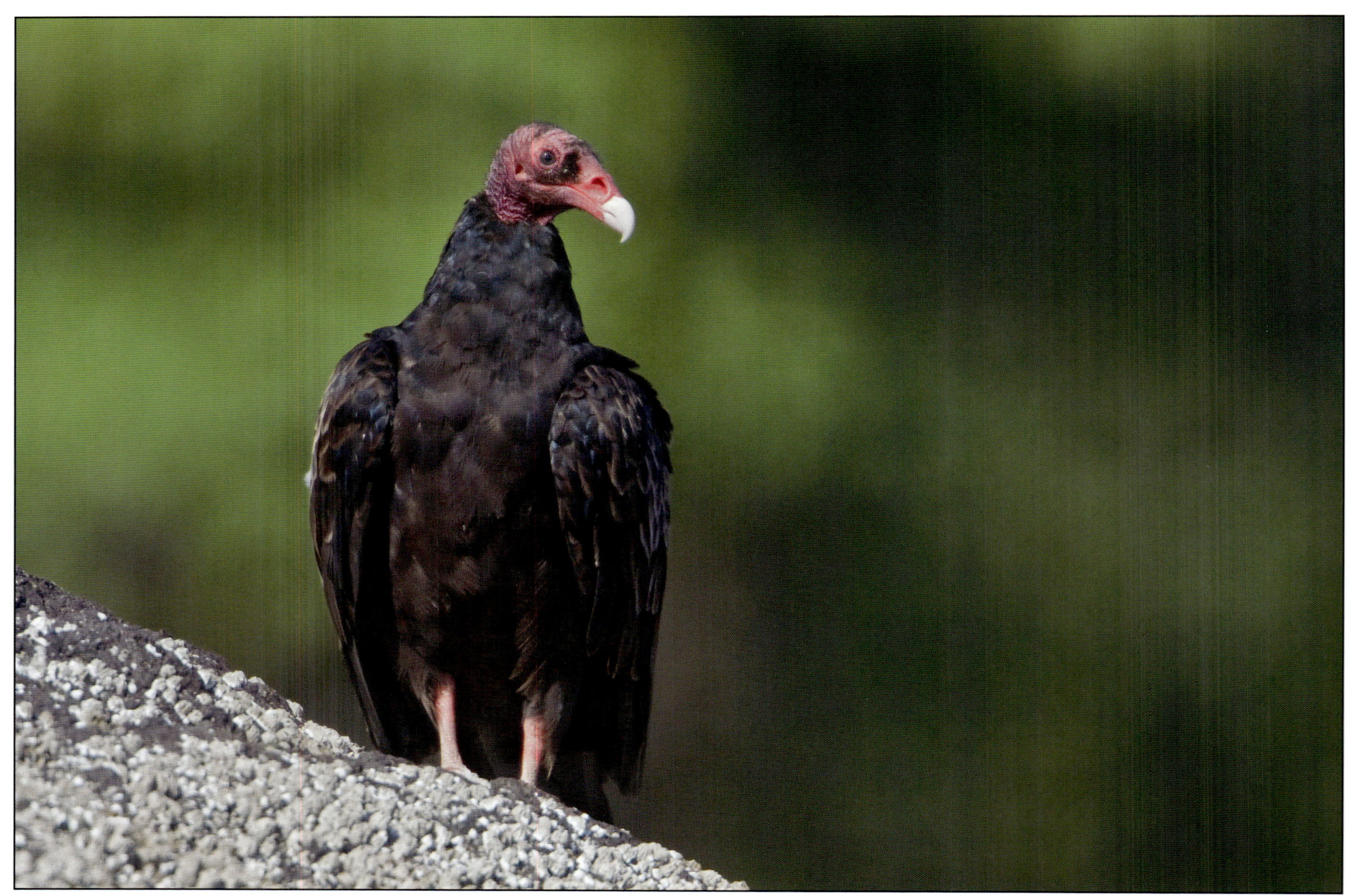

Most often seen soaring high overhead, the Turkey Vulture is a scavenger that is always on the lookout for an easy meal.

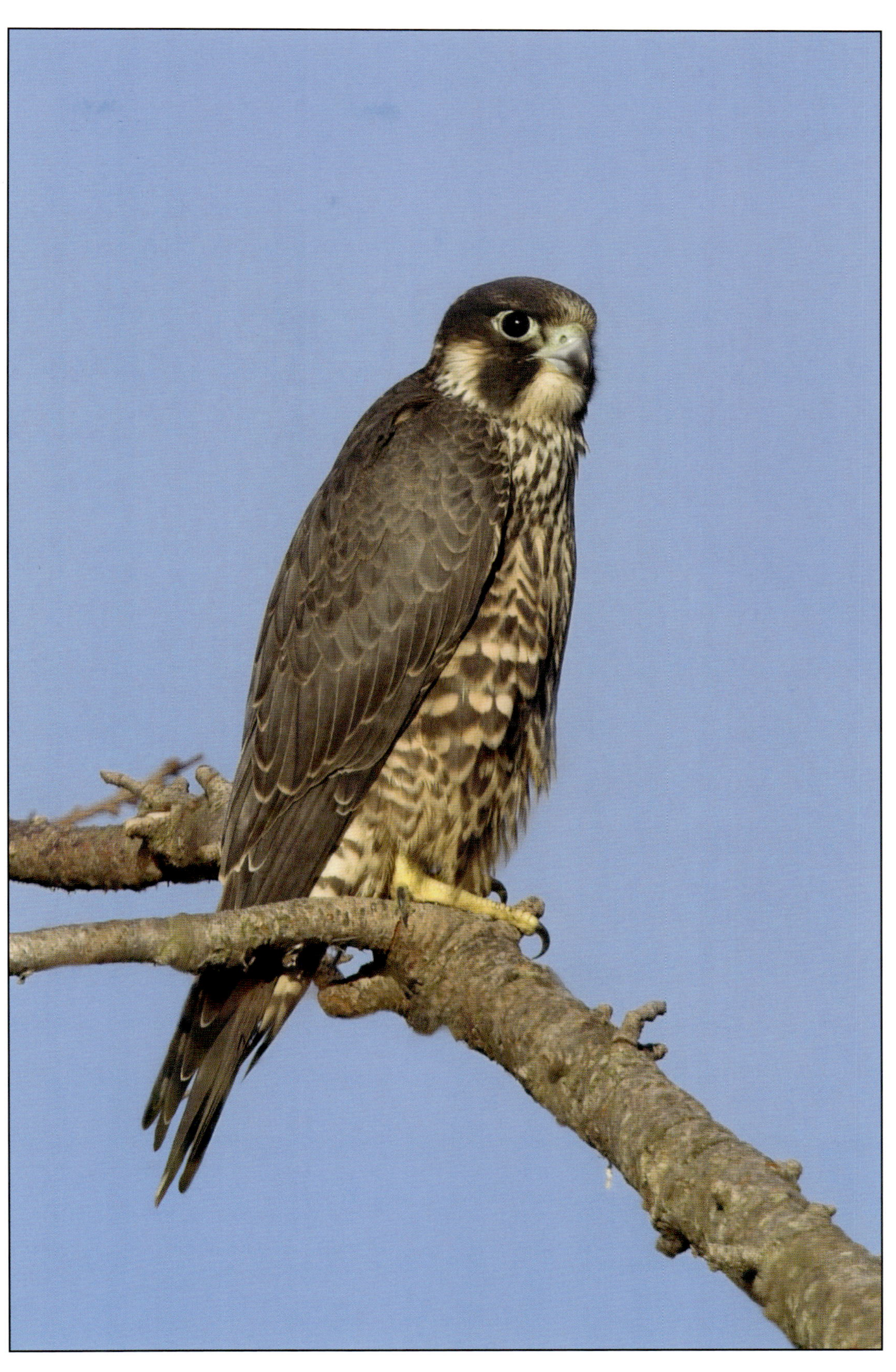

An alert Peregrine Falcon perches near the shoreline awaiting an unsuspecting shorebird during fall migration.

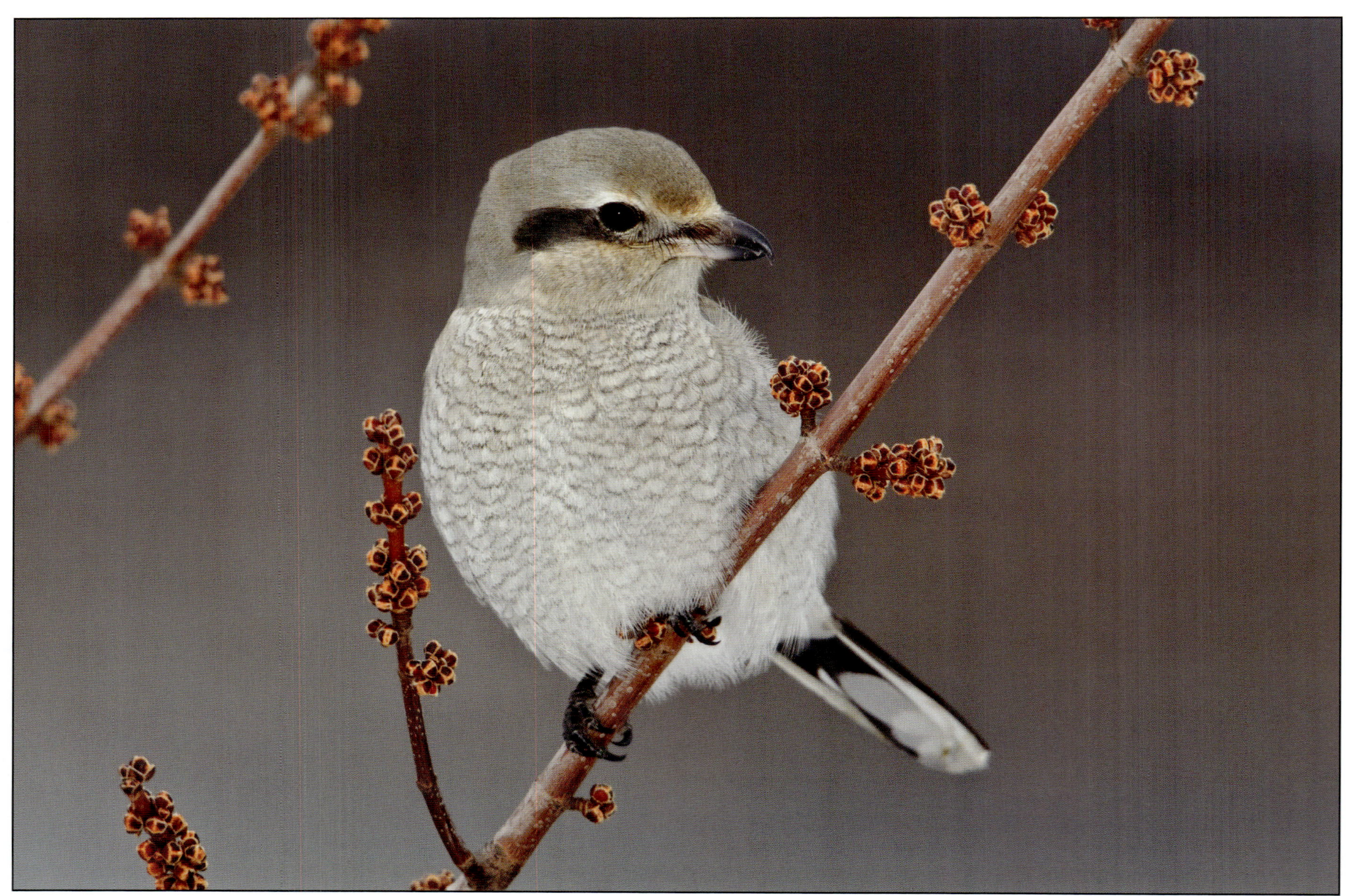

Known as the "butcher bird", Northern Shrikes often impale their prey on thorns or barbed wire before tearing them into bite-sized pieces.

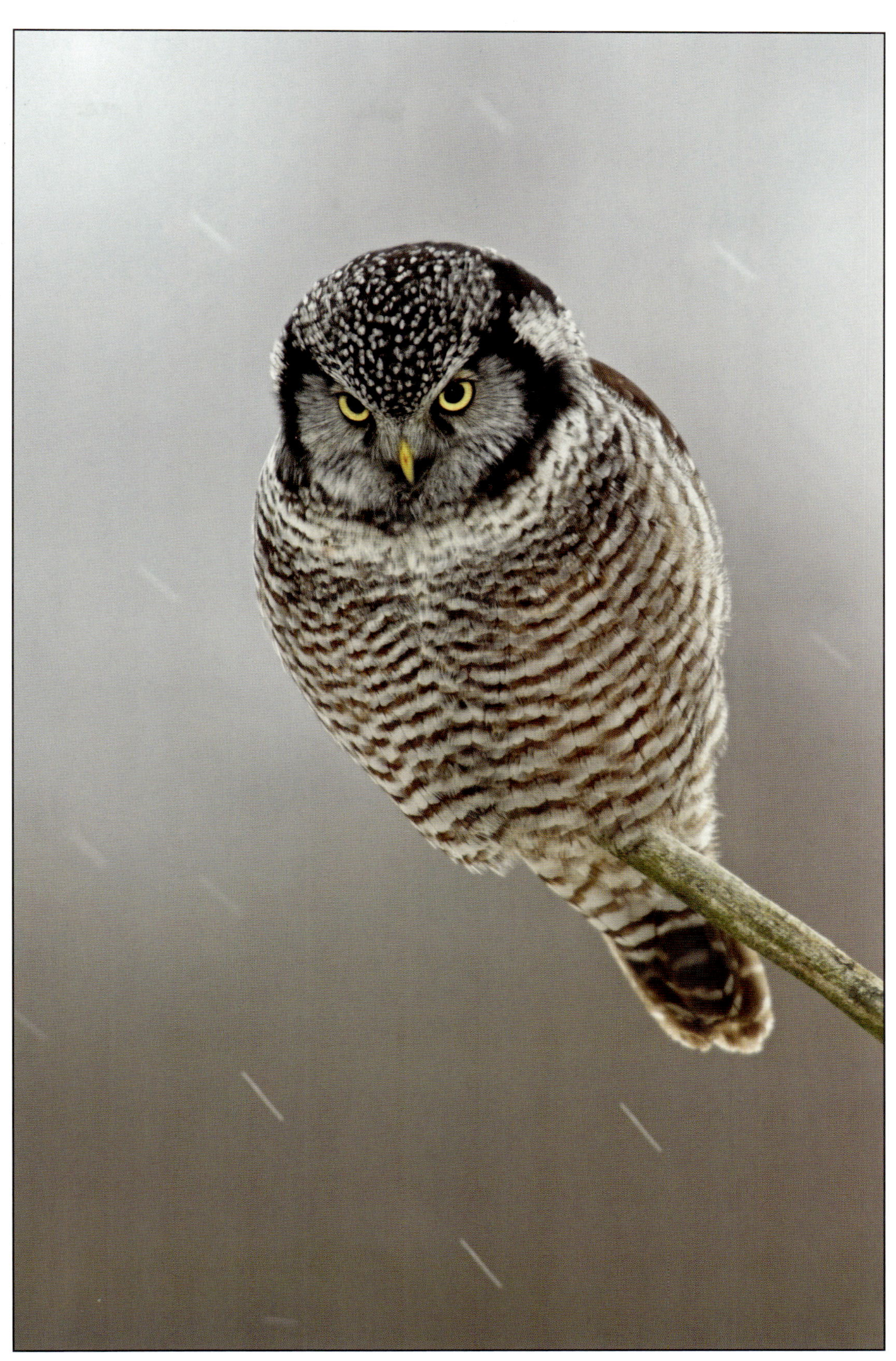

Although very rare on Vancouver Island, Northern Hawk-Owls are occasionally spotted away from their normal habitat in the northern parts of the Province.

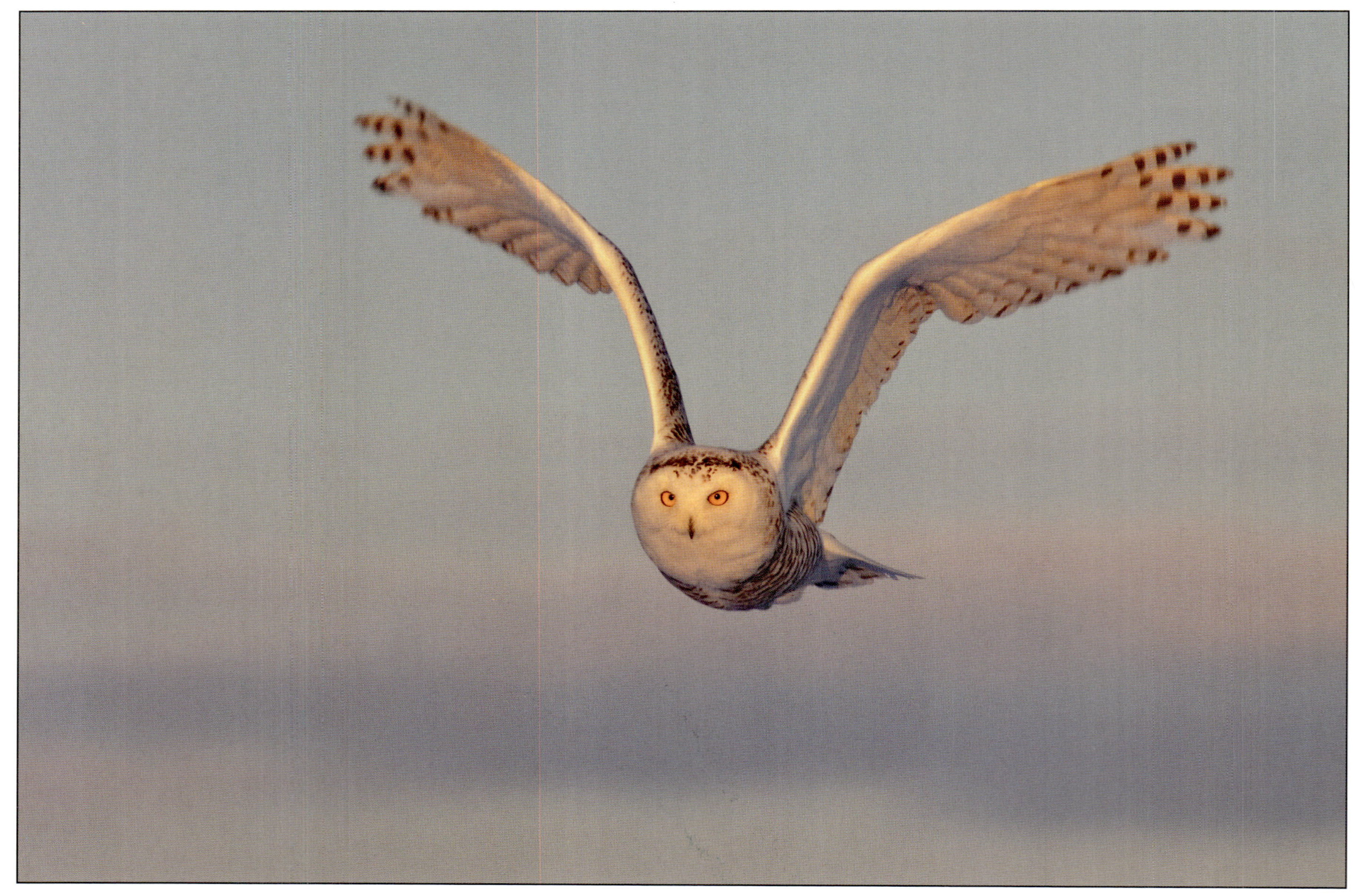

Snowy Owls are very rare visitors to Vancouver Island during the winter months.

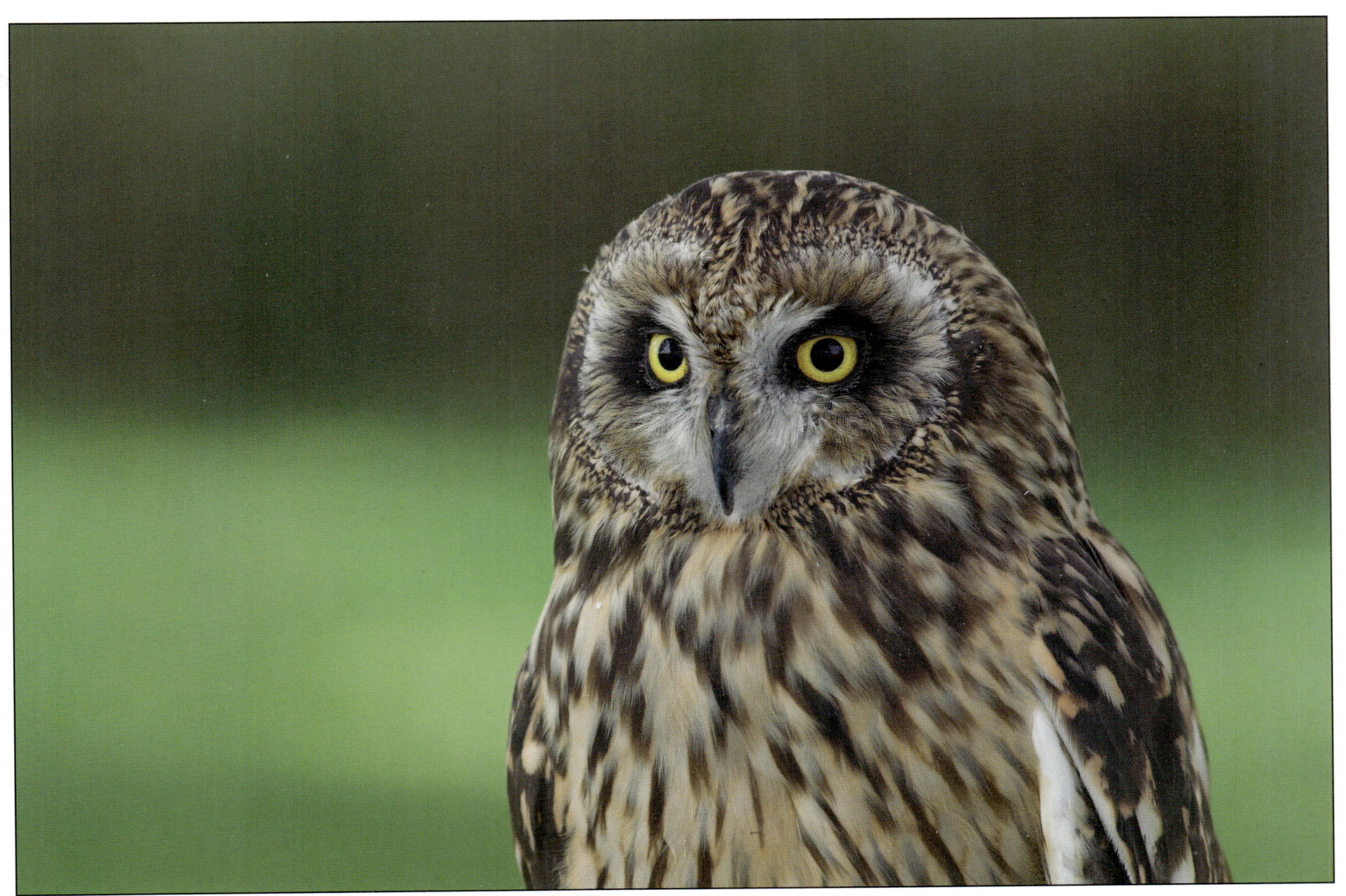

An owl of open areas, Short-eared Owls scan grasslands, estuaries and marshes for prey.

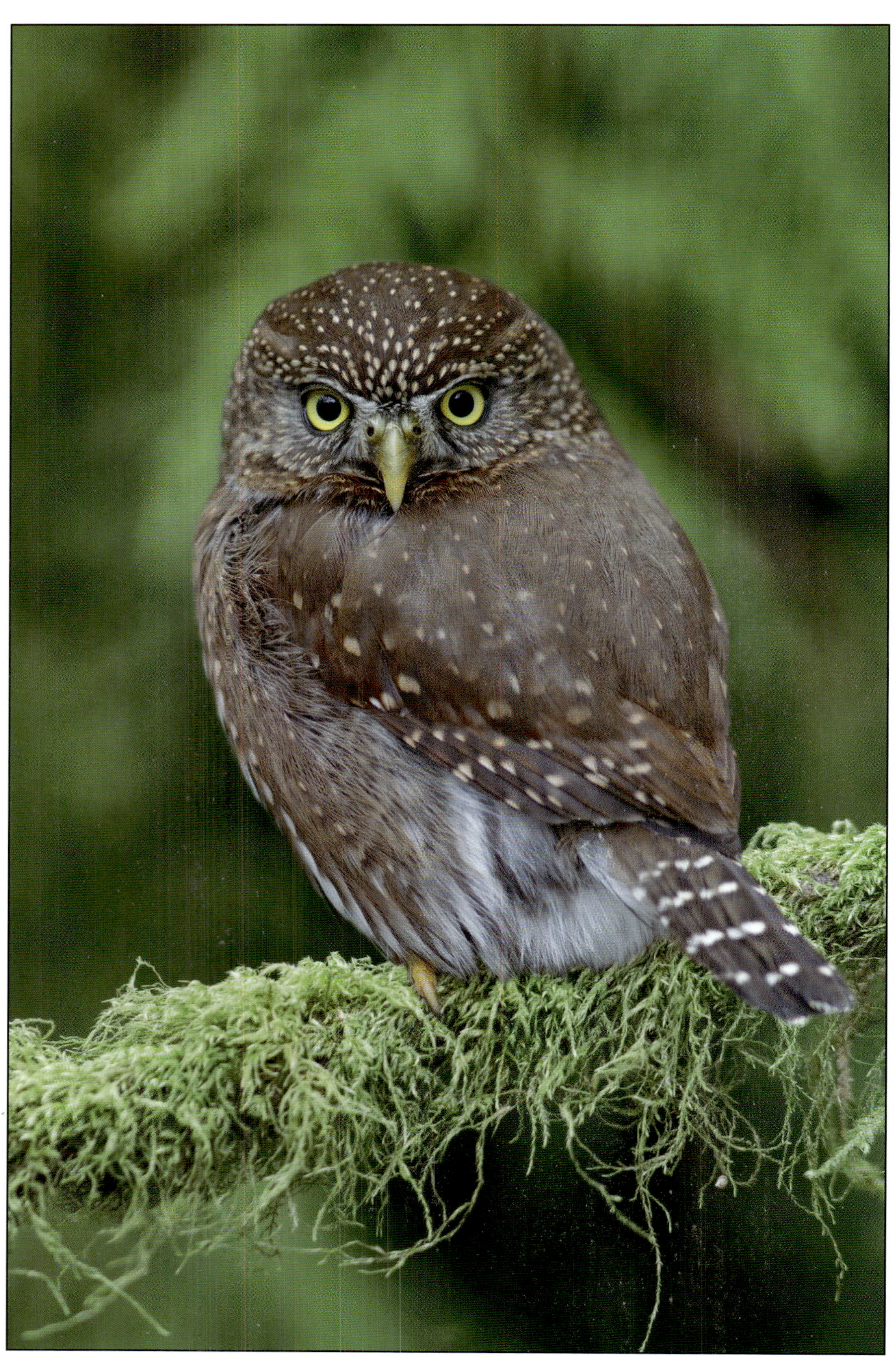

Although miniscule in size, the Northern Pygmy Owl is a ferocious diurnal hunter that inhabits the dense woodlands of Vancouver Island.

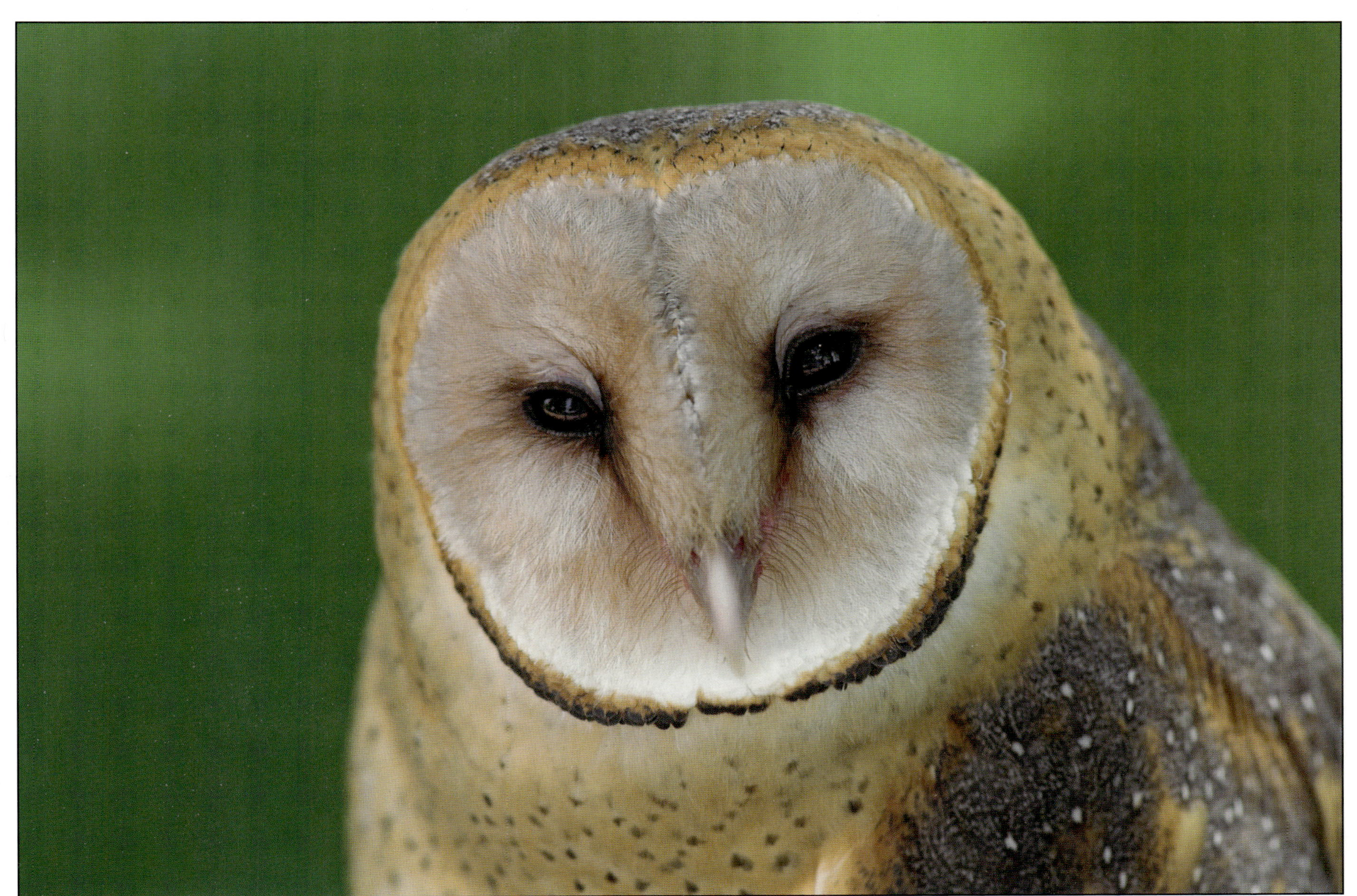

Named because they often roost in city or farm buildings during the day - the Barn Owl is a rarely encountered bird on southern Vancouver Island.

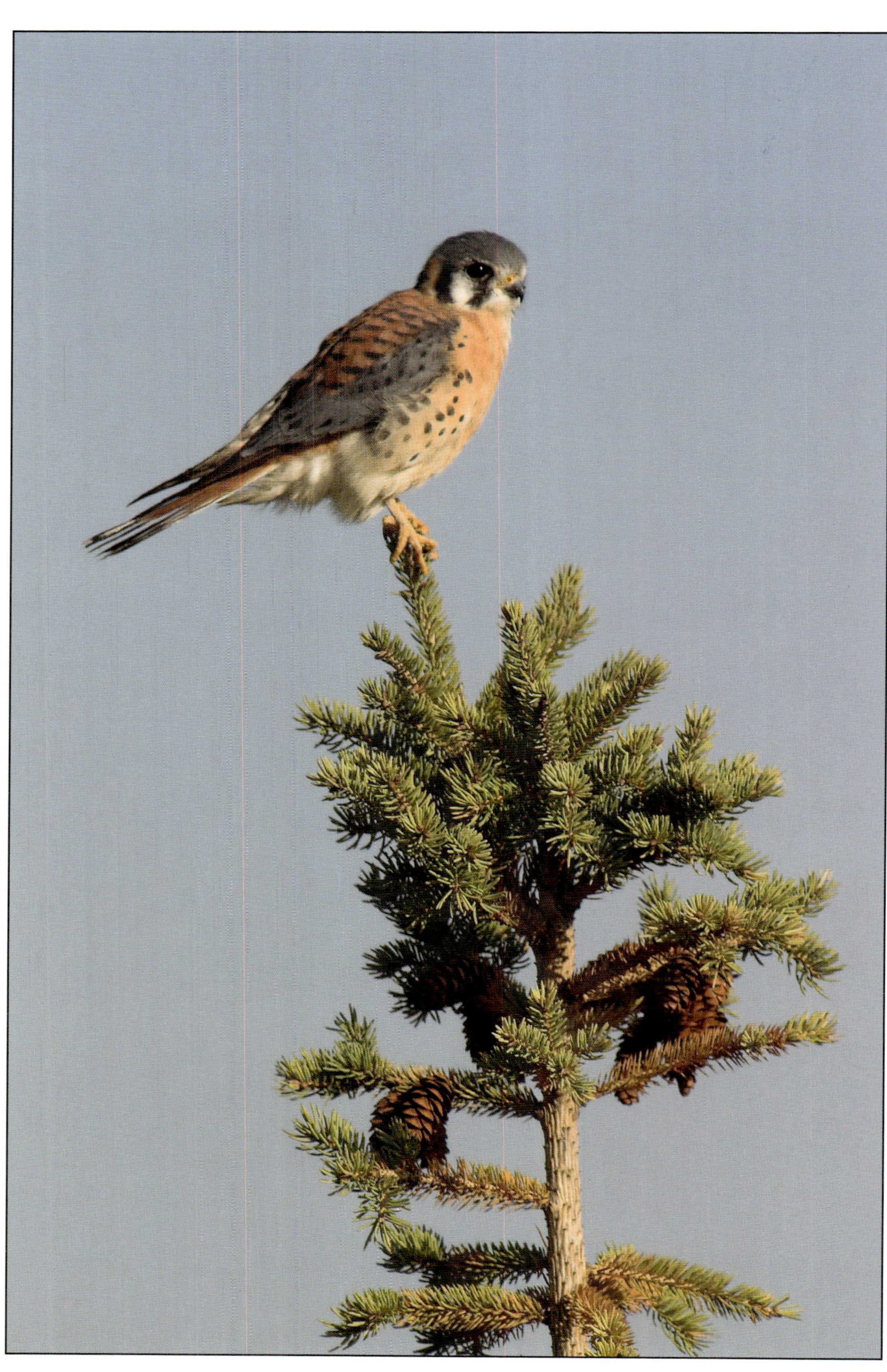

The smallest North American species of falcon, the American Kestrel can often be seen in open areas where it hovers before diving to the ground after insects or rodents.

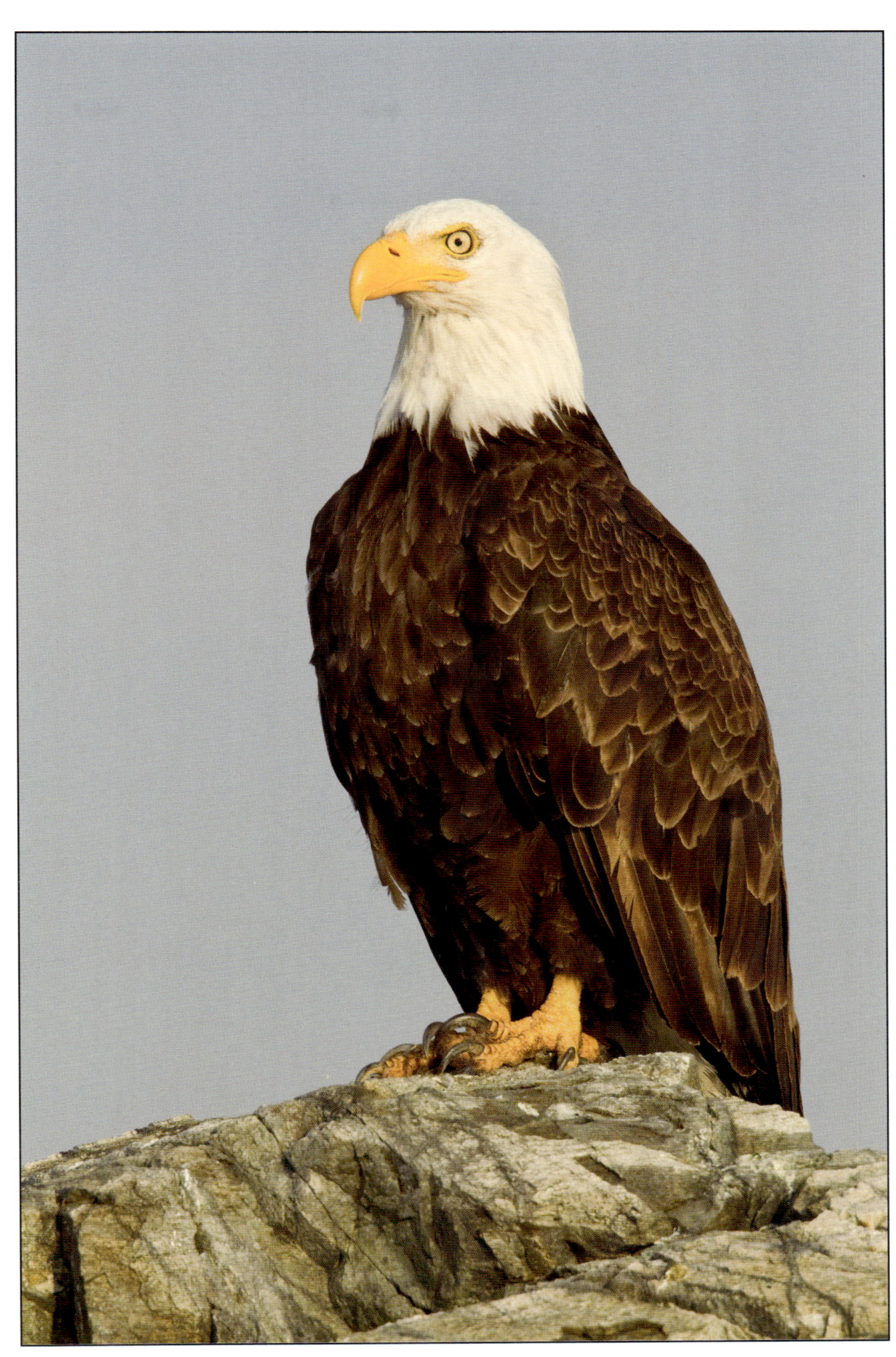

The majestic adult Bald Eagle is one of the most recognizable and symbolic birds in North America. These birds do not develop their characteristic white head until they reach five years of age.

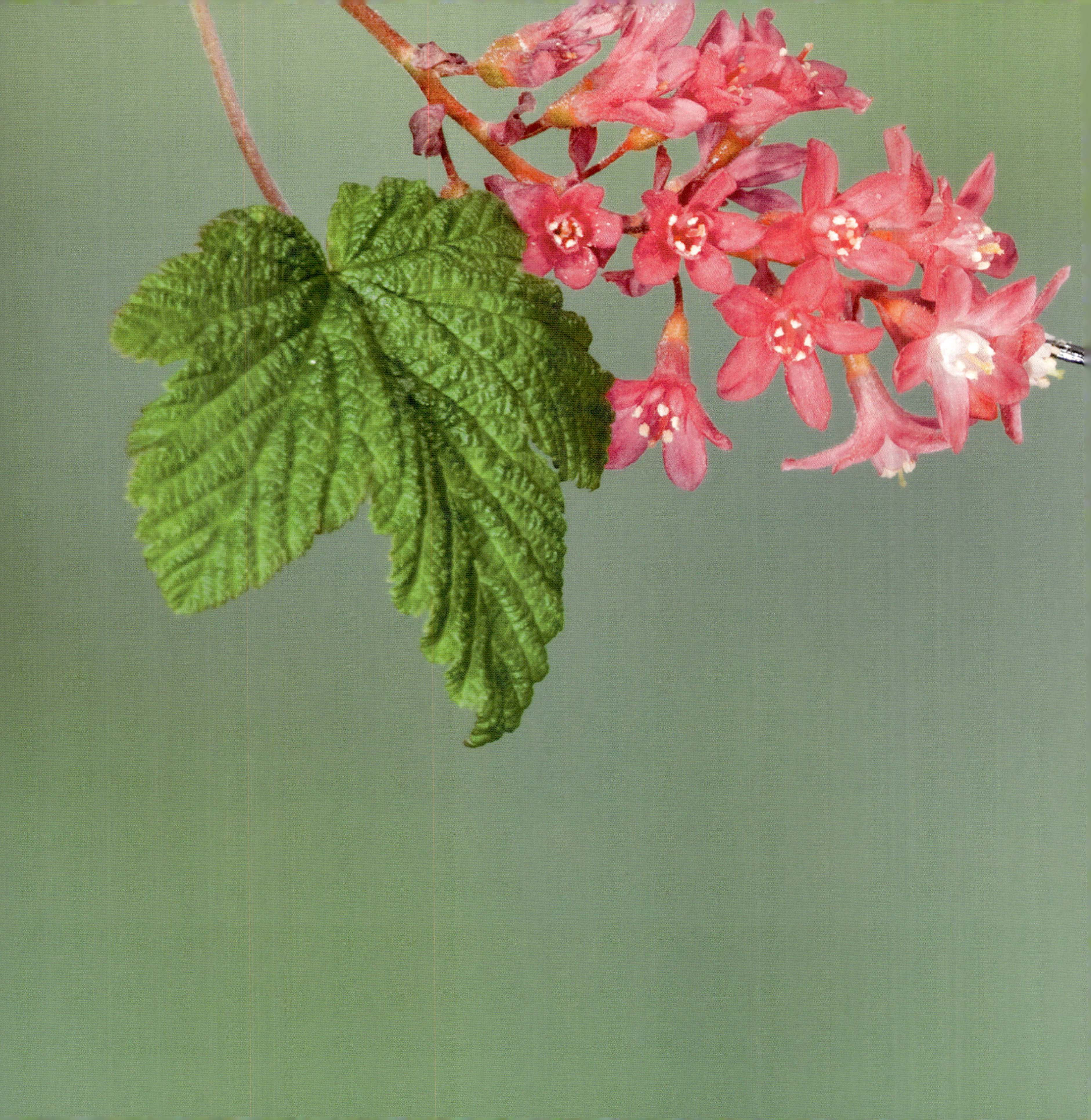

BACKYARD BIRDS

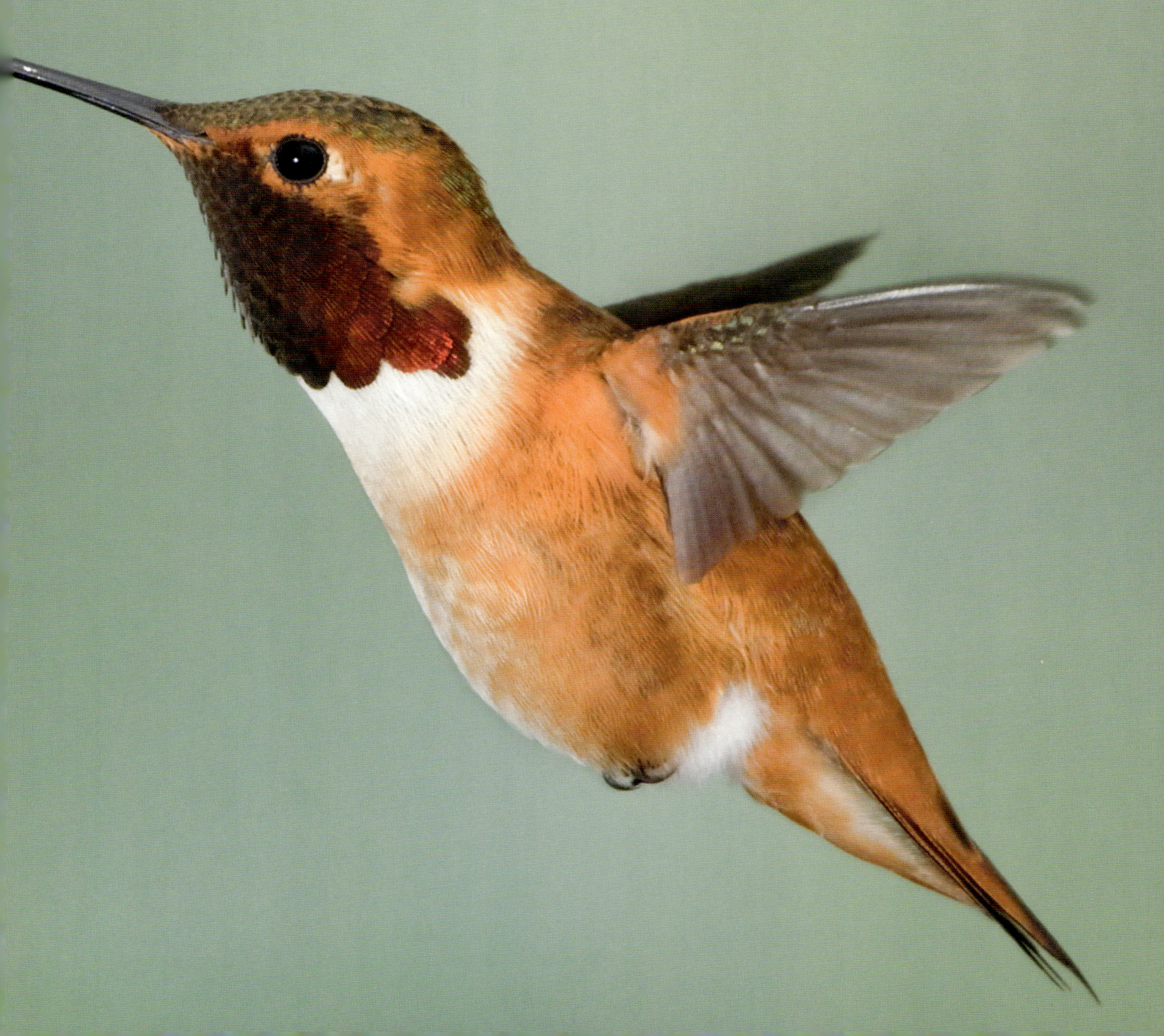

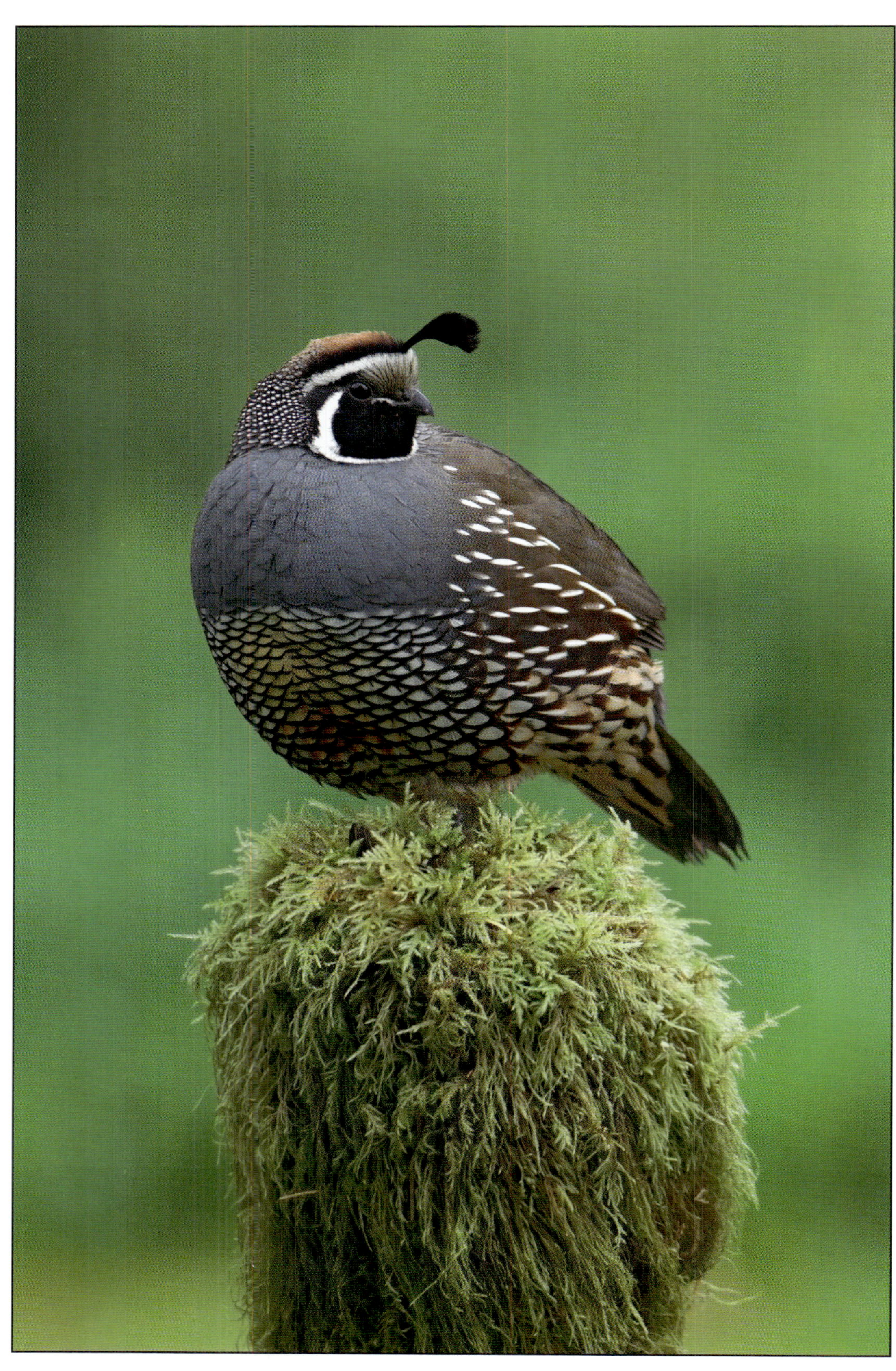

During the breeding season male California Quails often perch high off of the ground to watch over their mates.

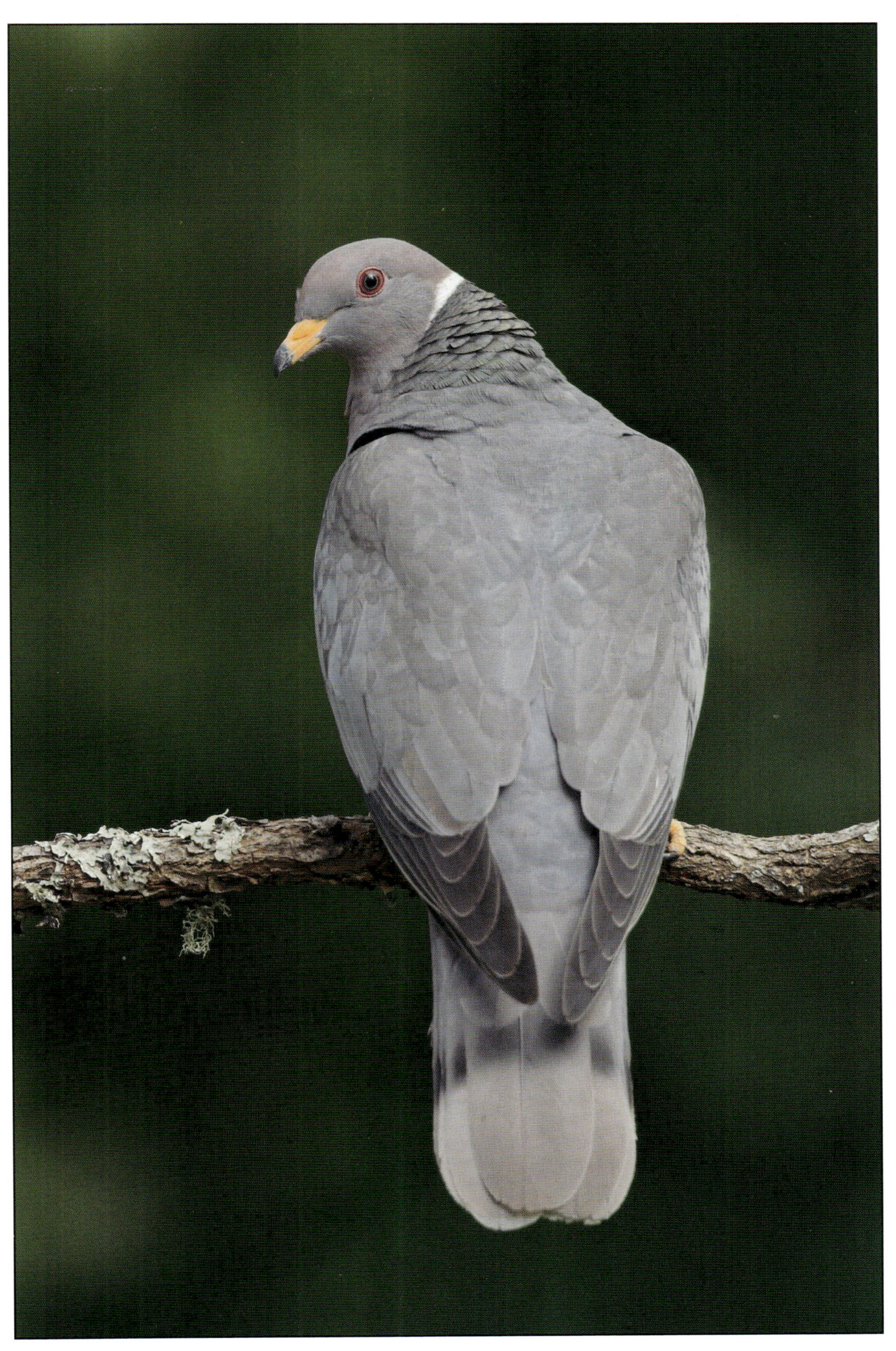

A Band-tailed Pigeon shows off its tail feathers for which it is named.

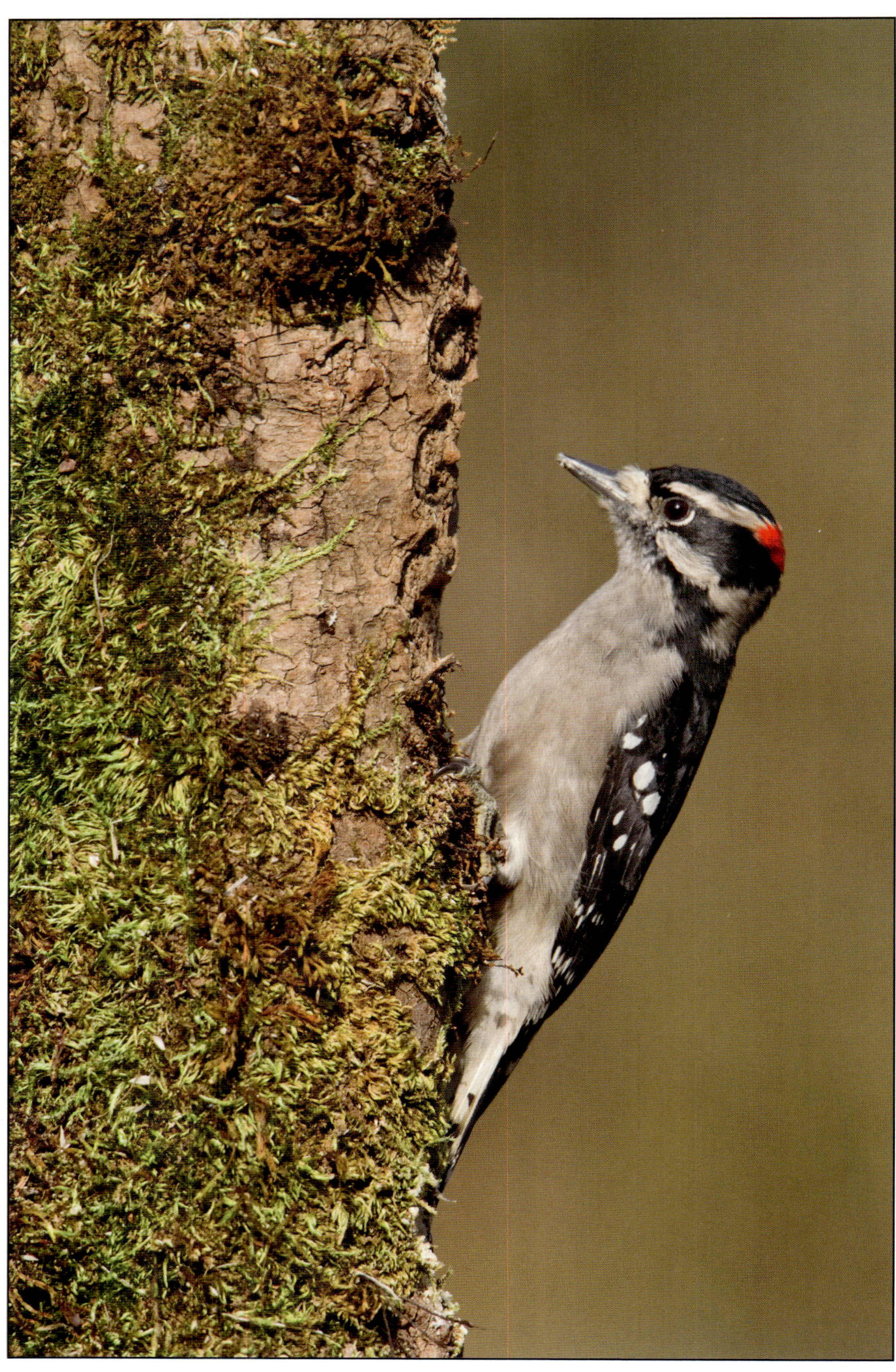

Especially attracted to suet feeders, Downy Woodpeckers are common visitors to backyards and parklands all over Vancouver Island.

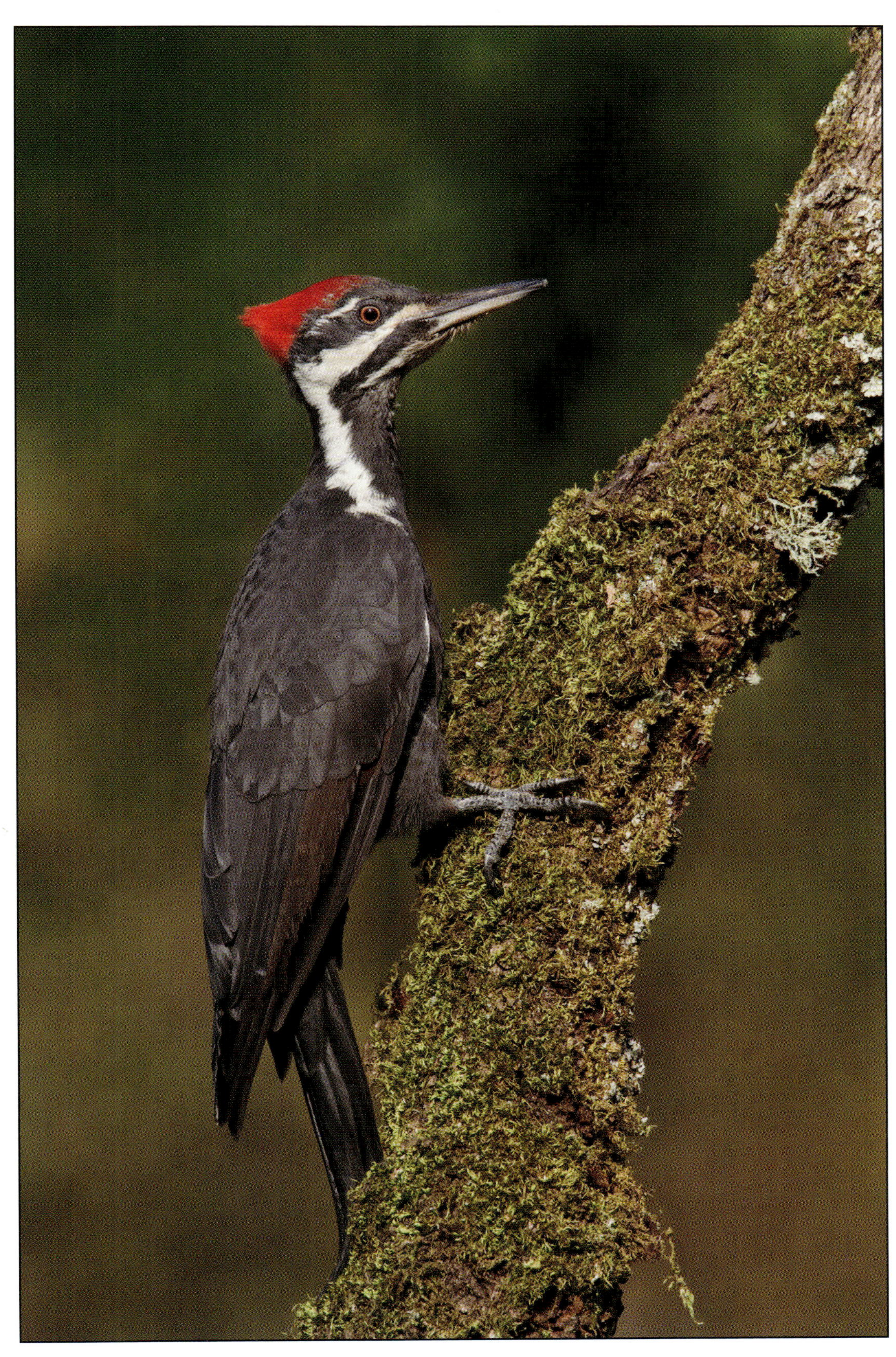

The powerful Pileated Woodpecker is the largest North American woodpecker species at up to 42 centimetres long.

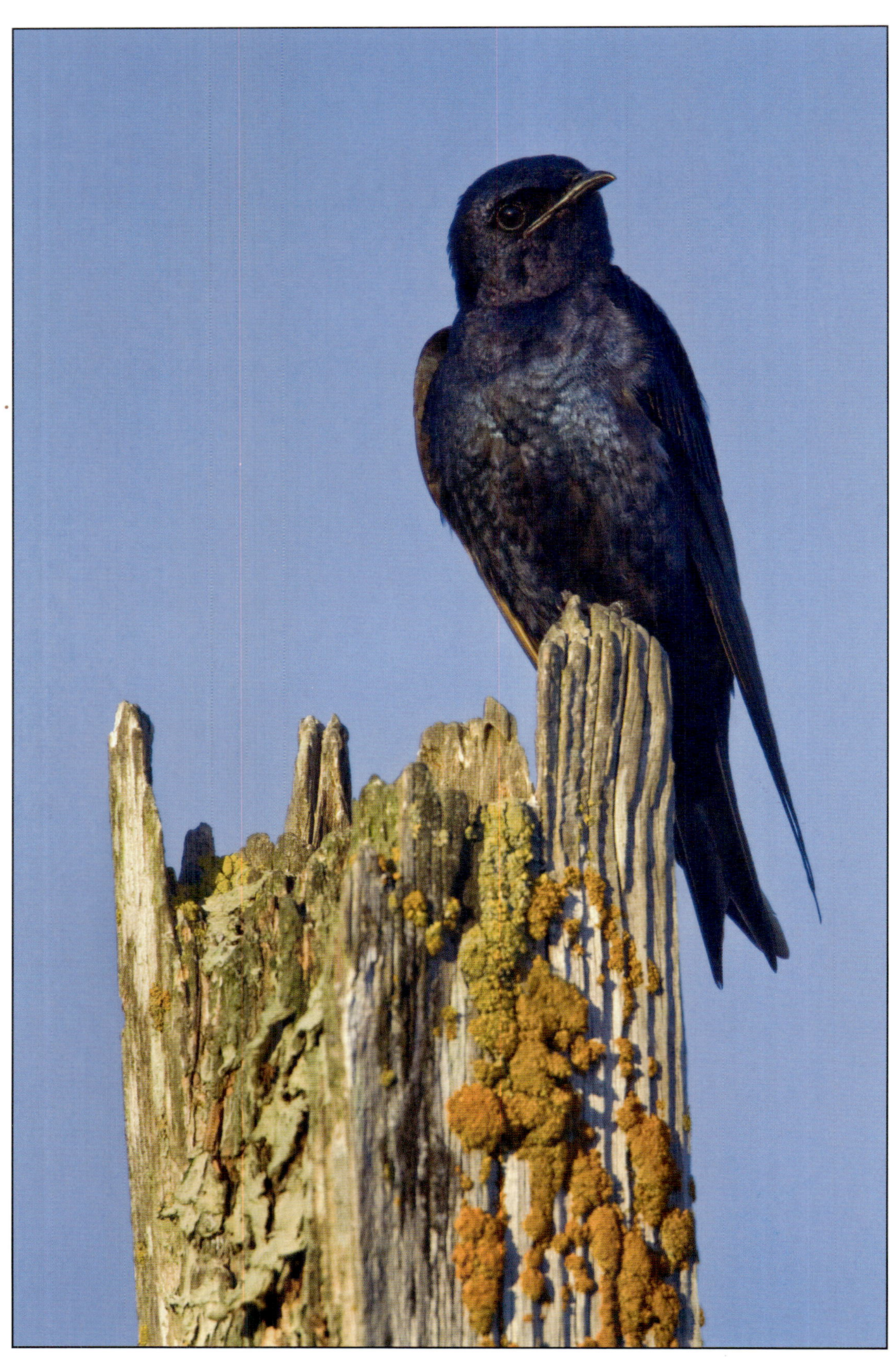

A male Purple Martin perches near a nest box where it hopes to raise a family. These birds have declined on Vancouver Island due to a lack of nest sites.

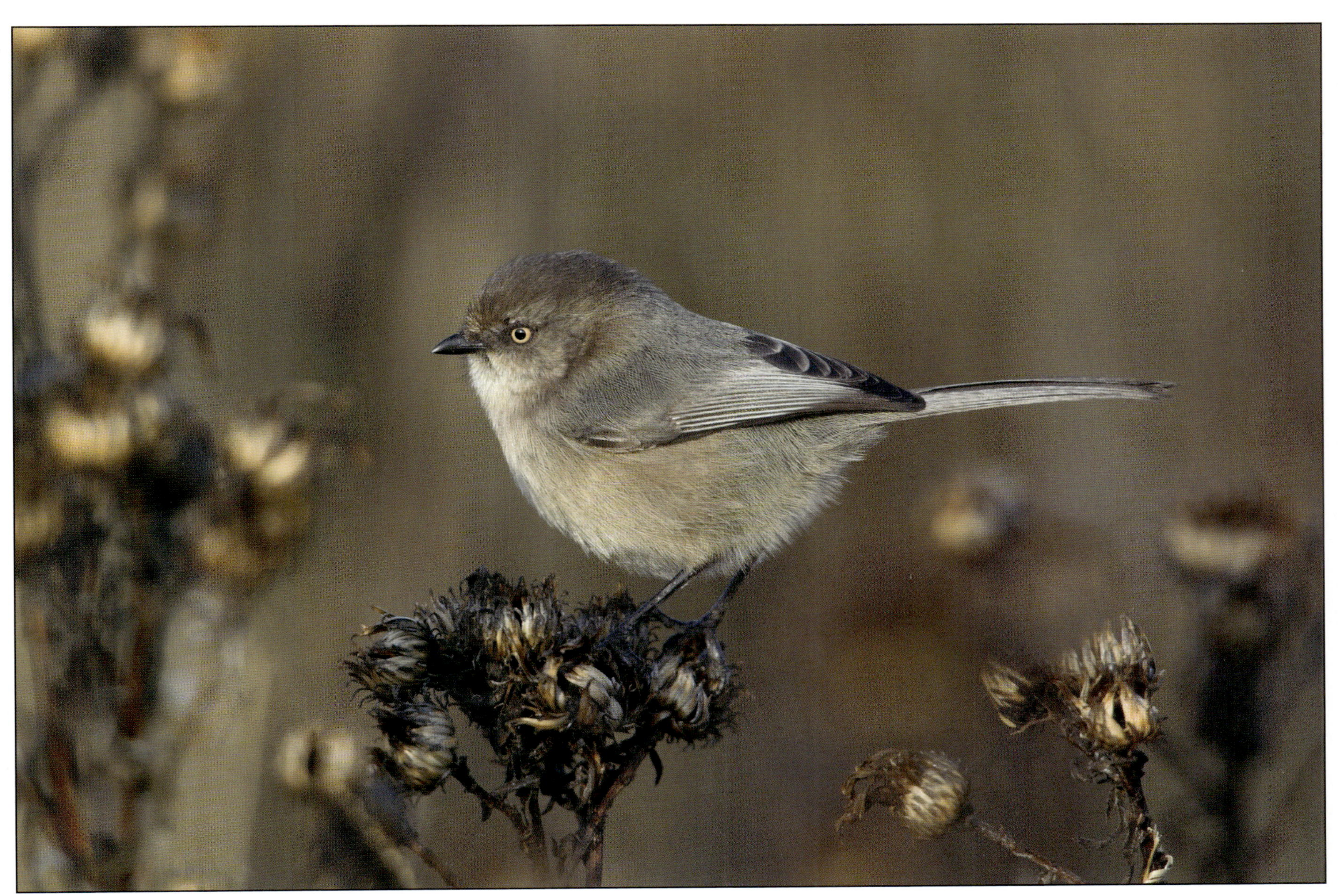

A curious Bushtit pauses momentarily while searching for insects on a dried flower.

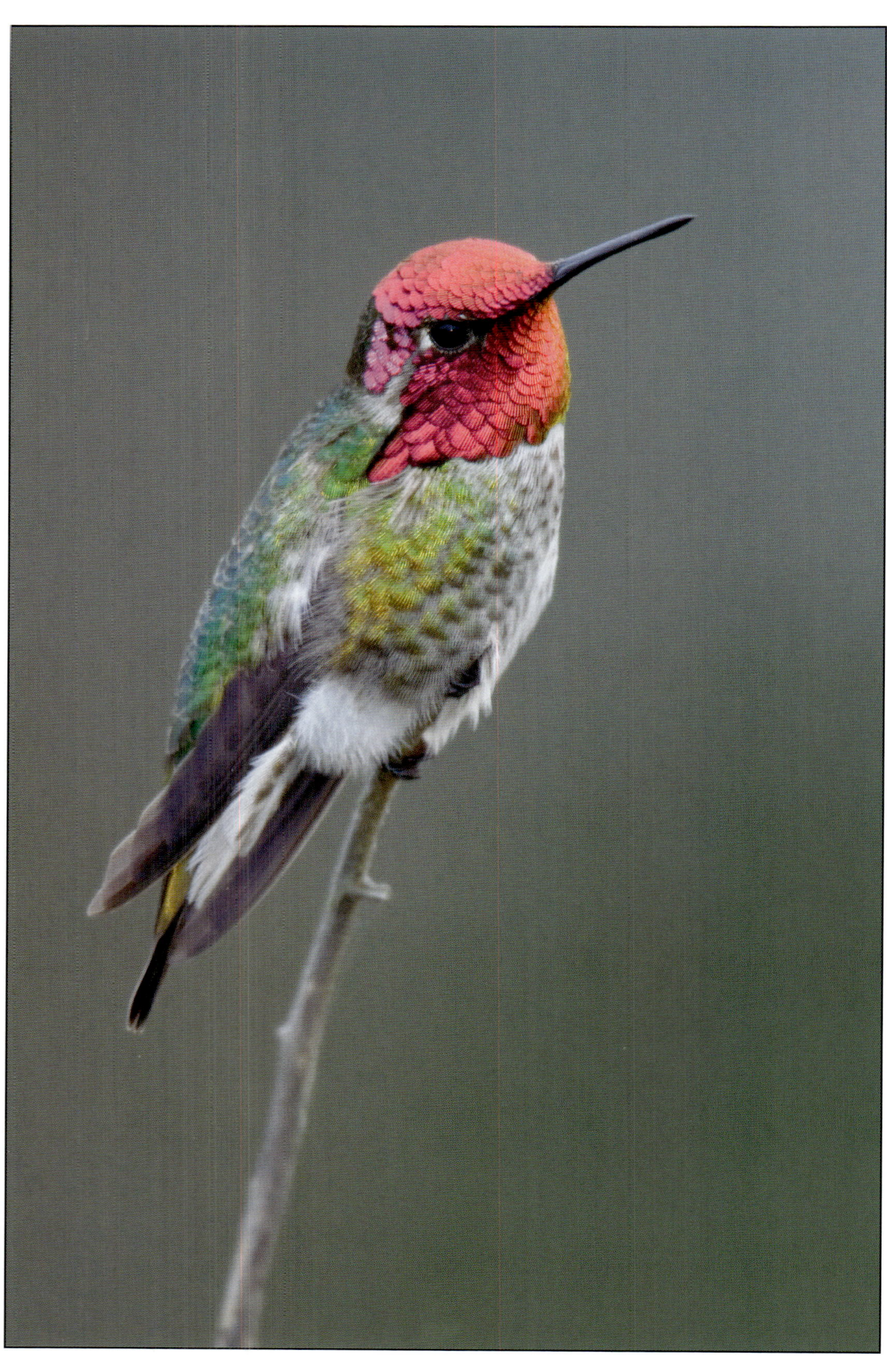

A male Anna's Hummingbird perches on a prominent branch to watch over its territory and call for a mate.

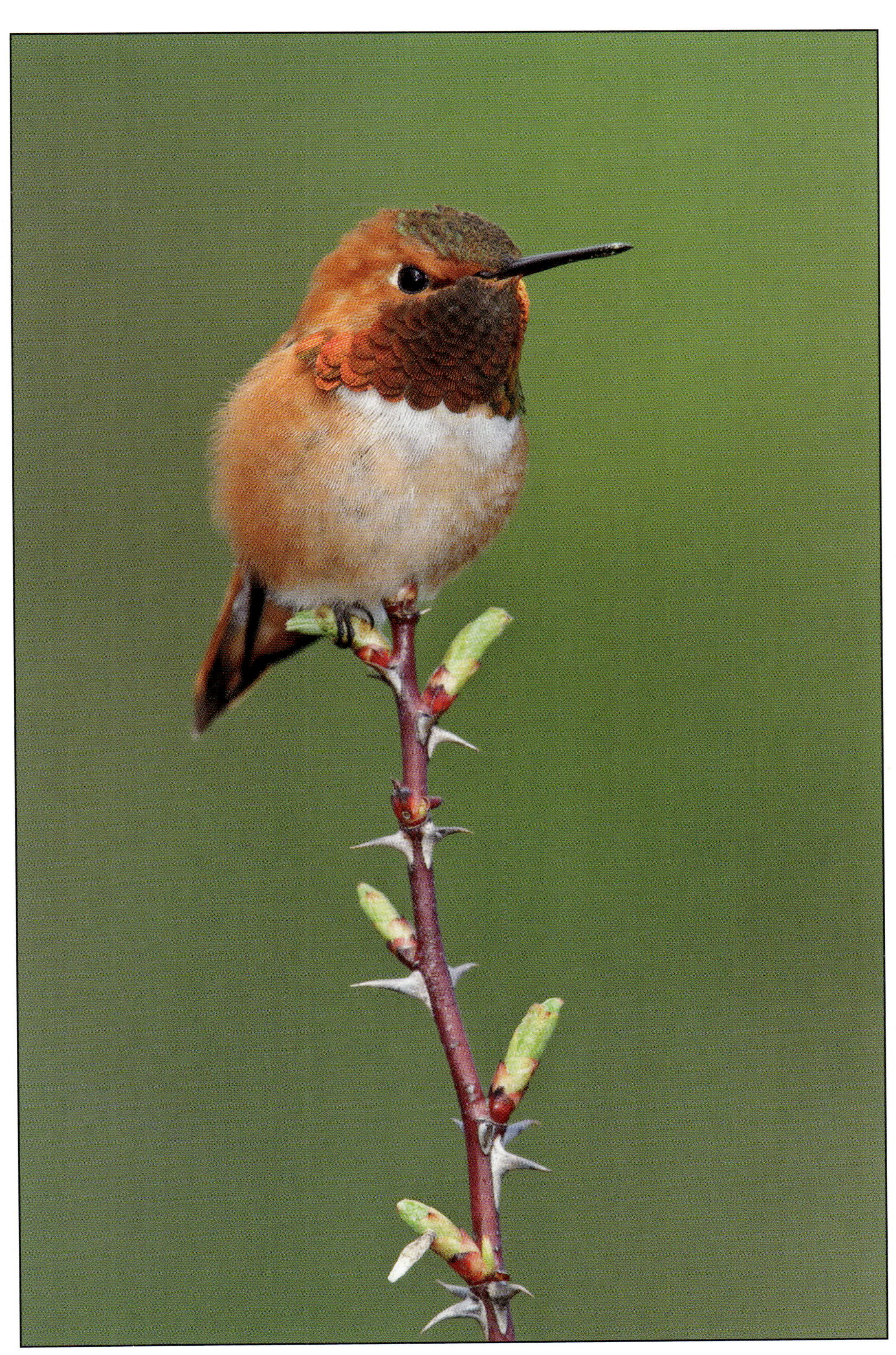

A male Rufous Hummingbird sits atop a thorny perch scanning his surroundings for the presence of potential intruders.

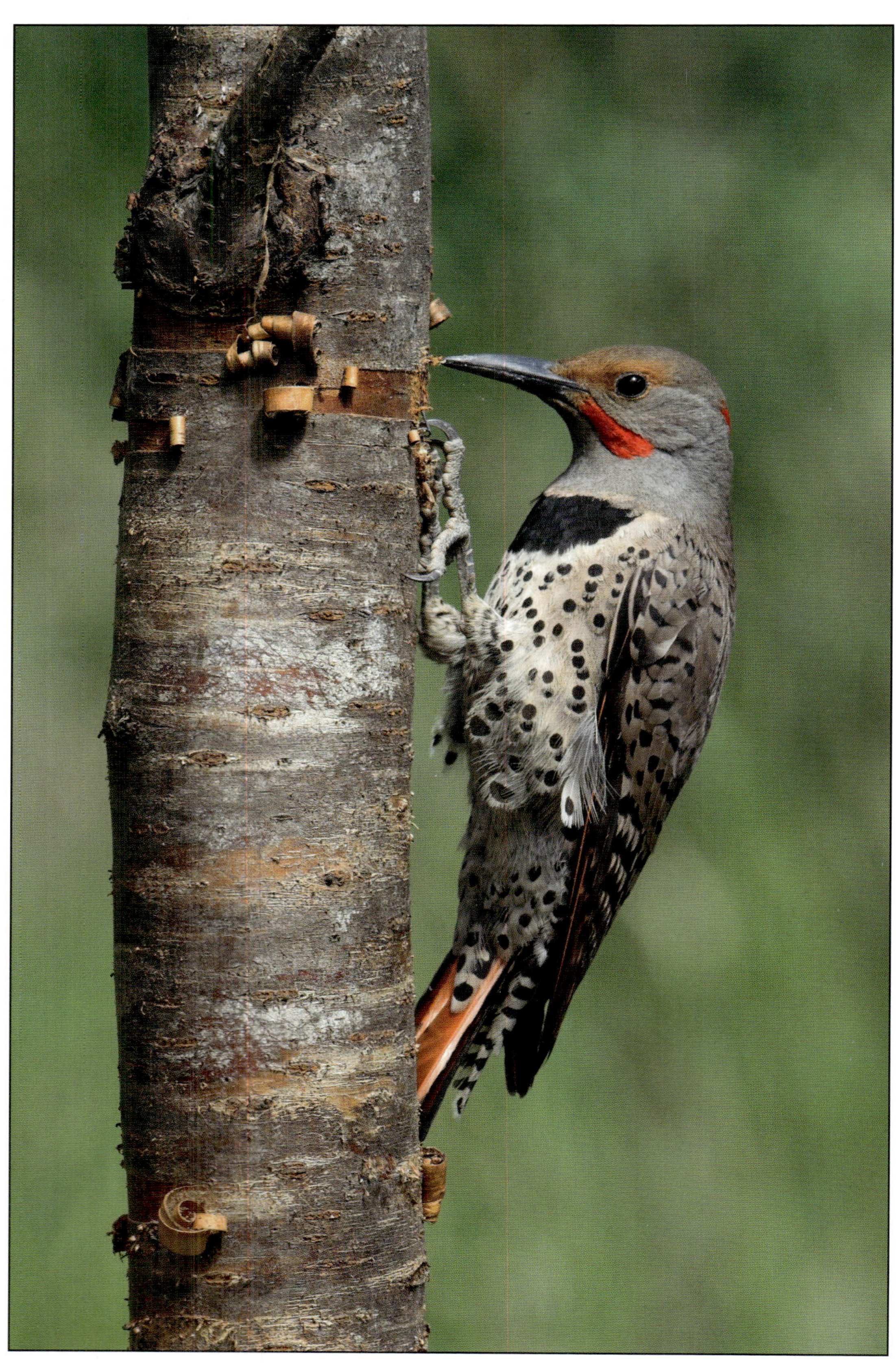

A Northern Flicker momentarily pauses his tree drilling activities in anticipation of discovering some tasty insects to feed upon.

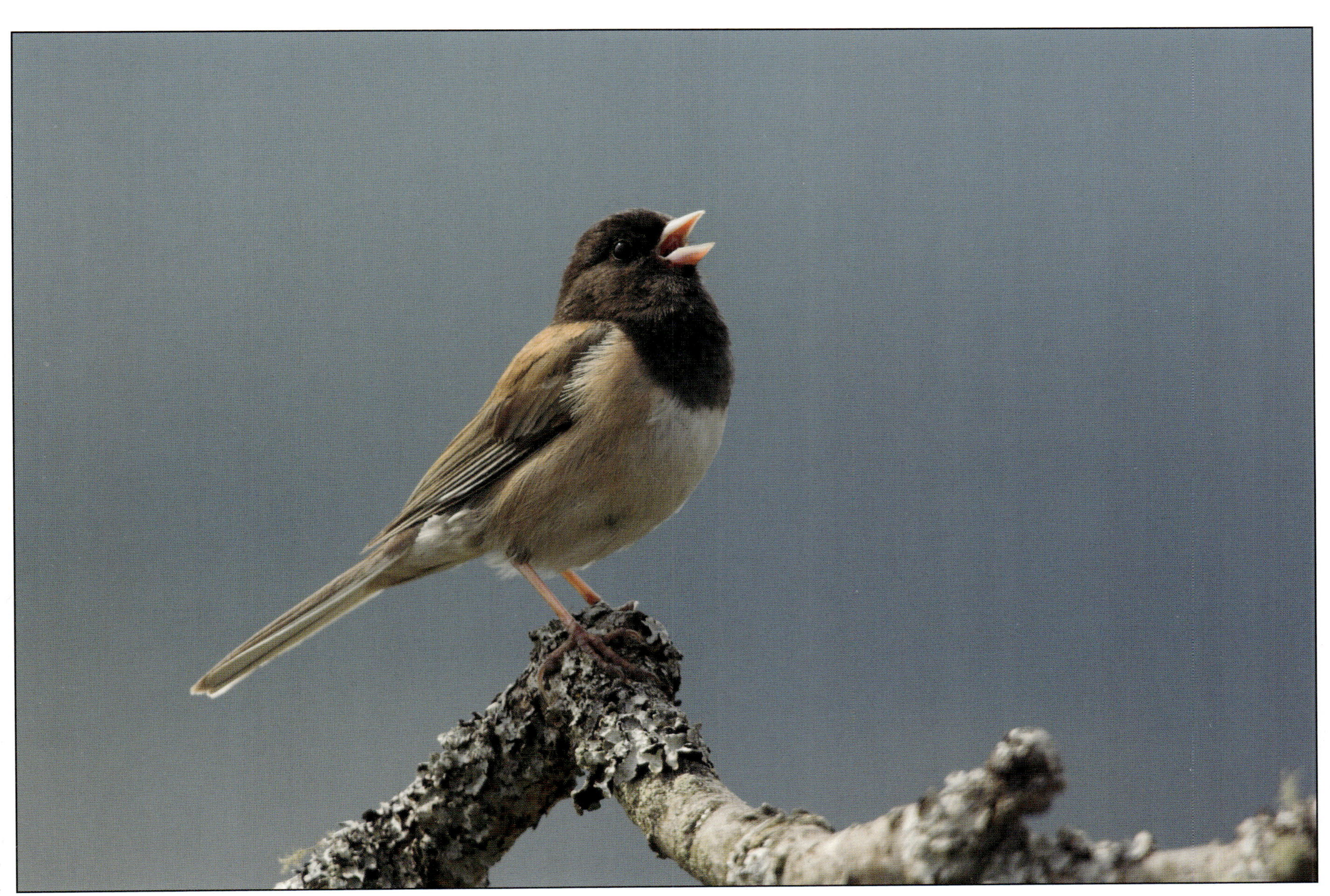

A Dark-eyed Junco sings a cheery song from a lichen-covered branch.

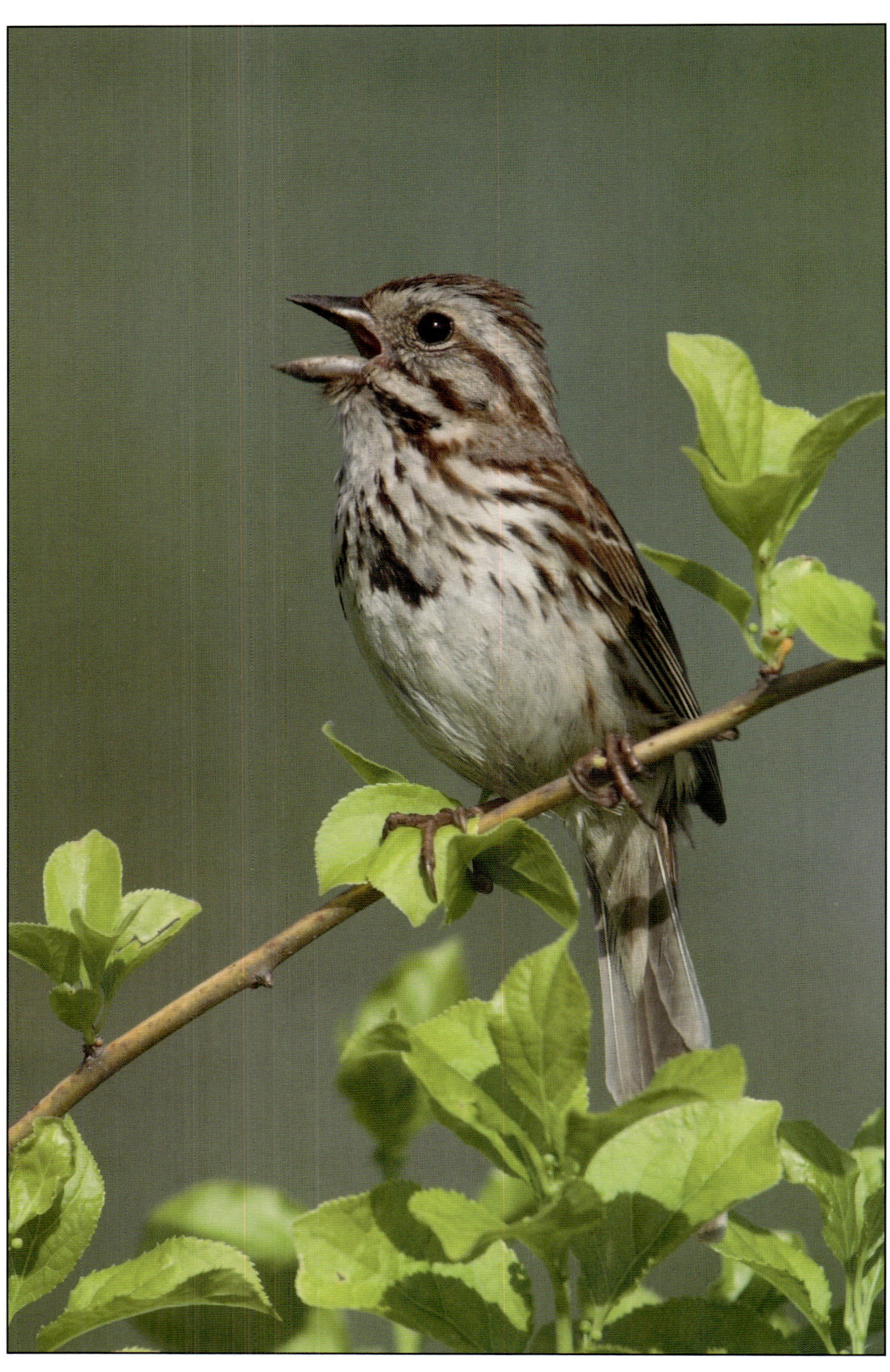

A Song Sparrow enthusiastically sings its song announcing that spring has arrived on Vancouver Island.

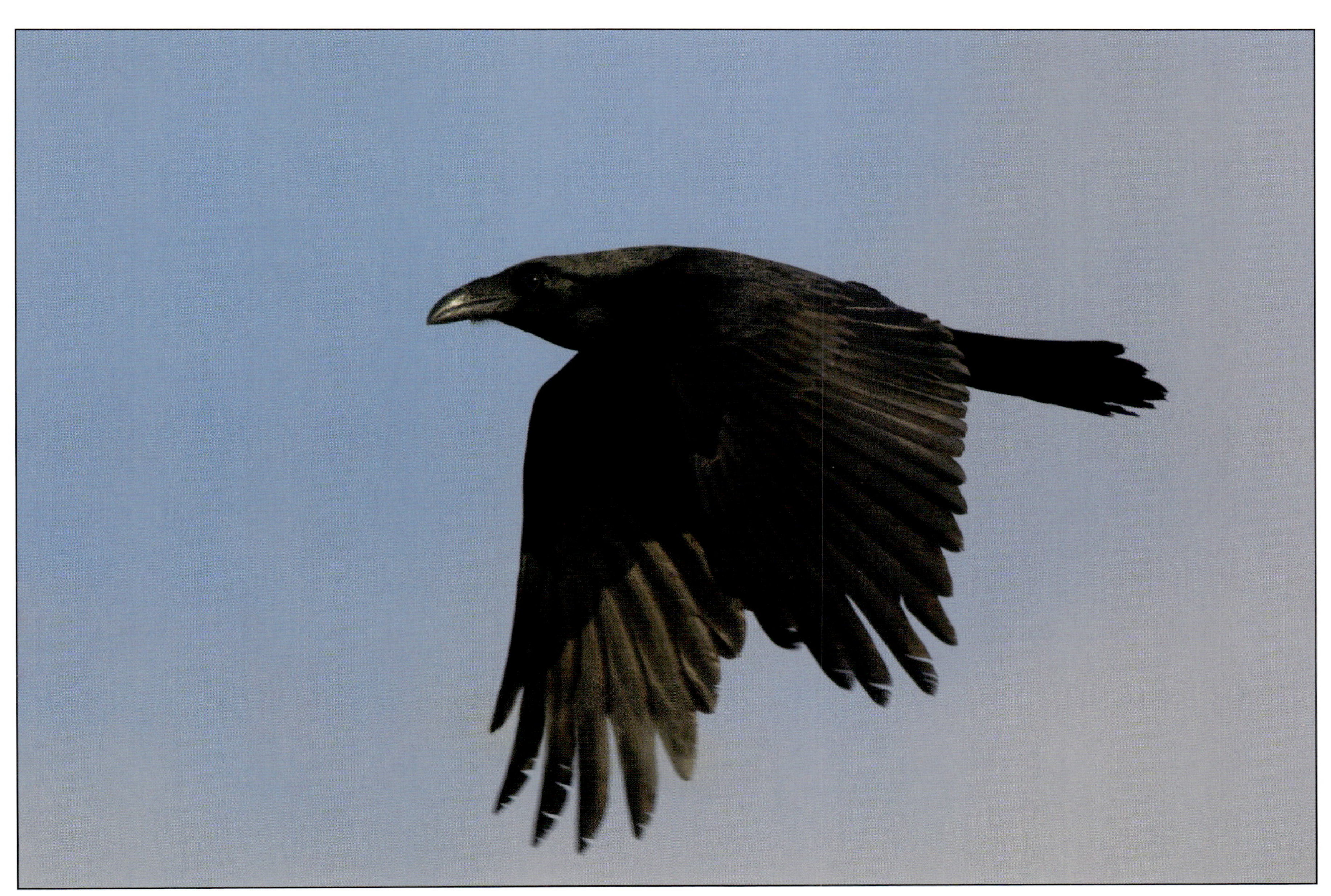

Common Ravens are prominently featured in the stories and artwork of First Nations cultures on Vancouver Island.

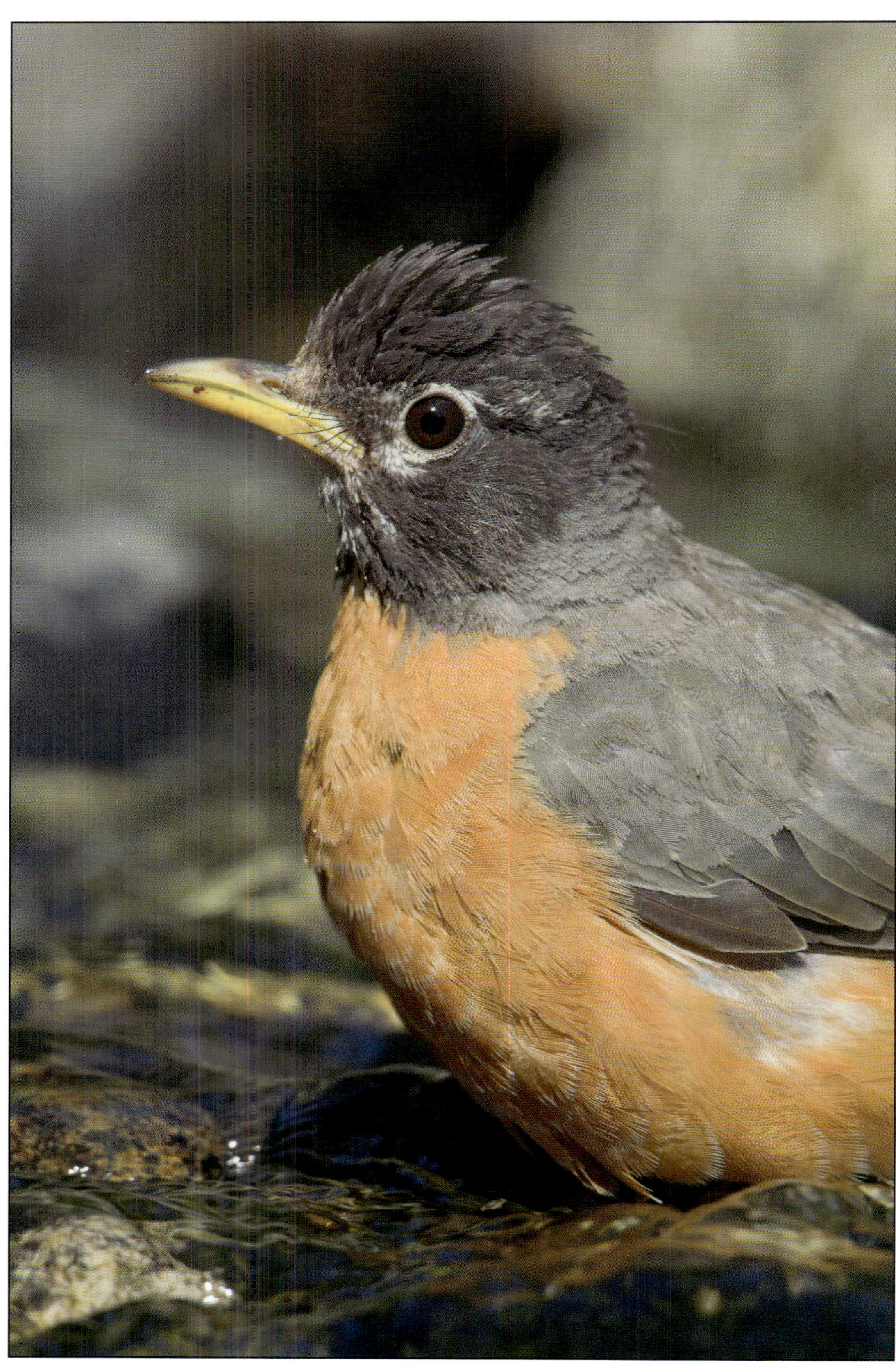

An American Robin takes a bath in a small stream on a hot summer's day.

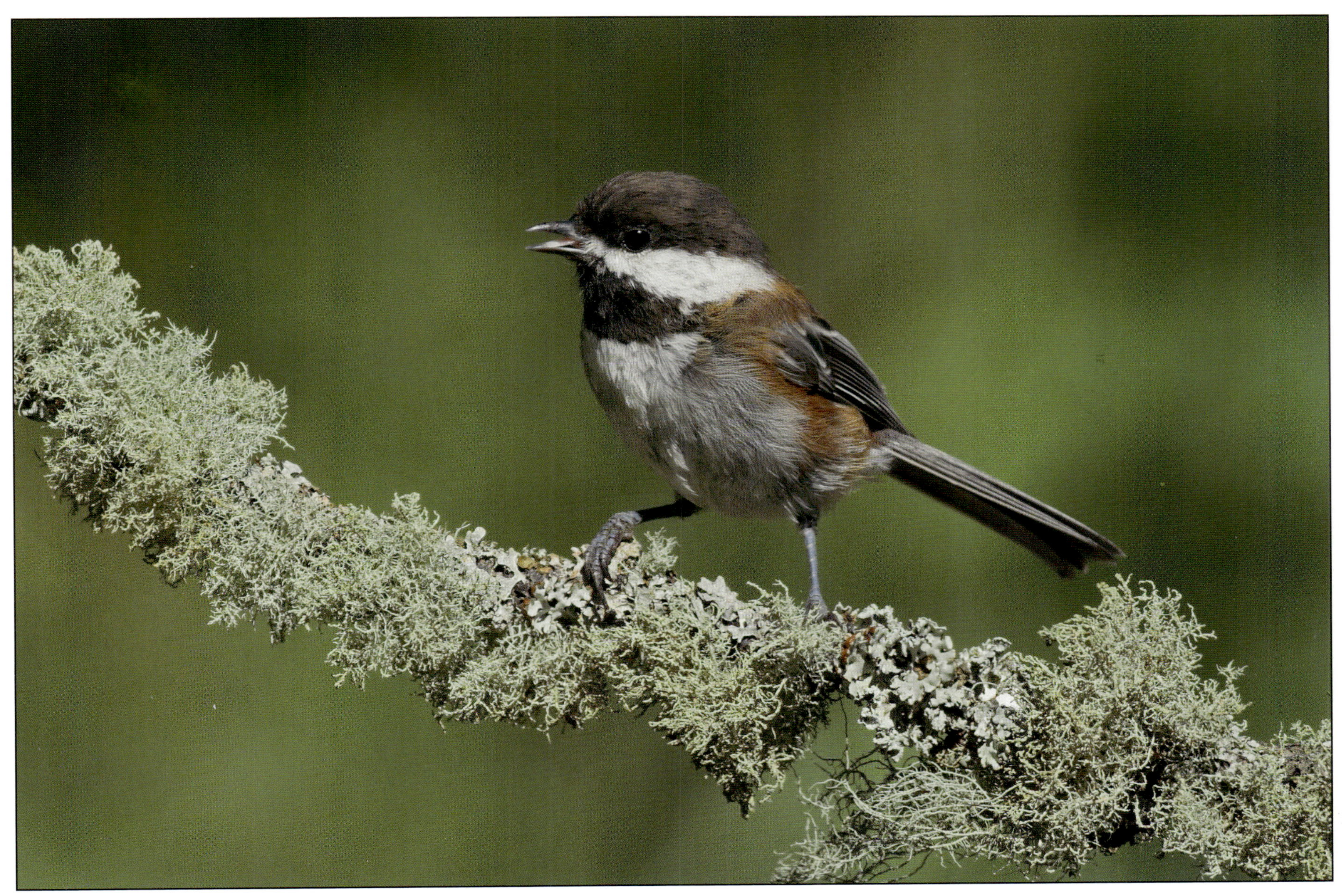

A Chestnut-backed Chickadee takes a break from feeding to sing its song from a lichen-covered perch.

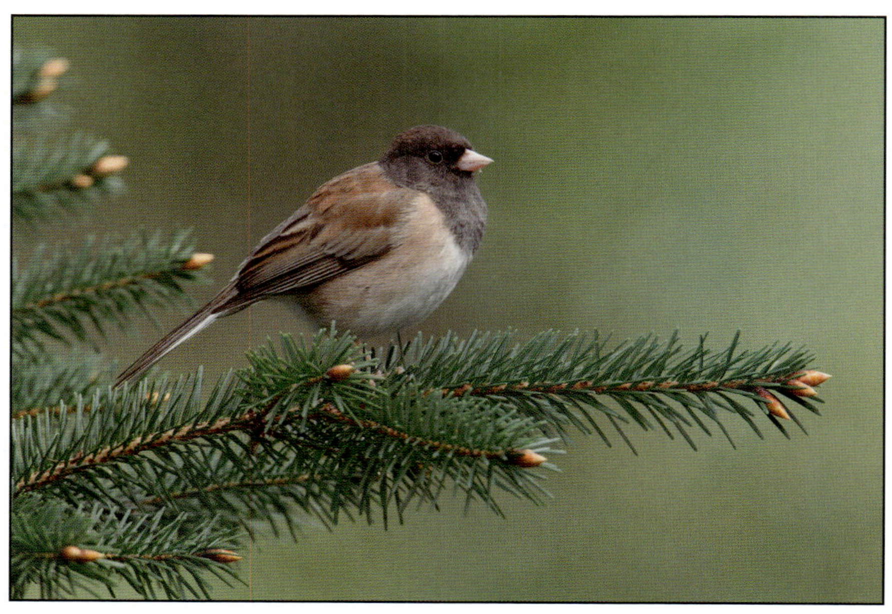

www.glennbartley.com

Designed and produced in Canada. Printed in China.

Library and Archives Canada Cataloguing in Publication Data

Bartley, Glenn, 1981 -

Birds of Vancouver Island: A Photographic Journey / Glenn Bartley

ISBN 978-0-9813212-1-9

1. Birds - Vancouver Island 2. Bird watching 3. Vancouver Island (B.C)